Taoism

GROWTH OF A RELIGION

Taoism

GROWTH OF A RELIGION

Isabelle Robinet

Translated by Phyllis Brooks

Stanford University Press
Stanford, California

Translated and adapted by Phyllis Brooks,
with the cooperation of Isabelle Robinet, from
Histoire du Taoïsme des origines au XIVe siècle
(Paris: Cerf, 1992)

Stanford University Press
Stanford, California
© 1997 by the Board of Trustees of the
Leland Stanford Junior University

Printed in the United States of America

CIP data appear at the end of the book

Stanford University Press publications
are distributed exclusively by Stanford
University Press within the United States,
Canada, Mexico, and Central America;
they are distributed exclusively by
Cambridge University Press
throughout the rest of the world.

Contents

Translator's Foreword

That Taoism is a composite religion is well known. Formed of many strands, it relies on no single supreme authority or fundamental holy book. In fact, there has been a long-standing tendency—both within and beyond China—to designate as "Taoist" all recorded Chinese traditional knowledge that was not part of official schemas or technical information, all that was different and, parenthetically, not Buddhist or Confucian. The multiplicity of Taoist traditions and texts has been one factor in the unwillingness of many even to accord it the title "religion."

This book, by one of the world's foremost scholars of Taoism, should remove any doubt that Taoism is a religion. It is an attempt to explain to a wide audience how, over a period of some sixteen centuries, various strands of thought, practice, and belief became woven together to form the Taoist religion. In preparing the English version, I have made some modifications to the ordering of the French text—for example, making part of the original Introduction the Author's Preface. Within chapters there has been some re-ordering of the presentation to fit English-language conventions, but Professor Robinet's exposition is so clear that I have had to make few changes in her actual wording. My hope is that the result is true to the original while permitting quick comprehension of the sometimes densely packed material.

In line with current usage, I have followed Professor Robinet's use of the *pinyin* system to transliterate all Chinese names and terms (except, of course, in the titles of books and articles that use other systems). I have preserved "Tao," "Taoism," and "Taoist" (rather than "Dao," and so on) since these words have entered ordinary English in this form. Pinyin transliterations may at first be disconcerting to those readers who have gleaned their knowledge of Taoism from sources using the traditional Wade-Giles system: Chuang Tzu become Zhuangzi in pinyin; *ch'i* (breath) and *ching* (sperm) become *qi* and *jing;* the *Ch'u-tz'u* (Songs of Chu) become the *Chuci.* To ease the transition, a certain number of familiar Wade-Giles terms are therefore listed in the index, with cross-references to their pinyin equivalents.

Constructing a history of the growth of a religion is necessarily a complex procedure. That the Chinese could even have a native religion, growing from indigenous roots, with a cosmology and pantheon that developed and changed through the ages, is an idea that has only now begun to take hold, even in scholarly circles. Until recent years, Taoism was usually studied as a "philosophy," as a way of viewing the world and humanity's place in it. To many it is still a sort of vaguely physico/spiritual-cum-ecological pattern of thinking adopted by elitist, often aristocratic hermits retiring from the world of affairs. Others see it only in terms of local cults to a myriad of deities, some representing chthonic forces and others euhemerized heroes. In any case, the general view has been that it is a mishmash of conflicting and jumbled beliefs and practices, without the coherence or form that marks the "true" religion. (The only other up-to-date short, popular presentation of Taoism as a great "world-class" religion is Anna Seidel's *Taoismus: die inoffizielle Hochreligion Chinas*—see the Suggestions for Further Readings for details.)

It was not until the late twentieth century that Western scholars started to appreciate Taoism as a complex religion worthy of study. Whatever the situation within China—and this book reveals the changing fortunes of Taoism within the great Chinese empire—there are complicated reasons behind the Western reluctance to accept Taoism as a religion on a par with Christianity, Islam, Judaism, or Buddhism. To begin with, to most nonspecialists, the very term "Chinese religion" is an oxymoron. When the West became aware of China in the sixteenth and seventeenth centuries, it was as the land of a ruling class of philosopher-sages on the one hand and benighted superstition-ridden peasants on the other. For most of the intervening centuries, China has been far away, and few Westerners have ventured there. Until very recently, those who did reach China were largely missionaries intent on rescuing the "heathen Chinese" or exploiters of one stripe or another with little interest in the practices or ways of thinking of the people they moved among.

Resident foreign scholars were few. Unlike India, where the British might shudder at certain aspects of Hinduism but could not deny that it was a religion, China was never closely administered or studied by "outsiders." Thus Taoism never underwent the scrutiny and close study that leads to the recognition of the "religious" nature of what at first contact might be labeled rank superstition.

In addition, the common Western view of China as a land of something called "philosophy" on the one hand and superstition on the other is a natural outgrowth of our unwillingness to concede serious religious thought to the "others." Orthodox Buddhism has dignity in Western eyes, and many Chinese have been Buddhists. To many, that was the only real religion the Chinese knew until the Christian missionaries arrived.

When French, English, and Scottish thinkers of the Enlightenment needed an exemplar for the rule of reason, however, Jesuit reports from China seemed to supply one. Even under the most rational order, rulers need guidance, and the belief arose in the West that the rulers of China guided their actions by sagely precepts thousands of years old. They also showed their good sense by suppressing superstition when it reared up in the form of enthusiastic popular cults that could lead the people from the path of reason.

The Chinese have bought this vision of themselves and their

ideal rulers as creatures of reason, East Asian Enlightenment figures guiding the superstitious masses. The model transfers itself
easily to the Marxist state. Religious practices can easily be labeled
"cults" and ruthlessly suppressed, whether in the fourth century
A.D. or the twentieth. It has taken the dedication of a few scholars,
scattered around the world (in China itself, in France, Japan, the
United States, and elsewhere), to start the rediscovery of the one
native Chinese religion, Taoism.

Yet the materials showing that it is a religion have all along
been there to be investigated. The *Daozang*, the great encyclope-
dic collection of sacred texts published in 1442, consists of more
than a thousand different works. To find one's way around this
body of data requires immense scholarship and patience. As Professor Robinet characterized it in the introduction to her earlier
work on Taoist meditation:

Imagine a situation in which a Christian *summa* had been put together, a
collection where we could find side by side St. Thomas Aquinas and Gilson,
but also all the hagiographies of Saint Theresa of Lisieux. The poems of St.
John of the Cross might show up next to medieval mystery plays and par-
ish hymns. There we would find the Gospels, the *Spiritual Exercises* of St.
Ignatius Loyola and *The Imitation of Christ*. The story of the Holy Grail and
the Latin works of Meister Eckhart and Basil Valentinus would appear be-
side the sermons of Bossuet, the writings of the hesychasts, along with
treatises on demonology, descriptions of local cults, and various rural superstitions. The result? An omnium-gatherum of which it would be said,
"This is Christianity."

Since, as we shall see, one fundamental definition of Taoism is
that it embraces everything in the Taoist canon, it is worth pausing
over the nature of this great collection. It includes the works of
philosophers like Laozi and Zhuangzi, pharmacopoeias, the oldest
Chinese work on medicine, lives of the saints, long ritual texts
larded with sympathetic magic, imaginary geographies, dietary
and hygienic prescriptions, anthologies of hymns, speculations on
hexagrams in the *Book of Change*, guides to meditation techniques, alchemical texts, and collections of moral precepts.

The *Daozang* is thus a huge accumulation of documents, and a
complete account of it remains to be made. Tables of contents

have been produced, but a table of contents in and of itself does not help us to understand the complexity of this body of texts. Some texts appear several times under different titles; others have the same title but different contents. Others contain within themselves versions of texts that appear elsewhere independently. Most of the texts are not signed or dated. Many are considered marginal to the great central schools and traditions of Taoism. For all these reasons, the confusion is even more complex than in the hypothetical Christian *summa* outlined above. The only points in common between certain texts that are called Taoist is that they are part of the *Daozang* and often, but not always, concerned with the quest for a particular kind of immortality, a yearning for something that lies beyond our knowledge and experience that sets the seeker apart as "different," not part of the mainstream of Chinese society.

Gradually the shape of the Taoist religion is being disinterred. Its various strands are being rewoven into a coherent whole. We have no trouble accepting that the enthusiastic gospel singing of a Southern Baptist congregation is a manifestation of the same religion as the chanted eucharist in an English cathedral—it's all Christianity. In the same way, the technicolor rituals of modern Taiwanese Taoism are linked to the lofty search for immortality of a Tang aspirant to enlightenment.

We would be intolerant of any depiction of Christianity as "incoherent and jumbled," because it lumped together the ritual of the Greek Orthodox church, the Catholicism of the celebrants at Chichicastanengo, and the stern doctrine of a Calvin or a Hus into a single, eternal phenomenon. We would rightly insist on discrimination and a sense of history. And to talk of Taoism only as a "way of thought" or a philosophy is to deny its nature as a religion offering the adept a pathway to salvation. The act of categorizing in one way implies the denial of another kind of definition. Fortunately our vision can be rectified.

This book undertakes this task, in its journey through time and across vast areas, both geographical and spiritual. It is a study of change, of permutation, of the alternation between group ritual and private devotion, between public acts of sacrifice and sanctification and individual strivings for salvation. It is a history of both a religion and the various churches that make it up, of cosmology and pontiffs, of ecstatic wanderings through the stars and the courting of gods through song and dance, of texts revealed in the kiss of a woman of jade and the careful bookkeeping of misdeeds and retribution.

I should like to acknowledge the help given to me by several people in the course of completing this translation. Foremost among them, despite his death five years ago, stands my husband, Edward Schafer, who encouraged me to translate this book in the first place, supported its acceptance by Stanford University Press, and, until his death, helped me over many obstacles along the way. It is to him that I owe most of the knowledge I have of things Chinese and things Taoist. Stephen Bokenkamp at Indiana University has been a sturdy right arm since that time, reading the first version of this manuscript and answering many of my questions. The late Anna Seidel gave me solid advice, and her "Chronicle of Taoist Studies" and Taoismus: die inoffizielle Hochreligion Chinas *have been constantly to hand as I translated this work. Other advice has reached me from Donald Harper at the University of Arizona, Franciscus Verellen of the Ecole Française d'Extrême-Orient (Paris), and R. J. Zwi Werblowsky of Hebrew University, Jerusalem. The punctilious and often inspired editing of John R. Ziemer at Stanford University Press has improved the text immeasurably. But the sternest watchdog over the quality of this translation has been Professor Robinet herself, both by mail and in the times we have spent together in her houses in Valpuiseaux and Cadenet.*

Phyllis Brooks
University of California, Berkeley

Author's Preface

In this history of Taoism I have tried, as succinctly as possible, to present the genealogy of this religious tradition: to show the wide varieties of factors that came into play over a long period of disconnected eras as well as the coherence of its development and its constant absorption and integration of outside contributions. My main aim has been to trace the major lines of doctrinal evolution rather than to retell the events that marked its history. Such a history of the religion still needs to be written, but at present it can only be sketched, given the current state of research in the field. Official Chinese historiographers are almost silent on the subject, since Taoism has always been considered a private matter, secondary to the official cult, except for the great ceremonies ordered by the emperor. It thus has no place in the dynastic annals, which are dedicated above all to giving an account of official political facts.

Within the growth of the Taoist religion, we shall see how certain recurrent themes are treated in different ways in different eras and by different sects: among these themes are the Ultimate Truth, immortality, the Sage, the genesis and the end of the world, retribution for good and evil acts, representations of heavens and hells, and the connections between the body and the spirit, between living and dead, between man and society, and between mystical experience and the social form of a religion. The organization of this book has been dictated by my concern to reveal the origins of these various trends. It is both chronological and thematic, but the chronology is somewhat fluid because of the way Taoism developed: as it assimilated new features in the course of its development, it never ceased to develop the old ones. Thus the Celestial Masters sect, which is chronologically the first to develop a structure, is treated at the outset (Chapter 3), but it continues to exist down to our day. The Shangqing tradition (Chapter 5) took shape during the fourth century A.D., but its glory years were under the Tang (618–907). The Lingbao sect (Chapter 6) emerged a little later, gave birth to an immense body of ritual that incorporated part of that of the Celestial Masters, and then grew even larger under the Song (960–1279). The movement toward consolidation that took place under the Tang and the influence from Buddhism, which came in during the same period (Chapter 7), actually had their beginnings much earlier, in the fourth and fifth centuries. Interior alchemy (Chapter 8), which developed mostly under the Song and the Yuan (from the tenth to fourteenth centuries), had begun in the eighth and ninth centuries and continues to be practiced today. Despite all this, the order I have adopted corresponds to a real chronology of events and lets me highlight major trends and their unfolding.

The reader should thus keep in mind that the various strands that make up the substance of Taoism interweave constantly and that each movement that appears retains the qualities of its predecessors and often contains the seed that will give rise to its successors. There were, as well, constant borrowings among the various sects and traditions. Even though in the following I present each of the practices and each of the major themes within the framework of the sect that developed it most markedly or that was its major initiator, no one sect can lay exclusive claim to any of these practices or themes. Thus, the ritual recitation of texts became important with the Lingbao movement, but it already existed from the beginning of the Celestial Masters school and continued to play a role in the Shangqing movement. Exorcistic practices were particularly characteristic of the Celestial Masters, but some Shangqing texts were also intended to exterminate and drive off demons as a prologue to other practices more typical of this movement. The healing procedures characteristic of the Celestial Masters also existed in other schools, and, far from being abandoned, the demonology behind these procedures has continued to be developed throughout the history of Taoism. The battle against popular cults began under the Celestial Masters, but continued during the Six Dynasties and the Tang and later. Methods of achieving longevity have existed at all times and in all schools; they will be discussed in Chapter 4 only because that chapter is dedicated to the movement that placed most importance on them.

As I trace the way the religion grew and developed, I have chosen to highlight only the most striking phenomena; this has necessitated many difficult choices: I did not want to overload a brief account of a subject that is still poorly known and that has not up to now been the object of any such summary. For this reason I have had to resign myself to many omissions. Still, I hope that this history of the development of Taoism will act as a guide to interested readers, leading them to deeper studies that have been made on certain points. An exhaustive bibliography on Taoist studies forms part of Anna Seidel's "Chronicle of Taoist Studies in the West, 1950–1990" (updated by Franciscus Verellen in 1995). Full references to these valuable guides appear at the beginning of Suggestions for Further Readings at the end of this work. This list mentions only works in Western languages relevant to each chapter of this book, but these works in turn guide the interested reader to those that exist in Chinese and Japanese.

Chronology

Dynasties	Cultural benchmarks	Taoism
	Confucius 551-479 B.C.	
Warring States 403-222 B.C.	*Chuci*, 3d-2d c. Han Feizi (ca. 233)	*Daodejing*, 4th-3d c. *Zhuangzi*, 4th-2d c.
Qin 221-206 B.C. Han 206 B.C.- A.D. 220	Emperor Wu 140-87 Formation of *fangshi* cosmology and the school of Yin-Yang and the Five Agents Dong Zhonshu 179?-104? B.C. Wang Chong A.D. 27-91	*Huang-Lao* school, 2d c. *Huainanzi*, early 2d c. Deification of Laozi, A.D. 166 *Laozi bianhua jing*, end 2d c. Celestial Masters, end 2d c.
Three Kingdoms 220-65	*Xuanzue*, Wang Bi 226-49	
Western Jin 265-316		
Six Dynasties, 316-589	Introduction of Buddhism among intelligentsia 4th c.	Ge Hong (ca. 280-ca. 343) Shangqing revelation, 365-70 Appearance of Lingbao texts, 397-402

Dynasties	Cultural benchmarks	Taoism
Sui 589-618	Great Buddhist schools, 6th-7th c.	Great anthologies of the 6th-8th c.
Tang 618-907		Sima Chengzhen 647-735 Chongxuan school: Cheng Xuanying, fl. 631-50 Du Guangting, 850-933
Five Dynasties 907-60		
Northern Song 960-1127	neo-Confucianism Zhou Dunyi 1017-73 Shao Yong 1011-77 Zhang Zai 1020-77 Cheng Hao 1032-85 Cheng Yi 1033-1108	New rituals "Interior alchemy": South: Zhang Boduan, d. 1082 Bo Yuchan, 1134?-1220? North: Wang Zhe 1123-1170 Qiu Chuji 1148-1227
Southern Song 1127-1279	Zhu Xi 1130-1200 Lu Xiangshan 1139-92	
Yuan 1279-1367		Chen Zhixu, fl. 1329-36

Taoism

GROWTH OF A RELIGION

Introduction
Definitions and Controlling Concepts

Definitions

In China Taoism is one of the "three teachings" (along with Buddhism and Confucianism). It took shape only gradually, during a slow gestation that was actually a progressive integration of various ancient lines of thought. No precise date can be set for its birth, and the integration of outside elements into the religion has never ceased. If we add to this the enrichment of Taoism throughout its history with new revelations or new inspirations, we can see how open a religion it is, constantly progressing and evolving, and how difficult it is not only to date its first appearance but also to define its boundaries. Thus we can legitimately say, along with Livia Kohn, that "Taoism has never been a unified religion, and has constantly consisted of a combination of teachings based on a variety of original revelations."[1] Thus it can be grasped only in its concrete manifestations, and it is meaningless to speak of Taoism as a whole. As I put this work together, however, I came to realize that if there is a single thread that runs through Taoism, it lies in its genealogy and in the cumulative and integrative process of its evolution.

One way to define its boundaries is by means of the Taoist Canon (*Daozang*). We could take it as axiomatic that all the texts in the Canon are Taoist texts and must be a part of any history of Taoism. This would not be completely erroneous, yet it would be necessary, on the evidence, to exclude certain of the texts; thus we would be left to wonder about our criteria. I hope to shed some light on this question in the course of this study.

As for the date of the birth of Taoism, this is obviously related to the definition we give this religion. Some people define it as the recognition by Cao Cao, in A.D. 215, of the Tianshi (Celestial Masters) church. This is a historical fact—attested, convenient, definite—but we cannot reduce the beginnings of Taoism simply to this church alone. Another possible date is that of the Shangqing (Great Purity) revelation between 365 and 370, since this revelation integrated and organized earlier data, which were then collected into a corpus that enjoyed an officially recognized status. Thus we have at least two separate dates corresponding to two complementary tendencies in Taoism. Both developed an organized form, and almost all subsequent Taoist traditions are descended from them in one way or to one degree or another.

However, we cannot rely on such formal, exterior criteria to assign a precise date to the appearance of Taoism precisely. Some scholars refuse to speak of "Taoism" before the development of a formal organization for the religion, but I believe that we must take into account the often marginal, informal nature of Taoism, which characterizes it more than any other single feature. In fact, we would be diminishing and betraying the religion if we did not take its marginality into consideration. It is thus absolutely necessary to reveal its multifarious origins and expose its roots if we want to understand its later structure and deep meaning.

Taoism is not like Confucianism, which has a civil status and can trace its origins to a single historical person recognized by everyone as a leader and to a precise set of classics that constituted the basis of its teaching throughout its history and evolution; Taoism has neither date nor place of birth. It has never stopped moving, transforming, absorbing. Its history shows us how ceaselessly it has proceeded by "recursive loops," taking up its past like a bundle under its arm in order to travel farther toward new horizons and, as it goes, gleaning all sorts of treasures along the way. We shall see that this pattern of development has made Taoism the most precious repository of one strain in China's cultural past, a past that remains alive in it, preserved in Taoism even when official doctrines discarded it.

During this account we shall often have to consider the question of the relationship between what are called "philosophical Taoism" and "religious Taoism." This distinction is much like the distinction between contemplative Taoism and the kind of Taoism seen as "purposeful," that is to say "involved" or "directed" (what I render as "practical" Taoism), concerned with the achievement of longevity. Much ink has been spilled on this matter, but usually, it must be admitted, by people who have not studied the texts of "religious Taoism." We shall see again and again that this division has no significance. I share the view that this is a nonexistent problem arising from only an apparent difference, one that exists in all religions and mystical systems—the difference between self-discipline (techniques, training, etc.) and either the results of this discipline or the speculations that can accompany or crown it. Clearly there is a difference between the person climbing a mountain and the person on the summit, between the mountain guide and his apprentice. Obviously sometimes the learner gets stuck halfway up or even turns back. Although some Westerners have used such differences to distinguish two separate currents in Taoism, this conclusion seems to me to derive from the fact that few in our culture are actively familiar with *techniques* that lead to mystical experience. As a result, we have trouble understanding the relationship between what may seem to be prosaic procedures and the ultimate goal behind them. Some adepts themselves forget this relationship, but there are plenty of Taoist masters to remind them of it. Certainly there were men, especially emperors, who sought only to increase their life span and improve their health, and others who were seeking only magical powers and, eventually, power over others. For our purposes it is unimportant to determine whether these were misappropriations of techniques originally intended to lead to ecstasy and mystical experience. All that is important here is that they were so used and that Zhuangzi himself knew them and alluded to them, clearly not by chance.

Thus, it is possible and appropriate to add another constituent to our definition of Taoism: the combination of or addition to techniques of immortality, with the ultimate aim of achieving an experience that is at least religious if not mystical. In the same way, it is arbitrary to separate, as some tend to do, the empirical approach to longevity techniques from the theoretical thought and the search for coherence that supports or controls them. Nothing objective can be said about such a separation except that the two endeavors have not always gone hand in hand. Ever since we humans began to think, right down to our own days of scientific research, we have always tended toward a dialogue between empiricism and theory: each in turn leads and advances the other, in a series of confirmations and refutations.

Another, similar question is the relationship of Taoists to the public arena, the world of men. Once again we see a dualism. Some Taoists have isolated themselves in retreats; others have not. We cannot, however, speak of fundamentally different currents. These are simply two possible options. Each individual may choose one or the other, according to temperament and depending on the period he lives in: in times of political troubles and insecurity, more people have always chosen to retire from the world. Such a choice can also depend on the level of spiritual development attained, a feature common to the history of all forms of mysticism. We shall see on several occasions how these two options are closely connected, just like the "philosophical" and "practical" aspects of Taoism.

Beneath its official, recognized form, even when it was established at court, Taoism has always led a secret life, at least in part. This happened both among the lower classes and among the educated, for whom an attachment to Taoism was a private affair. This secrecy makes it impossible for us to be sure we know everything about it. It is, however, proper and important, if we want to understand the form of this religion, not to limit it or dilute it, while keeping in mind its many faces and the immense and varied influence it has had.

It is not easy to set limits to our subject, let alone define it, given the delicate and shifting frontiers between Taoism and popular religion on the one hand and between Taoism and the thought of the intellectual elite on the other. The best basis for judgment, it seems to me, is to be found in the statements made by its most devoted spokesmen. Even if these are sometimes not completely sincere and yield to sociopolitical pressures, we can reach a satisfactory overall view by taking into account all these voices; the occasional contradictions and rare sectarian anathemas can be sorted out.

Unlike some Chinese historians, I insist on distinguishing Taoism from popular religion, in matters both of belief and of practice. I do this with confidence primarily because that is what the Taoists themselves do: their position is quite consistent. We need not accept the statements of those historians or others outside the religion who, either out of ignorance or for political reasons, tend to discredit Taoism by conflating it with unsystematic, popular religious movements. Such movements draw equally on Confucianism, Taoism, and Buddhism, and the Taoists decry them just as much as the Confucianists do. True, the relationships between the "three teachings" and popular beliefs have often been ambiguous. Various borrowings and dialogues have always gone on, as Rolf Stein has demonstrated.[2] Such interchanges between "popular religion" and "established religion" exist in all societies, as M. Meslin has so clearly explained.[3] This whole question of relationships is a vast one and would take too much time to debate within the framework of this book, which I want to keep to a modest size. I shall limit myself to noting here and there some mutual borrowings, but I will not take up the whole question of the absorption of local cults into certain types of Taoism. On this subject, the reader can consult the relevant works listed in the Suggestions for Further Readings at the end of this book.[4]

For the same reason I shall avoid lingering too long over certain aspects of Taoism that have been taken to be characteristic of the religion, but that, although they have certainly colored Taoism, actually belong to the whole corpus of things Chinese and are the property of a wide segment of the population that do not consider themselves to be Taoist in the least. Here I am referring to various matters of hygiene—techniques of breathing, gymnastics, and sexual practices. In this case, too, I shall defer to what the interested parties themselves say about these matters—the Taoists on the one hand and the practitioners of these techniques on the other hand.

It is hard to know precisely where Taoism starts and stops in the speculations of the Chinese intelligentsia. Some have considered the members of the Xuanxue (the School of Mystery) as "neo-Taoists," since Laozi and Zhuangzi are the basis of their studies. Obviously we cannot consider all the commentators on these authors as Taoists; that is not an adequate criterion. E. Zürcher has correctly drawn a line of demarcation between the authors of the Xuanxue and someone like Ji Kang (223–62), preoccupied with longevity techniques.[5] However, the border cannot be drawn neatly. Someone like Guo Xiang (d. 312), recognized as a member of the Xuanxue and much influenced by Zhuangzi, holds to a philosophy that is both naturalistic and mystical, very close to that of the Taoists. He is quite unlike Wang Bi (226–49), who seems to have been a speculative metaphysician and, as far as one can judge, never advocated any existential experience. On the other hand, all those in the neo-Taoist camp—Wang Bi, Guo Xiang, Ji Kang, and Ruan Ji (210–63)—despite their differences, emerged from a single tradition and a single milieu in which ideas were mutually exchanged. In fact, we could say that with neo-Taoism we are in the presence of undeniably Taoist influence and at the same time looking at a phenomenon that will have repercussions on Taoism itself (see Chapter 8). We are on the margin, where an atmosphere of give-and-take prevails, and we can consider this margin as part of the Taoist sphere of influence, even though I allude to it only in passing.

With the limits established, what common traits can we find in all Taoist traditions, or at least in enough of them to let us regard these traits as establishing essential connections among them?

Cosmology and Anthropology

The theoretical substrate and language of Taoism derive from the principles of the Yin-Yang school and the Five Agents, *wuxing*, also translated as "five elements." The definitive formulation of this cosmological system took place under the Han, on the basis of more ancient elements. These theories later became most highly developed and applied in the fields of Chinese medicine and Taoism (originally mingled).

The universe is constantly re-creating itself in a continuing evolution (one of its names is the "ten thousand transformations"). This is a constant process of genesis and development from a single component, the Primordial Breath, or Energy (*Yuanqi*), which is neither material nor spirit. Some historians translate *Qi*, "Breath," as "energy-matter," but this is not valid except in the case of a few authors from the eleventh and twelfth centuries on. This translation has led to the attribution of a form of materialism to Chinese thinkers, who almost unanimously (from Zhuangzi on) place Qi at the foundation of the world. But even though the word "materialism" still has some meaning in our day when the very idea of matter itself has been eroded, it meant nothing in ancient China. The only interpretation of the vague word "materialism" that could fit in this framework is that of "natural philosophy," which fits Taoism very well, along with, perhaps, all Chinese thought.

As a basic dynamic, Qi, which is neither matter nor spirit, existed before the world did, and everything that exists is only an aspect of it, in a lesser or greater state of condensation. Condensed, it becomes life; diluted, it is indefinite potential; this concept dates back to Zhuangzi and was reiterated by all classical Chinese thinkers down to the time of the neo-Confucianists in the Song. It is described as a force that expands and animates the world in a turning motion by which it spreads and distributes itself into every corner of space and time. It has no detectable existence outside the forms that it takes and their transformations; the "instruments" or beings that reveal it are its particularized forms, and when they disappear, they become Qi again. Qi does not "persist" alongside these manifestations; they *are* the forms it takes, and what it is. When they disappear, the Qi passes into another form; it is both a principle of unity and coherence that connects all things and a potential, an immanent life force in the world that is knowable only in the various changing aspects it assumes.

Thus, on the one hand, we have an energy distinct from concrete forms, without their exterior existence; it is the source of these forms, that is, it is indefinite and infinite potential, remaining when these concrete forms disappear. On the other hand, the concrete forms that this energy takes are nothing but Qi. Because of this dual possibility of residing in a form and going beyond it, Qi gives form to (*zao*) and transforms (*hua*) everything, in a two-sided operation, since it defines the fixed form but also changes it constantly. *Zaohua* is the Chinese equivalent of our word "creation," but it is a creation without a creator. The only constant reality is Qi *in its transformations*, the continuous coming and going between its undetectable, diluted state and its visible state, condensed into a defined being.

The transformations of this Breath began with its division into a pure, light breath, Yang, which moved upward and created Heaven, and an opaque, heavy breath, Yin, which moved downward and formed the Earth. The true nature of Heaven is to be pure and moving, and that of Earth is to be opaque and fixed. The pure and mobile Yang is the "yes," the Self, the principle of oneness (pure), of identity, of continuity, and thus of expansion and movement. The opaque and stable Yin is the opposing principle: it is the "no," the Other, the Two, which sets a limit on the expansion of the continuous. It is division, rupture, the different, the discontinuous, contraction, and immobility. In the *Yijing* (*Book of Change*), the Yang is represented by a solid line and is termed "rigid"; it is true to itself. The Yin, shown as a broken line, is called "bending"; it is openness to possibilities of difference. As a unit, the Yang "begins": all identity, every individual, begins in the One, in a principle of continuity, of identity with itself, opposing the Other, the different, which defines its limits. Thus the Yin "completes." One cannot exist alone; it needs the Other to show where it ends, to define its contours. This is why transparent, expansive Yang-Heaven holds a logical priority (it was formed first) over the opaque Yin-Earth, which was formed second, even though the one cannot exist without the other. (This "priority" is a matter of speaking; it does not refer to chronology.)

The world is a circle (or a sphere) divided along two planes. The vertical cleavage goes from north (seen as down below) to the south (up above): on the left-hand side is Yang, on the right-hand, Yin. The other cleavage is horizontal and marks off an upper half, which is Yang, from a lower half, which is Yin. As a result, the sphere is divided into four parts: the southeast is Yang, and the northwest is Yin; the other two parts are made up of Yin and Yang combined, with the northeast sector, according to the Chinese, that of Yang in Yin, and the southwest that of Yin in Yang.

Another such division sees two extreme poles, an upper and a lower one. The upper is marked by Heaven, pure Yang, and the lower, the Earth, pure Yin. They enclose an intermediate zone, the world of Man, made up of a union of Yin and Yang. In this world, there is no Yang without Yin, and, hence, neither pure Yin nor pure Yang. Thus Yin and Yang cannot truly be defined, as is sometimes done, in simple terms of darkness and light, feminine and masculine, passive and active principles, potentiality and actualization, turning inward and spreading outward, and the like. Rather, Yin and Yang are lines of force, directions whose nature is to cross and mingle, to play against and with each other, both self-generating and self-propelling, disappearing and alternating; and their function is to define a double syntax of polarity and ambiguity. Neither can exist at its extreme; at that point it reverses into its opposite, an idea the Chinese express by saying of the Yang that it gives birth to the Yin that it carries inside itself, and vice versa. We might well say that Yin and Yang are two extreme poles, two ideals with only a conceptual and didactic existence. They do not exist in the world, but all things tend toward them to one degree or another. They govern a liturgical division of the universe and its double generative process. They are the basis of the difference that gives rise to attraction, as well as of all development and the multiplicity produced through their combinations.

But Yang and Yin also testify to the basic Oneness that underlies the world, by the close correlation that binds them together.
They illustrate the dynamic of opposites, a dynamic that can be
seen only in pairs whose opposition shows in the law of alternation that governs their functioning. One member of the pair does
not operate at the same time as the other, in the same place, unless it is virtually within the other. When one dominates, the other
retreats into a state of potentiality, a stored, compressed, and in-
tensified force. All this occurs in a moving oscillation made up of
continual shifts from one to the other, from one toward the other.
Just as Qi is revealed only in the transitory forms that it takes, Yin
and Yang reveal themselves only in their exchanges. The rhythm
and principle of the play of Yin and Yang are essential in all of
Taoism, but the practitioners of interior alchemy have concentrated and reflected on their interactions to the greatest extent.[6]

When it comes to gods and the divine, yet another ambiguity
complicates the meaning of Yin and Yang. Heaven is the domain of
light, it is Yang, and so are the gods. Since they are invisible, they
belong as well to the realm of Yin, which is also that of hell, earth,
and the dead, the realm through which one reaches the celestial
domain. Taoists constantly confronted this ambiguity and its apparent contradictions. The Taoist must become Yin, concealed in
the divine darkness, and "feminine" or receptive to celestial infu-
sion, but at the same time Yang, pure light. Yin and Yang cannot
exist without each other. They are equals, yet Yang takes precedence. This paradox is easily resolved: seen horizontally as two
complementary poles in human life, they are clearly equals; if
aligned vertically, Yang is always upper and dominates Yin, an indication that the desired fate of the human being is transcendence
of self.

To Yin and Yang are added another set of rubrics, the Five
Agents: Wood (or vegetation), Fire, Earth, Metal (or minerals), and
Water. This system of categories divides and classifies the world in
both space and time, a strategic layout governing the organization
of the world into five "constellations" as well as the articulations
among them. Each of the five categories is defined by a set of
equivalences determined by one of the Five Agents. Thus, Wood,

Fire, Metal, and Water each govern one of the four sectors of the world: east-spring, south-summer, west-autumn, and north-winter, respectively. Earth is the center, providing cohesion to the whole. In the circle that makes up the round of the Five Agents, Earth controls transitions from one Agent to another, and it is located at the frontier that both joins and separates them: that is, Earth is where we cross from the areas of the Yang Agents (Wood and Fire) to those of the Yin Agents (Metal and Water), at the boundary of each of the sectors, the crossing points from one to another.

This system is combined with the Yin-Yang system, and Wood is called "young Yang," Fire "great Yang," Metal "young Yin," and Water "great Yin," with Earth as "central harmony." Like Yin and Yang, the Five Agents are "breaths," dynamic principles: according to the succession of the seasons or the path of the sun during the day, each in turn, in its "time" and "place," activates its sector. For example, in springtime and/or in the east, everything connected with the Wood category is particularly strong and active, whereas in summer, it is the turn of things belonging to Fire. Hence the universe is governed by a *changing equilibrium* in which the various forces that animate it are never equal, but dominate it in turn in alternating hegemonies. This equilibrium is founded in a balanced play of alliances and antagonisms among the Five Agents, which form a self-regulating system. The system inspires a sense of confidence in the normal course of nature, expressed in a mistrust of human intervention, the foundation for the Taoist "nonintervention" (*wuwei*).

All creatures are categorized, listed under one of these rubrics. All kinds of resonances and influences can be discovered in the system founded on this principle of classification, some of them opposing, some of them attracting. A basic guiding principle is that things which resemble each other go together. As a result, certain actions and interactions can be explained or predicted, both in space and in time, horizontally (from one end of the world to the other) as well as vertically (from earth to heaven).

We shall not delve more deeply into this aspect of Chinese cosmology here; its complicated operations have been widely studied by Western scholars, and many works provide details of the correspondences controlled by the rubrics. In Taoism, in which the Five Agents are deified in many forms, this system provides the structure both for meditation and for the liturgy, to which it supplies a syntax.

Taoist cosmological speculations have paid particular attention to the relationship between the One and the many and to the articulations of this relationship. In a direct line from Laozi, Taoists hold the idea (which later became a part of all Chinese thought) that the fundamental division of the world into two opposing tendencies, Yin and Yang, passes through another stage before giving rise to the "ten thousand beings": the Three, which is the union of the Two without which no life can exist. From the One (the Supreme One, the Taiyi, which resides in the Big Dipper) these tendencies pass, after the division into Two, to the Three, which gives life to earth. From there they go into either the Four (the four cardinal directions, the four trigrams) or the Five (the Five Agents), and then to the Six (the four cardinal points, plus up and down), the Seven (seven stars of the Big Dipper), the Eight (eight points on the wind rose), the Nine (eight plus one, culmination of the first numbers, totality, nine regions of the world), and then to the various astro-calendric categorizations: the Ten (ten cyclical signs), the Twelve (twelve calendrical signs), and 24 or 28 (24 "breaths" of the year, one per fortnight; 28 zodiacal constellations), and from there, to all sorts of multiples, especially of nine and twelve (for example, 360 for the 360 days of the year). A whole section of the Taoist pantheon takes its significance from this schema, and the role of the adept or priest lies thus in "descending" from the One to the many and then "going back up."

"That which is most precious in the world," Man, as a cosmic being, is the third term (his emblem is the number Three), on a par with Heaven and Earth, which cover and support him, enfold him, give birth to him, and nourish him like a mother and father. Made up of these two primordial Principles, he is the hybrid mediator, the element that both unites and separates them. The world was made when a man, Pan Gu or Laozi, grew from an egg and parted Heaven from Earth. In Chinese civilization, Man par excellence, the unique Man, is the Emperor; in Taoism, the meditating adept (not necessarily a male human being) is supposed to become this unique and total Man.

The universe is unified in both its substance, Breath, and its structure into Three (vertically) and Five (horizontally). Thus the human world and the physical human being must be constructed organically in the same way and are homologues of each other. The makeup of the human being parallels that of society and of the universe. The universe is a cosmic Man, a makanthropos, as illustrated by the myths of Laozi and Pan Gu—each with a body that both made and is the universe—and, in turn, each human being is a little universe. Each of us is made up of Yin and Yang— Yang on the outside and Yin within in the case of men, and the reverse for women. Yang is on the left side of the body and in the upper half, Yin on the right side and in the lower half, and each of the organs, internal or external (for example, the skin, eyes, and mouth) relates to one of the Five Agents. Each of the key numbers in the cosmogony enters into the organization of the body: two eyes, three parts of the body (head, chest, abdomen), four limbs, five "viscera," six internal organs connected to the viscera, seven and nine orifices, 360 joints (corresponding to the 360 days of the year), and so forth. The body's development and balance follow the same laws as the universe and obey the rules that govern the movement of the hours and the seasons.

The constituent parts of human beings are thus in a one-to-one relationship with Heaven and Earth. Our five "receptacles" (*zang*, usually translated "viscera")—in order, the liver, heart, spleen, lungs, and kidneys—are governed by the Five Agents; they are to us what the planets are to the celestial vault and the five cardinal mountain peaks to the Earth. Thus, we are related in a very precise way to that which is over our head and under our feet.

Beyond this, according to an ancient Chinese tradition that seems to have become widespread beginning in the third century B.C. and that appears both in the *Chuci* (The songs of Chu, an ancient collection of poetry) and in the Confucian classics, the human being has two kinds of soul: *hun* souls, which are Yang and of a heavenly nature, and *po*, which are Yin and earthly. These souls try to leave the body and return to their point of origin, with the *hun* souls going up to heaven and the *po* souls entering the earth. Here again are two dynamic principles that pull human beings upward and downward and that we must harmonize and maintain within our bodies, because they are the source of life. When these souls tear apart and escape, that is death.

The human body is also analogous to the organization of a nation, which was conceived as an organism throughout Chinese tradition. Many Taoist texts present this concept in a precise and developed way, relating each organ to an official, with the ruling organ, the heart, the homologue of the prince.

Circularity and Cycles

As we can see from the preceding discussion, the world is a closed whole, a sequence of nested enclosures in time and space, marked off by reference points that can be transposed from one scale to another. Everything is circular ("it turns and rebegins without end" is a constant Taoist leitmotiv). The end and the beginning join. Although the reference points are constants, ensuring rhythm and order, transformations are unceasing, and the possibilities of change through repetition, renewal, and rediscovery are innumerable. This is an *active* circular process: although the Taoist conception of the world and of time is cyclical and its followers see a constant return to alternations between the Yin and Yang forces, a repetitive unity conforming to a basic model, there is still a strong idea of progress, of stages, and of development, but more in the unfolding of the destiny of creatures, things, and events than in that of the world itself. This view is revealed in terms that express the idea of progress, such as *hua* "transform," *xiu* "exert oneself," *bian*, "change, metamorphosis," *lian*, "purification." Such terms are essential to Taoism and provide the raison d'être of its discipline: a constant renewal is under way, shown in the different successive forms taken by various versions of truth, the constantly changing appearances assumed by the gods, the idea of the progressive training of the individual human being who proceeds during this life toward a final consummation, which is the accomplishment of the "Divine Decree" (*ming*), of the mission of self-perfection that

Heaven has given that person. But this progress is also a Return. Because they are cyclical, the Taoist time and the Taoist world permit a new beginning, a rebirth. They are a time and a world of eternal transformations. The clearly enunciated nature of this circular time is that it is reversible, say the Taoists, unlike the ordinary time known by human beings, which permits no return and proceeds linearly toward a single end, death.

However, we have here not a closed circle, but rather a multitude of circles, of multiple worlds. The limited world opens out to the infinite, whose structure of nested enclosure lets us move from the greatest to the smallest and back, from the center to the periphery and back. It has a moving center, which is not a single point. One can move away from this center or approach it; it opens on the infinite that cannot be fixed but is, however, a fundamental benchmark. Perhaps one difference between this way of thinking and that of the Yin and Yang and the *Book of Change*—from which Taoism has otherwise drawn so much—lies in this idea of the Center, which is fundamental. In the *Book of Change*, the idea of the point of departure is most important. Obviously the distinction is full of shadings: the Taoist Center is also the point of Origin, and the Sage of the *Book of Change*, who is the one that sees the first movement of things, is situated in the Center. The difference is one of emphasis.

A world seen in terms of centering and outward radiation contrasts with that of the Confucians, in which things are ordered by layout and distribution, on the model of a pyramid rather than that of a circle. This difference is illustrated by the two different ways of representing the relationship of the One to the many. In Taoism, there are concentric circles, and a primordial Oneness *gives birth* to the Two, then the Three, and only then to the articulated many, arranged according to symbolic numbers. The neo-Confucians, following Shao Yong (1011–77) and supported in this by Zhu Xi (1130–1200), envisage squares arranged in flat layers placed on top of each other to form a pyramid, and a primordial Oneness that multiplies by *repeated divisions*, moving down from one to two, then to four, to eight, and so on, in a geometric progression. This difference can also be seen in conceptions of society: more hierarchical among the Confucians and more egalitarian among the Taoists.

The Taoist's Position in the Cosmos

In this dynamic world, which he himself has built, the Taoist sits at the center, as a kind of demiurge, a creating spirit: by locating, connecting, identifying, and naming, he gives meaning to the cosmos—not in order to intervene in its operations but in order to integrate himself into it and make it into a framework and tool of thought. His activity is one of understanding and questioning, which modifies the spirit and the being, setting up a relationship between reality and the individual, who gives meaning by interrelating and interacting.

Progressing toward an individual's spiritual salvation and physical health consists of returning to square one, to the Center, to take up the brand-new world, at the moment of its genesis, and follow its development in the right order and direction. Laozi frequently mentioned the return to the point of Origin, which forms another of the constant leitmotivs of Taoism, whatever its particular form: "return to the native village," "return to the One," "return to the Original father and mother," "return to the Pearl" (the origin of the world), return to the "state before Heaven and Earth," going back to the moment when movement and stillness are mingled, when everything perpetually produces everything and regenerates and reorganizes itself.

Then the Taoist builds a systematic whole, according to the comprehensive relational scheme provided by Yin and Yang and the Five Agents, a miniaturized world that provides him with an exemplar and exploratory model, one that can even be represented in a diagram, a sort of symbolic representation made up of space-time reference points making special use, among other guides, of astronomic and numerological benchmarks. As a cartographer and surveyor, he marks out the land, draws frontiers—that is, boundaries as places of transition and trading—and represents time and space in simple geometric schemas: square, octagon, and circle (moving from Earth to Heaven). Once he has this easily representable practical arrangement, one that can be made to function at several homologous levels, he populates it with gods and various concrete images. Finally he introduces the process of change.

In addition, he takes into account opening, going beyond, unthinkability, transcendence of the immanent Tao, the belief in immortality, and faith in another world, another truth, another body. Until the rise of neo-Confucianism around the eleventh century, Taoism (together with Buddhism, from roughly the fourth century when it clearly became part of Chinese thinking) formed the complement of classic Confucianism. Confucianism rejected the fantastic, the inexplicable, the distant (*yuan*, semantically close to *xuan* "mystery"), the incredible, and the extraordinary, all of which the Chinese felt to be Taoist notions. Here once again it is difficult to define Taoism and draw the line between it and primitive popular beliefs.

It is at this point of opening that we find the Taoist heaven, its pantheon, its paradises. The Taoist world is oriented not only toward the center but also upward, which are one and the same idea. The Taoist constructs the center and places himself there, but he must also ensure a bond between up and down, must ascend and descend again—which he does by using various symbolic instruments, such as divine cosmic entities or the trigrams.

Through and beyond the world, he rediscovers the Prime Mover. To do this, he must proceed by a conscious effort from his introduction into this world in which he both organizes himself and organizes the world, a world he reconciles to himself and assimilates and to which he reconciles himself. By contemplating himself and by locating himself in a correctly aligned geometric schema that represents the cosmos as a sort of mandala, he finally identifies himself correctly and ritually in relationship to the axis of the world. Further, by rediscovering the Prime Mover, he rediscovers the order of the world and his own relationship to it. The two movements go together. He must impose order on the world to reconcile it to himself and to reconcile himself with himself. Once he has done this, he can rediscover the Prime Mover that resides within all things, within himself, in the world and beyond. As he returns to the Prime Mover, he can understand and integrate the entire universe coherently.

The depth of the Confucian (especially the neo-Confucian) misunderstanding that Taoism opens a huge gap between the interior and exterior worlds,[7] exalting the former and debasing the latter, should be apparent. Although it starts from within the individual, the purpose of Taoism is to create a clear and close union between the interior and exterior world. The exterior world is understood above all as consisting of Nature, the cosmos, the natural world, and only secondarily of human society.

The Pantheon

The Taoist pantheon is vast and has grown constantly over the centuries, with each school, each revelation, adding its own gods to the older ones, who have usually been retained rather than replaced. Already in the fifth century, Tao Hongjing's (see Chapter 5) first effort at compiling a list of the Shangqing gods occupied 28 pages. Later lists are much longer. I shall not try to give a full account of this pantheon, but make only a few general comments.

With rare exceptions, Taoist gods are impersonal; the exceptions, however, did multiply as Taoism took on a more and more popular cast and local saints and legendary heroes were incorporated and blended into the pantheon. Unlike the popular saints, the gods, apart from Laozi himself, have no biographies except for purely ethereal, celestial, and impersonal ones.[8] They are distinguished more by descriptive titles than by names. Rather than individuals, they are the personification of roles. Even when they have a genealogy, like the daughters of the Queen Mother of the West, they are said to have been born from the "transformation of the Primordial Breath" and not from an embryo, unlike the spirits of the dead. A distinction must be made, however, between the gods of ritual and those of the body. Although the latter, because of their function, are gods with the same nature as the former, they nevertheless seem more familiar, more intimate. The gods of ritual are generally either abstract concepts, or hypostases of natural forces, among them the ancient gods of the earth, of the River, of the rain, and so on. Gradually three great gods emerged in ritual and formed the supreme triad. These are the Three Pure Ones: Yuanshi tianzun (the Venerable Celestial One of the Original Beginning), Daojun (Lord Dao), and Laojun (Lord Lao). They are clearly avatars of the three Lords, the patrons of the three great divisions of the *Daozang*, and are closely connected to the ancient fundamental triad of Three-One (*sanyi*) or Three Primordials (*sanyuan*).

We must make a basic distinction, however—one that is reflected in ritual—between the gods over whom the adept has power and those before whom he must bow. The situation of the adept and priest is a double one: on the one hand, he is the master of certain gods whom he assembles and puts to work in his service, and on the other, he must solicit them and receives sanctification from them. When it comes to the gods he commands, he is in the same position as the emperor vis-à-vis his officials and certain gods. But this power does not extend to the great celestial gods (who have no clearly defined functions), any more than the emperor has power over Shangdi (the emperor on high).[9]

Yet all these gods are really only one, or, according to another formula with the same general meaning, they are all emanations of a single instance, the Tao. Their multiplicity represents progressive differentiation from the Formlessness and the One that is the origin of all things. This differentiation follows the same plan as that of the cosmos: from one to three, to four or five, and so on up to 12,000 and more.

Such differentiated gods can reside in the body of the adept; they can enter, or they can emerge from it. There are those who emerge, like the four heraldic animals of the four cardinal points (dragon for the east, tiger for the west, phoenix for the south, and tortoise wrapped in a snake—or "dark warrior"—for the north), but sometimes they come from the four poles to enter the room of the devotee. What really matters is the coming and going, which makes manifest the path of communication between the interior and the exterior worlds.

Taoists and Society

More than just a pattern of belief or a doctrine, Taoism is a way of life. It is this perhaps that gives it its special nature. Over the centuries it has always remained the province of initiates who are the respectful possessors of revealed texts not divulged to the masses. Preaching plays no part in it, but replies are given to questions. It is an individual concern or, rather, the concern of various lines of priests. Because of this, it retains an elitist and marginal stigma, even though its activities take place among the people. Taoism has evolved in a world apart, like those it constructs in its meditations and ritual, a world always somehow marginal to society, within it but testifying to another world beyond.

The Taoist world is above all the world of nature rather than that of society. Taoists are renowned for this. Often hermits in distant mountains, they are the ones who taught the Chinese to appreciate landscapes with the feelings that we recognize as Chinese. Toward human society their attitude is more complex. Ji Kang (223–62), Ge Hong (ca. 280–ca. 343), and many others, especially during periods marked by political troubles, claimed that one could not seek immortality while living at the court. But Dongfang Shuo (154–93 B.C.), "the immortal exile on earth," councillor at the court of the Emperor Wu of the Han, believed that one could find immortality anywhere. There have been, as we shall see, Taoist masters who played an important role as advisers to emperors, whereas others—a classic theme in hagiographies—refused to go to the court, feigning illness when an emperor ordered them to appear. Still others put themselves above all society and the highest human authority, like the Old Man on the Riverside who gave striking proof of this when the emperor reproached him for not acceding to his requests. He rose physically into the air as he revealed his teaching, so demonstrating that he was no longer under imperial authority. Some masters initiated emperors into Taoist arcana, and others, great men like Ye Fashang (ca. 614–720) and Chen Tuan (ca. 906–89), refused to honor rulers' demands to reveal alchemical secrets and replied either that the search for the Philosopher's Stone was useless and dangerous or that it was not an emperor's province.

Appearances to the contrary, there was actually a close connection between exercises aimed at developing interior spiritual perfection and public rituals (both imperial and mass) to pacify spirits. This is attested in the work of a certain Bo Yuchan (fl. 1209–24), grand master of interior alchemy and a great ritualist. We shall see that for a great many Taoists good order in the universe corresponded to good order in the empire and the world of men, although the means of accomplishing this could differ radically from one school to another. Some recommended wise direction and counseling of the emperor; others advocated benign neglect, relying on the fact that order would come naturally if men did not interfere. Yet others called for great ritual propitiatory ceremonies. The goal of Taoism is often claimed to be that of simultaneously and in a single process bringing order to the individual and to the empire (expressed in the common axiom *zhishen zhiguo* "order one's person and govern the empire"). The sending to the emperor of Heshang gong's (fl. 170 A.D.) commentary on the *Daodejing* (the holy book attributed to Laozi) is one of the most famous examples of practicing this double principle and inspired a school of Taoist commentators on this work.

Furthermore, the emperor and the Taoist master also share a close, fundamental affinity, one that is often seen throughout Chinese history. As we shall see, Taoists possess objects whose sacred character resembles that of the talismans testifying to the legitimacy of the imperial power. Their talismans are said to have been passed down from ancient rulers (now viewed as mythical), making them in a way their spiritual successors. The investiture of a Taoist master is comparable to that of an emperor, for it places him at the center of the world, like the master of all humankind, and puts him in touch with celestial powers. This rite of investiture dates to the Zhou dynasty during the first millennium B.C., with roots in feudal rites of sworn allegiance and delegation of power.[10]

Finally, the popular nature of a certain level of Taoism puts it in the position of supplying an intermediary between the ruler and the people, who are supposed, according to Chinese belief, to be the mouthpiece for the divine will that legitimizes supreme power. On several occasions Taoist masters have been called on to confirm the legitimacy of a new emperor or a new dynasty by providing moral and religious support through a solemn enthroning.[11]

A creative power in his chamber, a prince in his body, the Taoist officiating at a ritual also plays a role like that of a sovereign and his representatives in the empire. The latter are ultimately "cult agents" charged with maintaining order both in the human domain and in nature, warding off natural scourges, rebellions, floods, and evil spirits. The Taoist, as we shall see, does the same thing in his liturgy. The Taoist's exorcistic function originally belonged to the government, either to the emperor or to the prefect, who had to protect the people against attacks of spirits that brought sicknesses or unleashed natural disasters.[12]

Taoist priests have always been an important element in the life of the people to whom, through their exorcisms, rituals, and healing, they bring an element of security in the battle against demons and disease. There are many accounts in novels or in collections of anecdotes accepted as true, such as the *Yijian zhi* of Hong Mai (1123–1202), of the presence and frequent positive intervention of Taoist priests in popular life, even when they are otherwise depicted as corrupt debauchees.

Taoism's natural propensity toward a certain marginal, sometimes anarchistic nature, the bonds that have always existed between it and the lower classes, and its claims to ensure the proper ordering of the world created a combination that often made it the starting point for uprisings inspired by Taoist-style ideologies. These revolts were most often against the greed of tax collectors. The first was that of the Five Bushels (see Chapter 3), which was followed, among others, by those of Sun En in A.D. 399 and Zhong Xiang in the twelfth century. This fact contributed to a certain mistrust on the part of those in authority, a mistrust that often led them to discredit and belittle Taoism, representing it as a mishmash of superstitions and magical practices.

The world of the Taoist is a "rational" world, in the wide sense sometimes given to that word. That is, it is organized according to a system that is logically conceivable because it is structured. It is also a symbolic world, in that it calls on a symbolic way of thinking. But myth properly speaking has little part in it, although some ancient myths have been integrated into it, and the myth of the Sage, central to the world of Taoism, forms an exception to this rule. The combination of these various tendencies—dream, structure, symbol—have permitted Taoism to be an intimate part of the birth and development of both Chinese science—medicine, astronomy, mathematical speculation—and letters and arts. Driven by a holistic worldview, it has reabsorbed and digested, regathered and amalgamated, and preserved and organized various strands of Chinese culture, from Laozi and Zhuangzi to the "skilled men," ancestors of scientific thought in China, from Chinese myth to certain Buddhist and Confucian phenomena—all without ever abandoning its own identity and coherence. It has thus become a constantly operating force coordinating and synthesizing Chinese traditions, beginning from its basis under the Han and then integrating more and more elements as they appeared. Taoism has impregnated all of Chinese civilization, not only poetry and painting (as is well known and has been abundantly demonstrated, even if much work remains to be done) but even Chan Buddhism (the Japanese Zen). Even more it has penetrated ways of thinking, especially with its ideas of the void, of exalting and giving life to the figure of the Holy Man, of reading the *Book of Change*, with which it has always been closely connected, and of using symbolically and actively the interplay of Yin and Yang, the trigrams, and the hexagrams.

1

The Warring States
(Fourth to Third Centuries B.C.)

The period of the fourth to third centuries B.C., a time of great intellectual vigor, saw the emergence of all the fundamental features of Chinese culture. This is also true of Taoism. For the moment, we need simply to mark four components that signal the beginnings of Taoism: "philosophical Taoism," techniques for achieving ecstasy (most clearly represented in the *Chuci* and the *Zhuangzi*), practices for achieving longevity and physical immortality, and, finally, exorcism. These four components often coexist in various proportions in the work of a single author or group.

Philosophical Taoism: Laozi and Zhuangzi

Laozi and Zhuangzi are the so-called fathers of Taoism. Liezi is often included in this grouping but is omitted here because the work bearing his name includes texts from widely separated dates and was actually compiled in the third to fourth centuries A.D. It also includes nothing that bears on the development of Taoism.

Laozi

Laozi may or may not have existed, but according to legend he was an archivist and soothsayer from the late Zhou dynasty. He is most commonly called Laozi, "Lord Lao," but also Lao Dan, supposedly his personal name, and Laojun, his name as a god. In any case, his position in the history of Taoism is ambiguous. Although some consider him the "father" of Taoism, others see him as only one sage or holy man among many others. On the other hand, as a god he is one of the triad of supreme gods of liturgical Taoism, and his person is surrounded by legends pregnant with meaning. Furthermore, the work attributed to him, called the *Daodejing* (also referred to, as are the works of Zhuangzi and Liezi, simply by its author's name, as the *Laozi*, or as the *Five Thousand Word Classic*), is constantly quoted, especially in texts on breathing techniques and interior alchemy. Even if he is not the dominant figure in Taoism that some Western readers have believed, Laozi is a major figure and the *Daodejing* an important source of Taoist references.

The title *Daodejing* means approximately "Book of the Way and Its Power (or Tao-given quality of a thing)" and seems to derive from the fact that the work is divided into two halves, one beginning with the word *dao* and the other with the word *de*, "power, charisma." It supposedly dates from the end of the fourth century or beginning of the third century B.C. The text was established around the end of the second century A.D., in the versions by Wang Bi and Heshang gong. Beginning in 737, it was raised to the rank of a classic and was taught officially. In a history of Taoism we are concerned with the *Daodejing* for its specific contribution to the religion and its significance in this regard among other currents of Chinese thought.

First of all, of course, it presents the idea of the Tao, a word that means "way" or "method" and by extension "rule of life" or "process." In the *Daodejing*, it takes on for the first time the meaning "Ultimate Truth." This Ultimate Truth, one and transcendent, is invisible, inaudible, imperceptible (*Daodejing* 14), not usable and not namable (*Daodejing* 1), an unmarked trail that one must travel to know. Located beyond all relationship of differentiation, all judgment, and all opposition, it is neutral. As such, its truth cannot be approached except apophatically, by negative statements. But it is also the source of all life, fertile (the "mother," *Daodejing* 1), widespread and universal ("pervasive," *tong*), rich in "promises," and the only sure reference point (*Daodejing* 25): in this it is no longer neutral but a positive way.

The term "Tao" would retain the meaning of absolute truth and is frequently employed in this sense throughout the Chinese tradition, not only by Taoists. But it is in this meaning that it would give its name to Taoism and, first of all, chronologically speaking, to "philosophical Taoism," to the *daojia* (literally, "school of the Tao"). In the bibliographical catalog of the *History of the Han*, the most ancient bibliography that we possess, *Daojia* is the title given to the category that includes the works of Laozi, Zhuangzi, Liezi, other works that refer to Laozi or are connected with the Yellow Emperor (Huangdi; see below), and finally some texts that have disappeared and about which we have little information—in all some 37 works. In this catalog a brief overview of the *daojia* defines it in terms very close to those used in the *Daodejing*.

The *Daodejing* also introduces a vision of the world that has remained the ideal of the Taoist sage: serenity, withdrawal from the "affairs" of the world, and rejection of established values as too abstract, relative, and incomplete, too conscious and artificial, in favor of a spontaneous way of life with none of those virtuous efforts at imitation that engender competition and vanity. If we let Nature operate in us and outside us, the world will go along very well on its own, since the hand and spirit of man only introduce disturbances into it. I do not intend to explain the whole philosophy of the *Daodejing* but only to sum up what later Taoism retained of it, and I will limit myself here to the ideas of the "spontaneous" (*ziran*) and non-action or non-intervention (*wuwei*), whose fundamental principles are presented in the Introduction.

Brief mention should, however, be made of the relativistic tendency of the *Daodejing*. The paired ideas of beauty and ugliness, good and evil, being and non-being, all imply and support each other, and each term has no meaning except in relation to the other. They are opposing logical concepts that exist only correlatively, every opposition implying correlation and membership in a common whole. Of course, this general idea can be found outside the *Daodejing*. It is one of the specific characteristics of Chinese thought found in the *Book of Change*, for example, and lies at the basis of the thought of the Yin-Yang and Five Agents schools. In the *Daodejing* different consequences are drawn from this idea, however. Whereas the *Book of Change* holds that man can know and even prevent coming events by understanding the laws of Yin and Yang, the *Daodejing* deduces that thought based on oppositions cannot arrive at the Ultimate Truth, which is One. This gives rise to the precept "Cease all thinking."

From this precept derives the notion of the void. In the *Daodejing* the idea is presented in a concrete fashion: it is the interstitial void that permits movement, the hollow in a vessel that is receptiveness (chap. 11); on the human level, it is mental and affective emptiness, the absence of prejudices and partialities, that lets things play out freely. We have here a functional and existential void. This is the first enunciation of the concept of the Void in China, an idea that would subsequently evolve and be further refined.

The fundamental lesson expressed in the *Daodejing* as it appears in Taoism is this: Ultimate Truth is one, working spontaneously with no need for conscious human intervention. Thought cannot reach it because thought is by nature dualistic; one can reach it only by letting it operate naturally. Thus, the *Daodejing* preaches emptiness and renunciation. It also gives us the image of the Sage, an image that will be greatly enriched and elaborated later. In the *Daodejing* he is above all a holy ruler, or a sort of demiurge, an anthropomorphized form of the Tao: as the unmoving director of the world, he ensures its well-being by his own unsuspected existence, by his inactivity, simply by placing himself at the central One.

In the *Daodejing* this image of the Sage is combined with a "primitivizing" tendency that is not unique to Laozi and is found in many currents of Chinese thought, including later Taoism. In a primordial, ideal human society, the ruler, here the Sage, does not intercede; natural law operates spontaneously and without impediments so that order is established harmoniously among human beings as well as between humans and Nature and humans and Heaven. Cosmogonic metaphors, connected with mythological themes—those of Chaos and of the Mother—call for a Return to the heart of primordial undifferentiation, to Childhood, and, on a social scale, to the happy and harmonious anarchy of our original condition.

This in brief constitutes the ideological or philosophical contribution of the *Daodejing* to Taoism. However, certain famous commentators and commentaries like Heshang gong (probably 2d c. A.D.), the *Xiang'er* (ca. late 2d c.) and the *Jiejie* (at the latest, beginning of the 4th c.) read the *Daodejing* differently. Their reading concentrates on a different aspect of the work, one that supplements the preceding summary without invalidating it. They read the *Daodejing* as the final intellectual result of practical efforts to achieve longevity, as a theoretical treatise referring to these practices and alluding to them in a coded form. It contains incomprehensible formulas over which commentators and translators have stumbled throughout the centuries—for example, "the spirit of the valley," the "obscure female." Such expressions, especially when we compare them with the text of documents recovered in recent archaeological excavations, may well contain allusions to longevity practices. The excavated texts dealing with long life date from the third and fourth centuries B.C. In addition, the *Daodejing*'s poetic, metrical form suggests that it acquired an incantatory power through the kind of rhythmic, repetitive recitation that strengthens a practice. It was intended to be sung and memorized, as it actually has been in certain religious sects. Thus we have plenty of evidence that this way of understanding the *Daodejing*, even if it does not exhaust the possibilities for interpretation, can no longer be ignored. If we do so, we run the risk of remaining ignorant of one of its dimensions.

The *Daodejing* is open to many interpretations and even demands them. Arthur Waley and R. G. Hendricks have shown that it contains plays on words and reveal the ambiguous nature of its language.[1] This reflects a recurrent attitude in Taoism. The text has been understood in different ways and according to all sorts of belief patterns: Legalist, Confucian, Buddhist, and Taoist. But, for our purposes, we can note that Taoist authors throughout the centuries have commented on, interpreted, and cited the *Daodejing* through the precise optic of their own Taoist practices, however varied they may be. For some Taoists, tradition leads them to see this work as containing allusions to longevity practices; for others it is the obscurity of its formulations that gives rise to this opinion. Its most enigmatic expressions have been the selections of choice for interpretations of this type. The "mysterious female" (chap. 6) has been the Heaven-Earth pair that, transposed into terms of breathing techniques, is that of the nose (Heaven) and the mouth (Earth). The expression "embrace the One" (chap. 22) has been used as the name for meditation exercises. *Mianmian ruo cun* from chapter 6 (meaning "continually—like a thread that unrolls—and constantly") was often cited to illustrate the continued imperceptible rhythm that breathing should take. Images like "know the white and hold onto the black" (chap. 28), this "confused thing born before Heaven and the Earth" (chap. 25), "indistinct and vague," in which "there is an image," "a very trustworthy essence" (chap. 21), and many others have evoked for Taoists either special meditation methods or certain phases in ascesis, or even the fundamental cosmological and anthropological data in their thought.

Zhuangzi

To Zhuangzi, who probably lived in the fourth century B.C., is attributed a work that bears his name and that, as is well known, ranks among the founding texts of Taoism. However, only part of it was probably written by him (the first seven chapters, according to the opinion of most scholars who have studied the matter). The rest was probably written in the third and second centuries B.C. The whole book is quite heterogeneous—a fact that can be explained in part by the writer's or writers' intent to mislead the reader—but it is considered in the Chinese tradition as a whole and has been accepted and studied as such. The version that we have today dates from its most famous commentator, Guo Xiang, who reconstructed and in part emended the original text. It is the only version known by the Chinese since that time, and it is on the basis of this version we shall examine the contributions of the *Zhuangzi* to Taoism. In order to keep our sights firmly fixed on this perspective, we must set aside some of the most important features of this text, one of the richest and most complex ever produced by the Chinese.

Zhuangzi takes up where Laozi left off on the themes of unity, serenity, and rejection of the world, but develops, systematizes, and gives them more strength and body. He distinguishes himself from Laozi by a greater tendency to interiorization. Sociopolitical concerns disappear, and non-action no longer has social or political connotations and becomes purely a state of consciousness. Rather than a dream of a golden age, the theme of unity becomes an aspiration to become one with the moving tide of life. A mystical element integrates and at the same time deepens the dialectical relativism of Laozi.

Undoubtedly the image of the Sage is the most important link that ties Zhuangzi to Taoist tradition. The dominant and probably the most characteristic feature of this image is the belief in the existence of beings in human form who are immortal and endowed with supernatural gifts. The *Zhuangzi* is the oldest extant text that gives us a vivid and precise description of them. Whereas the Sage of Laozi is an immense tutelary and exemplary being, to which some brief indications seem to give supernatural powers, in Zhuangzi's work the Sage takes on a whole new dimension, to the point, from our perspective, of constituting a positive pole, complementary to the negative pole represented by his whole apophatic, critical, and even destructive side. To the questions that Zhuangzi poses and leaves unanswered on the level of discourse and conceptualization, the Sage is the only reply, on another level, in a theological realm. Here again I discuss only those features of the Sage of Zhuangzi that seem to have specifically prefigured and probably inspired the Taoist Sage.

An analysis of the texts about the Sage in the *Zhuangzi* reveals that the Sage is characterized mainly by complete physical and mental freedom: he is outside this world, he wanders freely (*you*), enjoying himself at the four corners of the universe; he is one with the universe in its mystery of making no response, in his "nature beyond the norm," in the diversity that envelops him so completely that he draws from it an infinite capacity for change and varied responses, without destroying in the least his single, uni-

fying identity. Liberated from all moral, social, or political concerns, all metaphysical uneasiness, all concern for effectiveness,
all internal or external conflict, and all wants and desires, his spirit
is free and lives in perfect unity with himself and with everything.
He thus enjoys a completeness (or "integrity," *quan*) that gives him
great power, and he assumes a cosmic dimension. Logically, and
unlike the Sage of Laozi, he does not rule, even by non-action. To
list the descriptive terms most often applied to him, he is One, and
thus "alone" (*du*) and unique, "true" (for, according to Zhuangzi,
everything that depends on the external world is artificial), and
"heavenly" (*tian*), a term that also means "natural," as opposed to
"human," since man imposes on nature reference marks and tools
that have a utilitarian quality. He carries in himself his own source
of life, with which he is one.

The description of the Sage given by Zhuangzi in the first
chapters (accepted as the oldest in the book) is probably the earliest testimony not only to what would become the foundation of
all Taoist hagiographies, but also to what would become one of
the most powerful sources of the Taoist quest. The Sage rides on
the wind, or the "white clouds." His body never withers: "fire does
not burn him, and the water does not cover him." Neither hot
weather nor frost affect him, neither man nor beast can harm
him (chap. 6; see also chap. 17). In addition, he assumes a cosmic
dimension, a fundamental feature of the Sage throughout the history of Taoism. Zhuangzi gives memorable details about the Sage
that bear witness in a striking fashion to the contemporary existence of techniques for achieving longevity: "divine men" do not
eat the "five cereals," they inhale the wind and sip on the dew,
they ride clouds and air, they drive flying dragons and wander
beyond the four seas.

With this final description we come to a new element, taken up
at many points in the *Zhuangzi*, one that would become a characteristic feature of Taoism: mystic flights. Opening his work with
the magnificent flight of the giant phoenix, Zhuangzi alerts us
right away that this is an important theme, a key to his whole en-
deavor. On many occasions, his characters (Zi Qi, Lao Dan [that is,
Laozi], Nie Que, chaps. 2, 21, 22) fall into an ecstatic state, leaving

their bodies "like dead wood" or "lumps of earth," and their hearts (the seat of both intellectual and affective life) like "burned-out cinders."

Zhuangzi provides the mystical element of Taoism, revealed as an integration of the cosmos, unlike the structured system modeled on Yin-Yang and the Five Agents. This integration is worked out by establishing a spatiotemporal pattern based on distinctions and relations set by the workings of our world. It is an integration based on all being. This integration is not formal and objective and reveals itself not through any norms intended to establish and manifest it externally, but through an overflowing internal feeling that is the result of meditation and ecstasy. Zhuangzi, in this respect, contributes a fundamental complementary element that would almost always be superimposed on the other, more rational one. The mystical experience that he advocates is, in fact, the result of practicing the very exercises that he questions, that he sees it necessary to transcend. He is both the glorious, jubilant advocate of the results of these practices and the voice constantly reminding Taoists that they must go beyond them. This would be one of the roles he would fill for them: he represents the "rejection," the "forgetting" of these practices because he is the culmination that signals their abolition, and in that role he is always invoked by the masters as the one who justifies their practices by going beyond them.

Zhuangzi saw two principles as the basis of life, and they would have the same importance to the Taoists, as is shown in their shared view of vital mechanics. These basic elements are breath (*qi*) and "essence" (*jing*). Zhuangzi was the first who wrote that "life is a concentration of breath; when it concentrates itself, that is life, and when it disperses, that is death," a sentence repeated constantly by authors who often seem to have forgotten its source. This *qi*, this "breath," neither matter nor spirit, sole substance of the world, is the Primordial Breath of the Taoists, the object of most of their techniques for achieving longevity. The other element is *jing*, a term that would later take on various meanings; for now we may simply recall that Zhuangzi on many occasions insisted that in it is "the root of the body," (chap. 22), that "the Sage puts a high value on it," and that it must be kept "intact and whole" and must not "be agitated" (chap. 15).

Zhuangzi often stressed the quietism preached by Laozi: silence plus absence of thought. This is how Guang Chengzi advised the Yellow Emperor: "Do not look, do not listen, embrace your spirits in quietude, and your body will be correct of its own accord; be calm, be pure, do not exhaust your body, do not stir up your essence, and you will be able to live long; if your eyes see nothing, if your ears hear nothing, if your heart/mind knows nothing, your spirits will preserve your body, and your body will live long; take care of your interior, shut yourself off from the exterior; too much knowledge leads to destruction" (chap. 11; in Chinese thought, the heart was always the seat of both thought and emotions). The "heart/mind fast" ("Let your will be one; do not listen with your ears but with your heart/mind; do not listen with your heart but with your breath" [chap. 4]), the metaphor of the pure and undisturbed "mirror of the heart" (chap. 2) that can reflect the whole world in its entirety without distortion, "seated meditation" (*zuo-wang*, literally "sit and forget") in which one "abandons his body and its parts, rejects perceptual sharpness, leaves his form, drives away his knowledge, and becomes one with the Universal Greatness" (chap. 6)—these are also lessons that the Taoists would value highly.

The "heart/mind fast" is a corollary to a formula that Zhuangzi picked up from Laozi: "preserve the One." This became a key term in Taoism for various meditation techniques. Once again, Guang Chengzi taught this lesson to the Yellow Emperor: "I preserve the One," he said, "and remain in Harmony; thus I was able to reach the age of 1200 years" (chap. 11). And again Laozi replied to Confucius when asked how he entered an ecstatic state: "Achieve the One and identify yourself with it" (chap. 12). Bi Yi, echoing him, taught Nie Que, who immediately fell into ecstasy: "Let your body be right, your contemplation one, and Celestial Harmony will arrive; gather in your knowledge; let your acts be one, and the spirits will come into your dwelling" (chap. 22). We already have here, as in other passages of the *Zhuangzi*, all the principles of later Taoist contemplation: the "correct body" (*zheng*), which suggests a body that is both healthy and in the correct position for meditation, and the "coming of the spirits into the dwelling," which reminds us of the appearance of divine spirits, either in the meditation room or in the body of the Taoist, their "dwelling."

All this corresponds to the attitude of concentration and shutting out of the exterior world, the world of the senses—an act of retirement and breaking off that, in fact, is only the complement and preliminary state of the movement outward that opens onto the holy state of rejoicing in a continuous universe where there is no longer any interior or exterior. The closing of the world of the senses is a closing of the narrow world of the individual, the world limited by his sensory perceptions and his own thoughts, but at the same time an opening to cosmic unity through the cosmic "breath" ("do not listen with your ears, nor with your heart and mind, *xin*, but with the 'breath'"). Here are all the fundamentals of Taoist meditation.

Neglected during the Han, the *Zhuangzi* returned to high esteem during the third and fourth centuries A.D., especially once the Chinese had been brought face to face with Buddhist speculations. Zhuangzi has an important place within Taoism from the fourth century on: Ge Hong refers to him often as do, later, the Shangqing and other Taoist texts.

The "Chuci," the Wu, and the Fangshi

The *Chuci* and Ecstatic Journeys

Some of the features characteristic of Zhuangzi can be seen in another movement with which he shares certain affinities, to the point that it is possible and even probable that Zhuangzi is only the visible member of a once widespread movement that has left few traces; this other movement is that of the *Chuci*, the "Songs of Chu," which are our main evidence for its existence.[2]

These elegies, a group of poems dating from the third and second centuries B.C., are the product of the "shamanism" of the south of China, which possessed an autonomous culture; they reveal a form of religion quite different from that of northern China. The central individual is not the sovereign, or the head of the family, as in the official religion, but an inspired priest visited by a god with whom he or she enters into hierogamous relations of an undeniably amorous nature.

The poems seem to be the written remnant of the tradition of the *wu*, a term translated roughly as "shaman" or "sorcerer." These *wu*, although a feature of a religion very different from the official cults, had representatives among the priesthood of the court. According to the *Zhou li* (a work that seems to describe ritual practices under the Zhou dynasty), these priests (or, more often, priestesses) had to "sacrifice to the distant spirits," which they invoked and to whom they gave names, and to bring rain with dances. They also knew how to make themselves invisible and effected cures by means of medicinal plants, spells, and imprecatory formulas, *zhu*, a term later used to refer to Taoist invocations. Many Taoist practices descend in a direct line from this tradition, even though Taoists insist that they have no part of it.

The signs of the connection between the texts from this tradition and Taoism are many and often surprisingly precise. Here are only a few examples from the poems. The names of immortals like Chisongzi or Wang Qiao reappear among the legendary saints of Taoism. The poems allude to practices characteristic of later Taoism: the appearance of gods; mystical journeys of the soul in distant, mythical countries, which recall those of Zhuangzi and Liezi, or in heavenly lands (in the *Yuanyou*), where far from the dust of this world, the poet no longer sees anything, neither the sky above nor the earth below (a reference that will recur word for word in the Shangqing texts, the Taoist movement showing most influence from the *Chuci* tradition); and feeding on cosmic effluvia, to which Zhuangzi referred and which have names that will be the same in certain Taoist texts. The very name of the priestess possessed by a god, *lingbao*, is a term that quickly assumed, as we shall see, an enormous importance in Taoism.

The theme of the ecstatic journey in particular has played a major role in Chinese tradition under the aegis of Taoism. It is found in poetry, where it constitutes a genre all its own, and in all visual meditations of the Shangqing type, which appear almost everywhere in Taoist practices, both in solitary meditation and in the liturgy.

The *Fangshi*

The tradition of the *wu* shamans is connected to those persons known as *fangshi*, or *daoren* or *daoshi*—all terms that mean "man of techniques." Under the Han these terms, according to the perceptive insight of Kenneth DeWoskin, designated individuals one could term "outsiders," that is, those who were marginal or peripheral from the point of view of official Confucianist doctrine. They dedicated themselves to astrology, magic, medicine, divination, and geomancy, as well as to methods of achieving longevity and to ecstatic wanderings. Ideologically they were close to the School of Yin-Yang and the Five Agents and were usually solitary seekers who tried to find the laws behind natural phenomena. They were the possessors of a parallel wisdom, transmitted from master to disciple, either orally or by means of secret texts. Various lines of transmission can be traced, but these do not really constitute separate schools because the lines intersect: a single disciple did not hesitate to work under several masters and to follow various disciplines.

The genealogy of the *fangshi* is complex. They go back to the archivist-soothsayers of antiquity, one of whom supposedly was Laozi himself; under the Shang and the Zhou they were the only ones who knew divination and writing. The "magicians" of the northern countries of Yan and Qi described in the *Shiji* (Records of the grand historian)[3] may be considered among their ancestors (Chavannes, *Mémoires historiques*, 3: 436–37). In the late third century B.C., they "possessed techniques of immortality" and knew how to "break up, dissolve, and transform their bodies"—a practice the commentator expressly connects with Taoist practices of "deliverance from the corpse" (see below, p. 101).

The belief in physical immortality, later so characteristic of Taoism, dates to the eighth century B.C. and is attested by inscriptions on Shang bronzes. Various pre-Han works mention this belief. In the nation of Yan, it was strong enough that, in the fourth century B.C., kings even sent men in search of the isles of immortality, just as the emperors Shihuangdi of the Qin and Wu of the Han would do later. These isles of immortality, where plants that would guarantee longevity grew, are described in Taoist texts that have picked up the myth. Many of the legendary immortals of the Yan kingdom have entered Taoist hagiographies. About this time people seem to have begun to think that immortality could actually be achieved by taking drugs, the first step on the path toward alchemy.

No theoretical works from these Yan and Qi "magicians" survive, and until recently we have had only a few, brief historical mentions that did no more than suggest the nature of their practices and beliefs. Texts discovered in recent archaeological excavations, however, have given us better knowledge of their practices, and although the documents so far unearthed contain only fairly prosaic practical instructions stripped of any general theory, they confirm that longevity techniques much like those later associated with the Taoists definitely existed as early as the third century B.C.

Some of these documents discuss sexual and respiratory practices intended to lengthen life, and in terms close to those used centuries later. Thus some passages treat "sexual methods and regulation of the divine breath," intended to let one "see for a long time and live in parity with Heaven and Hearth," and "avoidance of cereals." There are many references to the circulation of sperm within the body, to the absorption of cosmic breaths that have the same names as those given in the *Chuci*, to "deliverance of the body," and to gymnastic movements imitating positions taken by animals—all just as Zhuangzi envisaged them, and as Ge Hong in the fourth century A.D., and many others would later describe them.

Exorcism was one of the particularly characteristic activities of the *fangshi*, just as it was among the *wu*. Sorcerers, called *lingbao* here too, are mentioned as chasing demons away, alongside the *fangxiang*, the official court exorcist. A recently unearthed third-century B.C. text contains, assembled into a collection, much of the data summarized above. In addition, mention is made of the "Step of Yu," an exorcistic "dance" that the Taoists continue to perform to this day. It dates at least to this period, along with the exorcistic postures found centuries later in texts on "Taoist gymnastics" (*daoyin*). This text also lets us reconstruct the connection between exorcistic practices intended to ward off harmful demons, and therapeutic practices intended to ensure good hygiene and good physical balance. We see, in other terms, the evolution of exorcism toward medicine, a shift from conceiving sickness as caused by demons to seeing sickness as the result of an imbalance. We also see a shift from demonology to angelology: in this text identification of demons is based on knowing their names, which are listed in specific registers. This idea anticipates Taoist techniques for mastering demons, gods, or spirits, also concretized in registers containing lists of the spirits' names.

The divinatory activities of the *fangshi* relied on cosmological and calendrical speculations. Under the Han these speculations would color the Chinese view of the world and then come to underlie that of the Taoists. During this period arose the system of correspondences based on the theory of the Five Agents and its connection with the sexagesimal calendar as well as with numbers and musical notes.

Guanzi

Three chapters of the *Guanzi*, a composite "philosophical" work of uncertain date but certainly pre-Han, allow us to point out once more the connection between "philosophical Taoism" and the techniques for achieving longevity, of which they provide a striking example. These three chapters, the "Nei ye" (Interior work; the esoteric tradition), which apparently date from the end of the fourth or the beginning of the third century B.C., along with two others with the title "Xin shu" (Art of the heart), join what has been called the "quietism" of Taoism with allusions to longevity practices. The idea of the Tao is almost the same as that in the *Daodejing*: ineffable, distant, impossible to locate in space, the Tao is "without root, without stem, without flowers or leaves." It is, however, the source of all life and close to everything. It cannot be understood by the senses, but may be comprehended by the "heart," which is the seat of thought and feelings. When the heart is free of all emotion, it is the equal of the Tao and is described in comparable terms. The Sage (*sheng ren*), as in the *Zhuangzi*, is at the same time moving, flexible, able to accommodate himself "to the times," but forever unchanged. Above he touches Heaven, and below, the Earth. He fills and knows completely the whole world.

The paths to this state of wisdom or holiness lie mainly in the "correction" (*zheng*) of the body (the term that Zhuangzi uses), the pacification of the heart (making it free of all emotion), concentration, and the control of the breath. These procedures are referred to later in Taoism by the classic terms "hold onto the One," "keep the One," "obtain the One," "keep the breath." As in all Taoist tradition, the body is compared to a nation and its organs to officials, with the heart as the "prince." Certain passages are close copies of passages in the *Zhuangzi*: "Can you concentrate yourself? . . . Can you be One?" (Rickett translation, 164). Others express basic axioms of Taoism: regularity of the breath is tied to peacefulness of the heart; spirits come spontaneously when interior peace reigns. The balanced life preached in this work (do not eat too much, do not think too much, do not be too abstemious) is one we shall see again and again in Taoism. Several comments suggest a transformation of the body: sight and hearing become acute, one of the qualities of the Sage; the "nine orifices" take on a universal dimension; the bones and tendons are strengthened. The main tools of this transformation are the "breath," which has a cosmic quality in its refined form of "essence" (*jing*); the heart/mind (*xin*), which, as we have seen, share qualities with the Tao when it is pure and quiet; and the "spiritual breath" (*lingqi*), which is in the heart and which is "so great that there is nothing outside it, and so small that there is nothing inside it," a clichéd phrase often used to describe the Tao.

Like the *Daodejing*, this text is also rhythmically composed as if it was intended to be sung and memorized, and its style is similar to that of the documents unearthed recently, mentioned above.

☯

This period is characterized by a great impetus to the trading of ideas among different movements: Confucianism, Legalism, Taoism, among others. It would be wrong to try to draw too clear a line at this time between these patterns of thought, which have continued to interact with each other. I have not addressed the well-known question of the flirtation between Legalism and Taoism because it left no traces in later Taoism. In the chapters that follow, we shall see interactions between Confucianism and Taoism, already detectable in the *Zhuangzi* and in the chapters of the *Guanzi* mentioned above. These interactions continue even today.

2

New Elements Under the Han

Taoism is the heir to many patterns of thought that developed and were prevalent during the Han dynasty (206 B.C.–A.D. 220). It consolidated the cosmological, theological, and anthropological speculations of the *fangshi* searching for immortality, respect for nonaction, and aspects of popular religion from throughout China and all social classes. At the court, people sought longevity and cultivated cosmological speculations. In the north, the territory of the former state of Qi was home to a Huang-Lao school and a center of the *fangshi*. In Sichuan the cult of Laozi was strong. Under the Han, the term "Taoism" (*daojia*) also designated, without clear distinction, seekers after immortality and their techniques (including Wang Chong [A.D. 27–91], for example; see the *Lunheng*, 7) along with the Huang-Lao movement (see the *Hanshu*).

Cosmological Speculations

One of the archaeological documents discussed at the end of the preceding chapter refers to a stove god, a being already mentioned by Zhuangzi. This leads us directly to the person of Li Shaojun. He lived at the time of Emperor Wu of Han (140–87) and knew, we are told by the *Shiji*,[1] the "art of the furnace" to summon spirits, the art of not needing to eat (also a Taoist practice), and the art of avoiding growing old. He is said to have melted cinnabar and turned it into gold with the help of the spirits he conjured up; immortality was assured those who ate from a dish made of this gold. This is the first recognized record of Chinese alchemy and apparently emerged from *fangshi* circles.

The *fangshi* also advised the emperor to make sacrifices to the Great Unity (Taiyi), to Heaven, and to Earth—a triad that prefigures that of the Taoists—as well as to the Five Emperors of the four cardinal directions and the center. He was also to carry a sacred standard bearing the image of the Big Dipper (the Bushel Measure) flanked by the sun and the moon.[2] Many of these gods had appeared in the *Chuci*, and the inspirers of this cult thus were connected with a more ancient religious current.

The *fangshi* flourished under Emperor Wu and other Han rulers. Their theories are closely tied to those in the *weishu* or *chenwei*, the esoteric "apocrypha" dedicated to the science of prophecy, of which they were the advocates. As the name of these texts indicates (*wei* in *weishu* means "woof thread"), they were claimed to be the hidden thread, the esoteric foundation, of the classical canon, the *jing* (this word could mean the warp thread of a fabric). They espoused an ideology that fit the times, one that has been called the "Confucianism of the Han" or the *jinwen*, the school of "new writings."[3] These writings were banned and burned at the end of the Han and survive only in fragments difficult to date. Studying them in conjunction with Taoist texts has proved profitable. The affinity between the subjects studied by the *fangshi* and those of interest to the Taoists was so great and lasted for so long that the distinction between these thinkers and the Taoists is not easy to make—to the point that many treatises on geomancy and divination that derive from *fangshi* practices have been incorporated into the *Daozang*, the Taoist canon.

The art of the *fangshi* and the ideology underlying the *weishu* apocrypha are based on a development and extremely complex application of the theories of Yin-Yang and the Five Agents schools. A comparable development and comparable applications are behind the language, codes, and a great many practices and beliefs of Taoism. The principle of the talisman or text as a token of the bond between gods and men and the power given by knowledge of the names of gods and demons, inherited from antiquity by the Taoists, came to them in the form they assumed in the *weishu*. The speculations on the *Book of Change* connected with this group, so popular under the Han, disappeared almost completely from the official scene in post-Han times but continued to be pursued actively within Taoist circles. The Taoists maintained this tradition and passed it to the Neo-Confucianists of the Song, who merely took up again a torch whose flame had been maintained (and is still maintained) by the Taoists.

Certain specific mythological features provide irrefutable proof of the influence of the *weishu* apocrypha on Taoism. Among these are the Taoists' citing of one of these texts, the *Sanhuang wen* (*Stories of the Three August Ones*), and the acceptance of the existence of *dixiazhu* (underground rulers). The *weishu* also mention plants or elixirs that confer immortality, which may be found in the mountains or delivered by "jade maidens." The names given for the emperors of the cardinal directions or gods of parts of the body are the same as those in certain Taoist texts. These important but scattered references suggest that the bases of Taoism were already in existence and fairly well established at this time and in this environment. This makes the disappearance of the *weishu* texts, of which we possess only fragments, all the more unfortunate. They could possibly have shed great light on the earliest period of Taoism. The germs of most of the beliefs and practices presented in the following chapters may well have existed already under the Han in *fangshi* circles.

We can say with certainty, however, that Taoist cosmology was rooted in that of the *fangshi* as it is expressed in the *weishu*, in the calendrical chapter of the *Hanshu* (*History of the Han*), and in certain divination tools like the *shi*, or diviner's compass. The representation of the workings of the world that grew up at this time was shaped to a large extent by divinatory concerns, following an ancient form of divination that can be traced to the Shang dynasty (second millennium B.C.). The system consists essentially of knowing the favorable time and place for any action. The universe is seen as constantly changing. What is good at one moment may not be good at another. An event, deed, or person takes on meaning in a given context, constructed according to a system of interrelations whose morphology must be discovered. These ideas gave rise to all kinds of speculations and "maps" of the world in which each sector of space had to be located in a given time. Under these conditions construction of the calendar gained added importance, and during this era calendar devisers and diviners were extremely active, probably encouraged by the official doctrine of the state—a kind of Confucianism impregnated with the theories of Yin-Yang and the Five Agents. These individuals established the foundations of what would become traditional Chinese cosmology, particularly that of Taoism. They sought to reconcile the many existing systems of dating and determining geographic directions in order to construct a coherent system, and they began to formulate the world geographies found in texts like the "Yueling" ("Monthly Ordinances," a kind of *Farmer's Almanac* incorporated into the *Liji*, the *Classic of Rituals*) or the *Huainanzi*, or in the tables of divination. Taoism owes much to these maps of the world and speculations on the world's genesis.

Here I shall briefly present only the part of this cosmology that presages Taoist cosmology. The slow gestation of the universe began from the Yuanqi, the Primordial Breath, and had many geneses, during which forms and matter gradually coalesced. The Three Originals (*sanyuan*)—of Heaven, Earth, and Man—preside over a tripartite division of the cosmos. Taking the place of the Polestar at the center of the sky is the Big Dipper, residence of the Supreme One, the Taiyi, whose rotation divides the world into nine sectors, the Nine Palaces (eight peripheral ones, for the eight points of the wind rose, and a central one), moving from the center toward the periphery. The Nine Palaces are related to the first nine numbers, and the eight palaces of the periphery to the eight Trigrams of the *Book of Change*;[4] they are surrounded by the twelve cyclical signs, which in turn are surrounded by the 28 constellations. The four corners of the world are the four gates, respectively, of demons or the moon in the northeast, of the earth in the southeast, of human beings or the sun in the southwest, and of Heaven in the northwest. On this cosmic plan, the distribution of the numbers related to the cardinal points follows several possible layouts. The system called *nayin* relates them to musical notes and is still found today in popular almanacs; it was the system most commonly adopted by the Taoists of the Celestial Masters and Shangqing schools, and the one used in their liturgy. This structure of the world is the one still revealed in the altar of the Taoist liturgy (see below, pp. 166–83).

The Huang-Lao Movement

The school called Huang-Lao, one of the most important links in the history of the building up of Taoism, also developed during the Han period. It took its name from the Huangdi (the Yellow Emperor) and from Laozi, both of whom were venerated as its patrons. Its was centered in the Qi country of the north (modern Shandong), whose ruling family claimed descent from Huangdi. A self-proclaimed descendant of Laozi had also moved there, and around 190 B.C. its chancellor practiced ruling by non-intervention, according to the precepts of Laozi.

Zhuangzi has given us an ambiguous image of Huangdi, sometimes making fun of him as an arrogant sovereign, dangerous in his excess of zeal in trying to bring order to the world, and sometimes presenting him as an enlightened disciple listening to teachings on longevity. We have already seen that several books attributed to him were regarded as Taoist. The tenor of these books, according to Ban Gu, the author of the *History of the Han*, resembled that of the *Daodejing*. The *Huainanzi* and the *Liezi* contain passages quoted as statements of Huangdi that are actually quotations from the *Zhuangzi* and the *Daodejing*; that is, they are attributed to three different individuals, Huangdi, Laozi, and Zhuangzi. The Huang-Lao school preached the renunciation of wealth, practiced recipes for longevity, and governed by non-intervention. Several magistrates under Emperor Wu of the Han, imitating the chancellor of Qi, tried to administrate by non-intervention.

During the Warring States period, certain Legalists like Shang Yang and Han Feizi had dedicated themselves to the study of the texts of both Huangdi and Laozi. They seem to have been trying to adapt Laozi's and Zhuangzi's principles of non-intervention and the transcendent dimension of the Tao, impracticable in their pure state, to the needs of human society in a more concrete and livable fashion. For example, they reconciled these concepts with more realistic ideas, such as the notion of "opportunity," introduced by the Legalists. The best source on these matters, for the Han dynasty, is the *Huainanzi*.[5]

The "Huainanzi"

The *Huainanzi,* compiled by a group of scholars working under the direction of the Prince of Huainan (180–122 B.C.), is a good source of information on Han cosmology and is representative of the attempts at syncretism that characterized this era. Its compilers tried to reconcile Taoist and Confucian ideals, correlating them with borrowings from Legalism, which were politically and socially more realistic. In addition, the cosmological substrate of the work, which harks back to the Yin-Yang school and the Five Agents, is Taoist. There are references to the Primordial Breath as origin of the world, an idea also present in the commentaries in the *weishu* apocrypha on the *Book of Change*, which date from the same period. We also find, however, an idea that would become a fundamental trait of Taoist cosmogenesis: the birth of the world from the division of this Breath into a pure and light breath that rose to form the sky and a heavy, opaque breath that sank to form the earth.

The figure that ensures the metaphysical, theoretical, and ontological coherence of the various existing ideologies and assembles them from within is the Sage. He is, more precisely, a Sage who reconciles the high spiritual spheres in which the Sage of Zhuangzi evolved and the more mundane sphere of a political man. In this role, he is derived from the Sage of the *Book of Change* and the Confucians, a cosmic civilizer and organizer. Huangdi has an interesting significance here: he is an emperor, unlike Laozi, who never presented himself as more than an adviser to rulers. The Sage of the *Huainanzi* is the incarnation of the Tao, of the Center-One. He both makes possible and protects the multitude in which the central unity is doubly reflected: it is made up of distinct units, and it forms a coherent, unified whole; it is the internal unity that all individual multiplicities must have. In this sense the Sage possesses all the qualities of a man of politics: he "distributes," "checks on details," "pays attention to small things, watches over the most minute . . . , guards the multiple facets," and "weighs opportunities." He knows how to judge human beings. He respects the hierarchies that give society its structural stability. "Flexible as leather and reeds," he knows how to change himself and adapt himself to needs and customs that change with the times. In sum, with the Tao rooted in his heart, he reconciles the mystic avoidance of knowledge, non-intervention, "non-utility," and purposelessness preached by Zhuangzi with the prudence and enlightened and canny wisdom needed in political matters by the man of affairs. His universality derives both from the universal presence of the Tao in all things and everywhere in all forms and from the polyvalent spirit of the statesman.

The Immortals

What was the relationship between philosophical non-action and the recipes for longevity that, at the beginning of our era, the skeptic philosopher Wang Chong specifically attributed to Taoism (*daojia*)? This question is difficult to answer because the connection seems to have evolved over time. We have seen that Zhuangzi preached the first as well as the second. Similarly Huangdi, in addition to his role as a cosmic ruler, was an important figure for the *fangshi* as the patron of medicine, alchemy, and longevity. He was thought to have attained immortality and flown away after having cast a magic tripod. There are also many indications that Laozi was a patron of physiological practices at this time. Furthermore, one center of the *fangshi* was located in Qi, an area where the Huang-Lao school was strong. It would seem, according to Anna

Seidel, that the doctrine of ruling by non-intervention gradually became less important than individual physiological practices.[6] Whatever the case may be, the term *huang-lao*, stripped of its political connotations, remained synonymous with "Taoism" until at least the Song, when it was often used with this meaning in works on "interior alchemy."

Both texts and archaeological finds reveal that the Han exalted immortality and the search for longevity. In those who pursued these ideas, we find again the hybrid mixture of two contradictory tendencies: the desire to remain young and live for a long time, and the search for something beyond ordinary life, for something marvelous that manifests itself in both extraordinary powers and different mental states. Hagiographies, drawn from historical documents or from more popular sources, describe these immortals (*xian*) or searchers for immortality. These texts were compiled from ancient sources telling of even older events, and they give us a vivid picture of the immortals.

Immortals prefer to live in hiding, far from the world, withdrawn into the mountains and often living in caves. Huangdi and Laozi are counted among them. They are masters of the rain and the wind, like the *wu* sorcerers, and, like the Sage of Zhuangzi, they can pass through fire without burning and through water without getting wet. These are signs that they know how to control Yin and Yang (water and rain, fire and wind). They move up and down with the clouds, as they please. They have wings, on which feathers grow, and they ride either cranes or fish (air-yang and water-yin). They know the future. They are masters of time and space. They can, at will, reduce the world to the size of a gourd, or turn a gourd into a world as vast as the universe. They are evanescent, disappearing and appearing in the wink of an eye. Like the immortals of Mount Gushi in the *Zhuangzi* and like the poet of the *Chuci*, they feed on breaths and vapors, as well as on flowers, seeds, and herbs. As healers, they compound drugs and practice respiratory and gymnastic exercises. They often look strange, with long ears and square pupils in their eyes. In a word, they conjoin the features of therapeutic exorcists, magicians, and immortals. They are characterized not by their moral qualities—paragons of morality are more a feature of Confucianism—but by their active, mystical participation in the natural workings of life and the world.

The Deification of Laozi

Beginning in the middle of the second century A.D., Laozi became deified. Until that time he had been more or less conflated with Huangdi and the god Taiyi. At this time, however, Laozi became the incarnation of the cosmic Sage of Taoism as he was depicted by Zhuangzi and later described in the *Huainanzi*. But certain interesting features had been added—features that reveal the incorporation of a cosmological, mythic element. Laozi lives in the Big Dipper, the center of the celestial sphere, descending and returning there. This gives him the status of an intermediary between Heaven and the human world. He is surrounded by the four heraldic animals of the four cardinal directions, a sign that he is the center. He changes according to the path of the sun and the seasons, assuming various guises at different times. Like the Tao, he can extend himself to the infinite and reduce himself to the minute.

This description is almost the same as that of the god Taiyi and reflects his role as central ruler and life giver, which is that of the sovereign in ancient China and that of the Taoist adept in meditation. The deified Laozi is a hypostasis of the Taoist cosmic Sage, the anthropomorphic form of the Tao mentioned above in connection with the *Daodejing*. But now he is more precisely imaged and accompanied by symbols that would be used by later Taoist texts and that constitute a large part of their language.

Popular Religion

The study of Huangdi leads down another trail, that of popular religion. An analysis by Anna Seidel of extant Han funerary texts reveals that the supreme god was called either the "celestial emperor" or "yellow emperor" (*huangdi*), or even the "yellow god of the Big Dipper." Examination of these texts reveals many interesting things. Besides this mention of the Big Dipper, we find an envoy of the supreme god, a monster armed to the teeth, surrounded by the heraldic animals of the four cardinal directions and helped by demons who mete out the justice of the supreme god. In them we can see the prototype of the protective and exorcistic demons of Taoism.

No less significant is the maintenance of registers of life and death by the Five Emperors of the Five Peaks, the five famous mountains of Taoism. Note the bureaucratic aspect of this popular form of religion. Besides the reference to these registers that control the length of life and the date of death, we find in funerary texts the exact phrase that closes official documents under the Han: *ru lüling*, "as [it is written] in the decrees and ordinances" a phrase adopted by the Celestial Masters and incorporated into liturgical texts down to the present.

The strongly exorcistic nature of this popular religion has a connotation that is both judicial and moral. Absolution for misdeeds plays an important part in it, especially for those that trouble the spirits of the earth by building houses or digging tombs. Absolution requires a request for pardon intended to pacify the wrathful spirits. The length of life and the date of death are tied to moral behavior, and the term "deliverance" (*jie*, which we will meet again in the meaning "deliverance from the corpse") carries with it the ideas of imprisonment in subterranean hells as well as of atonement for misdeeds. Here, unlike beliefs among the elite, who had been exposed to classic texts, the *hun* and *po* souls pass underground together, like the souls described later in the *Taipingjing* (*Classic of Great Peace*), an early Taoist text.

The "Laozi bianhua jing"

The *Laozi bianhua jing* (*Book of Transformations of Laozi*), also studied by Seidel, survives only in one version, found at Dunhuang, with many lacunae and mistakes. It appears to date from the late second century A.D. and to have come from a popular source in Sichuan, whose beliefs it records. As its title indicates, it deals with the transformations of Laozi, a deified Laozi described at times by the same words used to describe the Tao: he "shapes" the world, his existence predates that of the universe and goes back to the beginning of all beings, and he has a cosmic stature. This god Laozi is immortal and constantly transforms himself, either on a cosmic level as he follows the revolutions of the stars or on a human level by adopting various identities among us.

In his successive human guises since the beginning of time, he has played the role of wise counselor and instructor of emperors. As a savior god, he announces to the people that he will intervene in order to re-establish order at the end of the Han dynasty: he thus has, to a certain degree, a revolutionary nature. In addition he takes shape inside the body of the meditating adept. He advocates a purity free from all desire and all intentional action. He preaches the recitation of the "five thousand words" (another name for the *Daodejing*) and the confession of sins.

We can see in this text some fundamental traits that will persist throughout the history of Taoism. The delineation of the Sage becomes more precise. Like the Tao, of which he is only the anthropomorphized form, he has a double nature. One is dark and hidden, primordial. The other is shining, open, and active. His actions take place on three levels. On the cosmic level, he shapes the earth and the sky and makes the stars revolve. On the personal level, he is the object of meditation by the adept and identifies with the adept. The third level is sociopolitical: he incarnates himself to advise and direct emperors and to save the people at times of great disorder, and he preaches good behavior. This last aspect will be found throughout the history of Taoism. Taken up again under the Six Dynasties (222–589), the theme of the successive reincarnations of Laozi would develop greatly under the Tang and again under the Song. It provided an outline for a whole view of the history of Taoism: all its elements were gathered under the aegis of Laozi, and he was presented, in his different rebirths and under different forms, as the single revealer of all the teachings and the founder of all the schools of the religion.

3

The Celestial Masters

Historical Background

The second century A.D. witnessed a series of events important in the history of Taoism. A form of Taoism with a truly collective spirit, different from that of the independent, more or less legendary and anonymous *fangshi* we have seen up to now, appeared. Many of the elements we have been looking at recur, and this new Taoism was to a certain degree an extension of earlier phenomena. The new, essential feature, however, is that Taoism now acquired an organized form.

With the eclipse of the Huang-Lao movement, pushed into a secondary position by the installation of Confucianism as the state cult, a cleavage arose between the official doctrine and the more marginal Taoistic movements, which survived to a great extent among women and peasants. Two distinct but parallel movements sharing features then appeared: the Yellow Turbans movement in central and eastern China, and the Five Bushels of Rice (Wudou mi dao) movement, later to become the Celestial Masters school, in Sichuan. Led by Zhang Jue, the Yellow Turbans attracted masses of adepts, and through it "multitudes were cured." In A.D. 184 the group instigated an uprising that threatened the Han dynasty, which the Yellow Turbans regarded as decadent. Their adepts venerated the Yellow God and believed in a new era under the reign of a "Yellow Heaven." Yellow is the color of the Earth Agent. According to the sequence accepted by the School of the Five Agents for the creation of each of the reigning agents from the previous one, the yellow Earth agent arises after that of Fire, the red agent ruling over the destiny of the Han dynasty. In honor of the Yellow Heaven, adepts wore the yellow turbans that gave the movement its name.

The idyllic era that they anticipated would be that of the Great Peace (Taiping—whence another name for this movement: The Way of Great Peace, Taiping dao). This idea goes back to the Chinese notion of a utopia, a golden age (*datong*), of harmony, peace, wisdom, and equality. Traces of this idea are found in the classics, but the concept does not seem to be of Confucian origin. It is characterized by descriptions of an ideal state located in the west, the Da Qin (which has, incidentally, been identified with the Roman empire). Throughout the Han, a political faction from the Qi region had tried to impose on the court a doctrine of Great Peace, and this spread among the people once the official powers were discredited. A new messianic element arose with this movement. The era of peace was no longer located in an infinitely distant past. It was yet to come, and soon—in the year 184 to be precise. In this millenarian doctrine, 184 was designated as the *jiazi* year, the first year in the sixty-year cycle, a fact that gave it a special character, somewhat like the year 1000 in our tradition.

The Yellow Turbans were finally crushed by the Han authorities. Perhaps this is why the Taoists (for example, the Shangqing school, in the *Zhen'gao*—see Chapter 5) later disowned them. But despite their eclipse, their practices persisted: cures through the confession of sins and meditational retreats; the recitation of sacred texts; an ecclesiastical hierarchy based on the Chinese triad of Heaven, Earth, and Man, already part of Confucian doctrine; and veneration of the god Huanglao. All these practices were close to those of the Celestial Masters, who also adopted the Yellow Turbans' sacred book, the *Taipingjing* (or a similar work under the same name). In addition, like the Celestial Masters movement, the Yellow Turbans maintained the Taoistic ideal of the Sage-ruler who also functions as religious leader.

The Five Bushels of Rice movement, later to become the Celestial Masters movement, arose about the same time. In A.D. 142, Laozi appeared to Zhang Daoling, a man who aligned himself with the *fangshi* group, belonged to the class of small landowners, and had withdrawn into the mountains of Sichuan. Laozi, as we have seen, had been venerated among the people as a great holy man and was deified a little later, in 165, under the title Taishang Laojun (the very high Lord Lao). Laozi brought to Zhang Daoling a new law, the *Orthodox One* (*Zhengyi*) of the Authority of the Sworn Oath, that was to propagate the rule of the Three Heavens, deliver the world from the decadence caused by the evil Six Heavens, and re-establish in its perfect state the "seed people," the chosen people. Rather than overthrowing the Han dynasty, the aim seems to have been to establish an interregnum based on a religious ideology. This interregnum would prepare the way for a renewed, virtuous dynasty. The god Laojun had removed the mandate of Heaven from the emperor and given the Celestial Master the responsibility of ruling the chosen people. The Celestial Master was thus the god's earthly vicar.

At first this movement was called the doctrine (*dao*, "path") of the Five Bushel Measures after the contribution of five bushels of rice required of each of its adepts. It spread widely and rapidly, particularly under the direction of first the son of Zhang Daoling and then his grandson Zhang Lu (fl. 190-220). In Sichuan they organized a truly independent state, which, thanks to the taxes levied on the faithful, enjoyed both political and financial autonomy. In 215, Zhang Lu, who seems never to have laid claim to the throne, handed over his power to Cao Cao (155-220), legitimized by the deified Laozi. Although Cao Cao never became emperor, his son took the throne as the first ruler of the Wei. In return, Zhang was given titles and an income and was brought to the capital. Subsequently he gained many adherents. Citing a passage from the *Zhuangzi* as a license to act, his heirs adopted the title Celestial Master and claimed the role of instructor and guide since Laozi's earthly incarnations came to an end.

This was the first organized form of Taoism. Also called Zhengyi, from the name of its revelation, the movement prospered. By the third century A.D., it counted among its members and protectors many powerful families as it moved up to the aristocracy from the lower class and peasant circles where it first developed. Despite the appearance at various times of new lines of masters, the original organization has survived to modern times, led by a line of hereditary Celestial Masters, the descendants of Zhang Lu, who continue to maintain their ascendancy and preside over this church.

A variety of written sources lets us reconstruct the beliefs, practices, and organization of this movement. Some, like Buddhist texts of the fifth and sixth centuries, should be read with skepticism, given their polemic nature. They can be supplemented and corrected in part on the basis of other historical texts, which unfortunately give only fragmentary information. To these may be added a few specifically Taoist texts.

Organization

Like the Yellow Turbans, the adepts of the Path of the Five Bushels of Rice believed in a golden age and hoped to bring about a perfect state ruled by religion and morality. This ideal guided the state organization they established in Sichuan, under the rule of a line of Celestial Masters. The first three of these leaders, the founders of the movement, were worshiped in the same way as ancestors. The state was divided into 24 regions, seats of both administrative and religious power. They were called *zhi* (later, in Tang times, the name was changed to *hua*, because of a taboo on the word *zhi*). Each of the 24 *zhi* was connected with one of the Five Agents, one of the 24 periods of the year, one of the 28 zodiacal constellations (in two cases with two of them, and in one case with three), and with the signs of the sexagesimal cycle. All the faithful belonged to one of the districts, according to their birth signs. Each district was administered by 24 officials, who had under their command 240 armies of spirits, made up of 2,400 generals, 2,400 officers, and 240,000 soldiers. This administrative system, governed by Han cosmological schemas, was infused with an archaicizing spirit close to that of the state that Wang Mang, founder of the short-lived Xin dynasty (A.D. 9–25) between the Former and Latter Han dynasties, had wanted to establish: it reflected a utopian system described in the *Ritual of Zhou* (*Zhouli*). At the same time it was inspired by an ideal of village communal life.

The bureaucratic spirit, traces of which we have already seen in Han popular religion, shaped the system, with administration and religion going hand in hand. The religious hierarchy adopted titles from the Han establishment: *jijiu* (libationer), *zhubu* (recorder), *ling* (director), and so on. The spells and requests addressed to the gods followed the model of administrative deeds and like them drew their warrant from specifically named codes. The faithful were grouped by families, with each one attached to a district. Registers of civil status were kept by families and in each of the districts. Any change in civil status had to be entered and was accompanied by contributions in kind from the faithful. These registers matched those that the gods keep. The effectiveness of requests directed to the gods depended on the registers' accuracy, and they were updated periodically at great assemblies (on the seventh day of the first and seventh months, and the fifteenth of the tenth month). The registers recorded in detail the civic status of each party, identifying him or her exactly. The registers also served as talismans, and the contributions made to bring them up to date, called "wages of faith," established a connection among the faithful, the master, and the gods who preside over fate. In addition, as Rolf Stein has written, "the ideal of communal life, with its morality and its relatively insulated life," remained influential, and it is revealed, for example, in the institution of the local community leader, who was elected for his wisdom and integrity.

Neophytes were called "demons available for forced labor" (or just "demons"). Those who led groups were called "instructors" or *jijiu*. New members seem to have been instructed by a catechism of the kind found in the *Xiang'er*, a commentary on the *Daodejing* attributed to Zhang Lu, a work dedicated to spreading the "true path" and launching anathemas against fallacious doctrines. The One that must be "preserved" is the deified Laozi and his teaching. The *Xiang'er* wars against "common and false forms of magic" that give a name and an appearance to the Tao and to the One, and turn it into a meditation method. (Here the *Xiang'er* is probably echoing the battles that pitted the Celestial Masters against other tendencies, such as those recorded in the *Laozi bianhua jing*.) The *Xiang'er* thus provides indications of the antiquity of visual meditation techniques that would be greatly developed later on.

The *jijiu* handled both religious and administrative duties. They received tax payments in kind (rice, fabrics, paper, brushes, mats, and so on) and set up "honor-system inns" along the highways. These were somewhat like the official way stations of the Han. Rice and meat were provided for travelers, who were supposed not to eat more than was needed to satisfy hunger, under pain of punishment by the spirits. Some of the "demon officials" were charged with seeing that the sick prayed and with drawing up on their behalf petitions addressed to the triple administration of Heaven, Earth, and Water. In fact, the primary skill, and main function, of the Celestial Master priests was their ability to direct petitions and to send them to the divine powers.

The faithful, male and female, were assigned to levels in the hierarchy according to merit; the highest were ordained as masters (*daoshi*) and received the "register." The texts compare the ceremony of ordination in this office to the investiture of a king. The register was a list of those spirits the new master had the power to command and defined the master's rank not only in the ecclesiastical hierarchy but also in the celestial bureaucracy.

Religious Practices

Law and morality were one. The gods, some of whom were of popular origin, like the gods of the earth and the hearth, watched for and recorded misdeeds such as drunkenness, debauchery, and theft. These had to be expiated by confession, often public, and by penances that consisted of community service, such as road repair, or a retreat (into "purity chambers") to encourage the sinner to reflect. Sickness was seen as a punishment for sin and treated by religious methods like confession or the use of holy water. The faithful recited sacred texts, the *Daodejing* in particular, and practiced "embryonic" breathing and abstention from cereals. On fixed dates, especially at the equinoxes, group ceremonies were carried out, usually in the open air. On these occasions the masters disseminated their teachings, precepts, and prohibitions. The ceremonies brought the faithful together in assemblies (*hui*) or "fasts" (*zhai*), a word borrowed from the official religion and used even in modern times to designate Taoist ceremonies. These assemblies were the prototypes of later Taoist liturgical ceremonies (*zhai* or *jiao*).

The ceremonies were often punctuated by communal meals; on occasion these were true agapes. They were a legacy of ancient practices often connected with the cult of the household gods, the gods of the earth, or those of tombs. (One had to make recompense for digging a tomb by a rite of contrition toward the earth god molested during the construction.) Such meals were called "kitchens" and often took place at times of change in civil status (births, deaths) or in order to avert evil and bring "happinesses." In any case, such meals were held at the beginning of the year and on the occasion of the "assemblies" of the Three Administrations. The participants observed a strict hierarchy, with merit and seniority in the path prevailing over social class. The meals consisted of three kinds of food: snacks, alcohol, and rice. Alcohol was controlled to avoid abuse, and its role in these functions explains the group leaders' title of "libationers." These meals were communal, with the number of participants fixed by decree, at least in principle. Food and drink were also offered to the gods present, as well as to the faithful. The "kitchens" disappeared as such around the sixth century but would continue in the form of "offerings" made the gods as thanks for favors received.

Among the assemblies were the festivals of the Three Administrations (*sanguan*)—Heaven, Earth, and Water—in charge of checking on human doings and sanctioning them. These took place three times a year. Participants in the assemblies cured sickness

by addressing petitions in triplicate to the *sanguan*: the one to
Heaven had to be burned and so was carried toward the celestial
realms by the smoke; the second, addressed to the Earth, was
buried; and the third, addressed to the Water, was submerged.
This procedure would be maintained in many Taoist ritual practices, and other schools, such as the Shangqing, would adopt it.

A description of one of the fasts, the Fast of Mud and Charcoal
(*tutan zhai*), survives in an anthology dating from the sixth century (*Wushangbiyao*, summarized by J. Lagerwey, pp. 156–58), although in a form edited and reworked by Lu Xiujing in the fifth
century. It has been translated in part and commented on by Maspero (pp. 381–82 in Kierman's translation).[1] This was a ritual of
contrition carried out by adepts daubed with mud and charcoal as
a sign of penitence. They lay down with a piece of jade in their
mouths and their hands tied behind their backs, like criminals.
The ritual was intended to ask forgiveness for sins committed by
the participants' family members (both living and dead), by the
participants themselves, by "the entire people," and "by all people
and animals on earth." It was thus a ritual of universal salvation. A
long litany of sins was recited, the gods of the five and ten directions were invoked, and the ritual ended with a rite preserved
down to modern times in which the priest supervises the "leaving
of the officials" (*chuguan*). He charges his bodily spirits to carry to
the heavenly deities the prayer he has drawn up in the form of a
memorandum accompanying the confessions of the penitents.

Much has been written about Taoist sexual ceremonies. The
Buddhists of the sixth century delighted in denouncing them and
presenting these ceremonies as orgies in order to discredit the
Taoists. In fact, as Rolf Stein has shown, sexual rites were strictly
controlled. After three days of fasting, each participant had to
mate with a male or female partner chosen by the master, according to an order of precedence that left no opportunity for individual initiative. Precedence was established by the religious master
according to acquired merit. A text of this movement reveals details that match closely those in citations and descriptions made
by outside observers in the sixth century; it dates, at the very lat-

est, to the same time as these witnesses' accounts. The ceremonies began with a fast and prayers, accompanied by breathing exercises, visual meditation, and repeated invocations of the main bodily divinities and the higher gods, who would succor the participants throughout. The purpose of the ceremonies was to inscribe the names of the participants in the registers of life. The loosening of belts, clothing, and hair by the master symbolized explicitly the "loosening of the bonds of the adept" and was the prelude to a choreographed dance representing the Nine Palaces of the magic square. This square was related to Han calendrical speculations and divination, and it connected the eight trigrams of the *Book of Change*, the nine points in space (four cardinal directions, four intermediary directions, and the center), and the first nine numbers. The square was indicated by the positions of the interlaced fingers of the partners and then by the positions of their feet and toes. The symbolic dance brought together a man and a woman called "Yang" and "Yin" or "Heaven" and "Earth," thus giving them a cosmic dimension. Their hierogamic union was understood as the beginning of the process of creation of an immortal's body.

As Marc Kalinowski has clearly shown, this dance applied a blueprint marked out in both space and time, ordered and numbered according to a procedure that belonged to a cultural milieu common both to the Confucianism of the period and to Taoism. It was a rite of initiation permitting entry into the church of the Celestial Masters, but not on a level with ordination. To be precise, this rite, through the intermediary of the symbolism of the primary numbers, consisted in reconstructing the human body according to a plan of the cosmos along the lines of the construction of the world by the Great Yu. In some ways this dance, based on the pattern of the cosmic square, is reminiscent of the many rites of "pacing the stars" in later meditations of the Shangqing movement. The same terms show up (the "threads of Heaven" and the "network of Earth"), but the information in the texts left by the Celestial Masters is too vague to permit us to know precisely what the terms meant to them.

Finally, other textual remnants mention the ritual of entry into the chapel, or "purity chamber." Such chapels were built in imitation of those that the Confucianists constructed for reading the classics and had to follow precise rules regarding dimensions and furnishings. Each adept was supposed to have one at home. The importance of this visionary ritual, which we have in a version transmitted via the Shangqing school, lies in the fact that it constitutes the kernel of what would become Taoist ritual. Short and simple compared with what would come later, it contains the seed of many principles and practices further developed by later generations. It was not a sacrifice but, as Ursula-Angelika Cedzich has shown, an administrative procedure intended to establish communication with the beyond and to transmit to the Jade Emperor, the supreme god, a prayer carried by divine messengers emitted by the body of the officiant, who at the same time invoked cosmic and heavenly powers to come into him, which he then sent back to the skies. These powers are mainly the original Celestial Masters and their wives, along with the three Primordial Breaths. The officiant prays that they will irrigate and make fruitful his body, ward off evils, cure sicknesses when the ceremony is performed for this purpose, deliver the souls of his ancestors back to seven generations, and make of him a "flying immortal." The ritual ends with the snuffing of the incense lamp, accompanied by the "thanking" of the mediating powers invoked and a "proclamation of their merits." We have here a complete basic outline of Taoist liturgy of later centuries.

Battle Against Popular Religion

One of the roles and aims of the Celestial Masters was to battle against popular religion. Clearly they incorporated into their own practice and beliefs many elements of this religion, a practice that turned out to be decisive in their later battles. In their opposition to popular religion, the Celestial Masters reflect a general attitude common in Taoism throughout its history, one it shares with Confucianism. Taoism has often openly borrowed from Confucianism and Buddhism, saying that the ultimate goal of these two religions is the same as its own. The only groups that the Taoists explicitly deny are "extremist cults" and "shamans" (*wu*), even though they did use the latter as their agents.

The Celestial Masters saw a need to correct existing relations between the people and the sacred. They exposed charlatans and healers who abused the credulity of the people and messiahs who claimed to incarnate Laozi. They sought to channel religious fervor, which was running wild in many forms of belief: in miracles; in the worship of local, "minor" gods not in the official lists (rocks, trees, tombs, or dead people other than ancestors, and so on); in mediums possessed by "demons" (*gui*); in prophets and soothsayers; and in animal sacrifices, dances and chants, and banquets and drinking bouts (literally "meats and wines"). All these practices, designated under the general terms "wrong paths" or "extremist cults" (an expression that would quickly come to include Buddhist cults), could be found among all strata of society, including the imperial court. According to historical sources, Zhang Lu himself, along with his mother, seems to have followed such practices. But the appearance of the deified Laozi (Taishang Laojun) was destined to put an end to these excesses by establishing the reign of the pure Three Heavens and consigning to hell the faulty Six Heavens connected with the cults offered to "other" gods. One of the meanings given to the word *zheng*, "correct," which is part of the other name of the Celestial Masters school, Zhengyi ("Correct One") is "orthodox," in the sense of "under control, regulated," in contrast to everything that is anarchical. The "correct" spirits were those of the Celestial Masters.

Two basic means were used in the battle against popular religion. The first was the regimented, bureaucratic, and hierarchized aspect of the sect's relations with the divine: a ritual governed by strictly fixed, formal rules. In contrast with the practices of the *fangshi* and unlike the mediums, a single priest mediated between the adept and the spirits, filling the role of a scribe, like a licensed bureaucrat. There were both a well-established hierarchy and fixed religious districts. Registers contained an exact record of the adepts and the merits that would determine their longevity.

Both the ecclesiastical hierarchy and the administrative districts Zhang Lu had organized were retained. In addition, a large number of the texts belonging to this school—which date from the second to the fifth centuries—are dedicated to laying out in detail the exact stylized and ritualized form that must be given to prayers and requests addressed to the gods. The Celestial Masters became the greatest specialists in this art. These texts often resemble instruction manuals prepared for the use of priests. They include forms with blanks for the insertion of the name of the priest, the name of the adept, and the place and circumstances of the ceremony. Communication with the spirits had, moreover, a judicial aspect. (The term that designates the ritual is *fa*, or "law.") This recalls procedures in Han popular religion mentioned earlier. The nature of the requests reveals the concerns of the followers of this school: drought, tigers, sickness, invasions of locusts, possession, death, liturgical festivals, birth, repose for the dead, and so on.

The other weapon used in the battle against popular cults was a campaign of vilification, a kind of exorcism. Church leaders described the popular gods as demons and blamed all the evils and afflictions humanity suffers on them. The agents of disease were the ancient shamans (*wu*) or medium-sorcerers, or the popular household gods of posts, of corners of the house, of metal utensils, of wells, and of the hearth, or other ancient nature deities like the Count of the River. Dark spirits of the invisible world, they came from beyond the grave to molest the living; the land of the dead gave birth to all evils. Henceforward, it was war. Using old practices to their advantage, the Celestial Masters assumed an exorcistic role that connected them once more, despite claims to the contrary, to the ancient *wu* shamans.

The Masters sought, however, to establish an independent identity and affirm their uniqueness and authority, and to this end they worked on two levels. On the one hand, they inherited and took over the ancient powers of the *wu*. On the other, they set themselves off from them in the eyes of the literate by battling against popular beliefs and practices that were actually very close to their own. To accomplish this task, they called on armies of spirit warriors. The chief of the opposing demons was described as a creature with armor of copper and teeth of iron. They drew up impressive lists of such demons (like the *Nuqing guilu*, 790),[2] among whom were ancient *wu* shamans, along with their exact names and descriptions. They then unmasked and accused these spirits—far from being beneficent and worthy of cults, even propitiatory cults, they deserved to be expelled. They warded them off in a menacing fashion by making use of all the weapons at their disposal: talismans, sacred writings, formulaic curses (*zhu*), the power of their breath (Qi), and help from the gods. Transformed into military leaders, as indicated by some of their titles ("soldiers of the demons," "generals," and so on), they either punished and drove off the demons and evil spirits or else forced them to submit and turned them into minor gods. In the rout, they tried to check and reduce the ancient cults offered to ancestors, gods of the earth, and the god of the hearth; since abolition was impossible, they instead integrated these cults into their own ends. They did, however, limit offerings to vegetable products ("pure" offerings, excluding meat and money) and restrict the number of offerings to five a year for ancestors and two for the gods of the earth and the hearth. They made high claims that the Tao, their path, "loves life and hates death," and they adopted the ancient division between heaven and life on the one hand and the underworld and death on the other. This opposition was reinforced by the contrast between their ordered religion and the "wild cults" and between the heavenly officials of the nine heavens charged with maintaining the "registers of life" containing the names of the living and those of the six underworld realms, dark gods of the invisible world who keep the registers of death.

This aspect of the Celestial Masters, as bureaucrats and exorcists, admittedly does not seem in tune with the naturalist philosophy, with its respect for the rhythms of nature and their complex balance, generally characteristic of Taoism. Nevertheless, it has not disappeared from the religion and constantly recurs in the texts.

Morality

To be inscribed in the registers of life and increase the number of years they might live, adepts had above all to behave virtuously; any slips were penalized by a shortening of life that might extend to their descendants. The morality to be observed was fairly ordinary, except on some points. One should aid the poor and the oppressed, covet neither riches nor fame, consume meat and wine only in moderation, recite sacred texts in a "purity chamber" built according to the rules, observe the Confucian virtues—humaneness, loyalty, justice, respect toward parents and old people. One must "not desert one's family" (this suggests rejection of the life of the hermit) and must not unlawfully divulge religious teachings (a rule that would be developed in detail later). Some features reflect a village morality of good communal behavior: one must not pollute or divert rivers, stop up wells, light fires on open land, or disturb birds on their nests. Respect for animals and slaves (the latter were not to be marked on their faces) was also called for, along with certain specific religious commands that we shall encounter in more detail later: "nourish one's breath," "avoid cereals," "preserve the One," and carry out breathing exercises. The search for universal well-being persisted; for example, it was recommended that one not burn incense simply on one's own behalf but for "the greater peace of the entire world." A note of mistrust of the authorities shows up, recalling the autonomist and village antecedents of this religious movement: adepts should not be too friendly with imperial officials. The higher virtues were in line with those called for by Laozi: flexibility, femininity and humility, nonaction, and quietism.

The texts tell us that in their advance toward salvation, adepts were divided into three classes that foreshadow later Taoist classifications. On the lowest level were those who could not or did not intend to achieve anything but longer lives; above them were the "divine men," about whom no details are given. (Apparently two of the three classes announced were conflated into the second group.)

Cosmology and Pantheon

This system rested on a cosmology that, even if it is nowhere presented systematically, can be deduced in its major lines. This presentation cannot be seen as doctrinal; contradictions within the texts preclude this.

The Tao is at the origin of the world, emerging from nothing, resting on nothing, and transforming spontaneously (*Santian neijie*, DZ 1205, 1.2a). It is "at the same time square and round, with nothing outside it." Men live in it, like fish in water, without recognizing that it surrounds them (*Zhengyi fawen tianshi jiaojie kejing*, DZ 789, 8a). Here is how a text dating from around the third century puts it:

The great Tao embraces Heaven and Earth, nourishes all lives, governs the myriad workings [of the world]. Formless, imageless, confusedly and obscurely [*hunhun dundun*, a kind of onomatopoeia recalling primordial Chaos], spontaneously, It gives birth to the myriad species. Men cannot name It, and all that exists from Heaven and Earth is engendered and killed off by It. The Tao confers [life] by means of subtle breaths of three colors, which are the Xuan, Yuan, and Shi breaths. The Xuan [dark, mysterious] breath is blue-green and forms the Sky; the Shi [inceptive, gestative] breath is yellow and forms the Earth; the Yuan [primal] breath is white and forms the Tao. (DZ 789, 12a)

The Tao, continues this text, has given birth to Heaven, which has given birth to the Earth, which has given birth to Humanity (following the outline of the process as it is given in the *Daodejing*). These three Breaths, related to the three heavens of Qingwei, Yuyu, and Dachi (DZ 796; 807; 1354, 14b), have each in turn given birth to three further breaths so as to form nine (the "nine heavens") which correspond to the nine orifices of the nine breaths of the human body. When these latter are in good order, so are the five viscera; it follows that corporeal spirits are then also in good condition.

The *Santian neijie jing*, dating from the fifth century (cited above), contains traces of a battle against the Buddhism derived from the Chinese form of Hinayana (Little Vehicle) Buddhism on the grounds that it teaches only that one should "sit and count one's breaths." This presages a recurring criticism of Buddhism by the Taoists. The text also reviews part of the cosmology we are now considering. The place of human beings in the universe is complementary to that of the Earth and Heaven, which can never "establish themselves" without the existence of Man. A world without human beings would be like a belly without gods. But without Heaven and Earth, people cannot live. In other terms, just as the spirits are the animating forces in the body, humanity animates the universe. Conversely, humanity is to Heaven and Earth as the body is to the spirits: the foundation supporting their power. Thus, human beings participate in the cosmic order and their misdeeds have repercussions there in the same way as do those of the Heavens (eclipses) and the Earth (floods).

The supreme god, in this text, is the Great Man of the Dao and the De (Daodezhangren), born before the Primordial Breath. He is followed by the great gods of the Celestial Masters and then by several forms of "primordial chaos," the *youming* ("dark"), the *kongdong* ("empty cleft"), and the "great void" (*taiwu*). This theme of multiple versions of chaos, proceeding one from the other, is also found in the *Liezi* and was discussed in the Han *weishu* apocrypha. It is constantly returned to in Taoism to illustrate a slow, progressive generating process. These various forms of chaos underwent change and gave rise to the three Primordial Breaths (Xuan, Yuan, and Shi). These fused to form the Jade Maiden Xuanmiao (Dark Wonder), who gave birth to Laojun (the deified Laozi) through her left side, an inverted replica of the birth of the Buddha. Laojun spread the three breaths, which, in their original state of chaotic fusion, looked like a yellow egg that then separated out into three: the Xuan breath, light and pure, moved upward to form the sky; the Shi breath, heavy and turbulent, moved down to form the earth (this scheme follows that of the *Huainanzi*); and the Yuan breath flowed out to form water and the stars. Then, with the Breath of Central Harmony, Laojun went on to create the universe and propagate the "three ways" to educate "heavenly people": the pure, Yang way was destined for China; the others, with their Yin quality, for the 81 barbarian peoples. Then comes the series of reincarnations of Laozi as instructor of rulers mentioned above. The account is much like that in the *Shenxian zhuan* (a work coming from a movement close to the *fangshi*). Going back into his mother, Laozi was born a second time, during the reign of King Wuding of the Shang dynasty (ca. fourteenth century B.C.), and then again in many different periods, to play the role of adviser to the emperors.

Later, much would be made of this theme of Laozi being reborn over the centuries in order to play the role of master to the rulers of antiquity, and it would be greatly developed. The Celestial Masters presented themselves as the heirs to ancient kings, whose place they assumed when a decadent dynasty could no longer fulfill its mission of keeping the Tao circulating. They received from Laozi the Way to rule people and command demons, to establish dioceses (and thus build a church), and to spread the "three Breaths" thanks to the "Breath of the Correct One by authority of the Sworn Oath" (DZ 789, 14b). This is revealed in certain formulas in which the list of merits to be acquired includes "helping the nation" (*zhuguo*; e.g., DZ 1301, 16b). In actual fact, the Celestial Masters, after setting up an operating state government in Sichuan and then failing at it, renounced the political role they had seen as their calling and moved in the direction of interiorization. Their role as the guide of rulers then took on a completely symbolic and religious meaning.

The extremely complex and extensive pantheon of the Celestial Masters is known to us from texts specifically dedicated to listing the names and appearance of gods and demons: cosmic deities, star gods (especially those of the Dipper and the five planets), gods of the four cardinal points and the center, and gods of the cyclical signs, which were spatiotemporal benchmarks depicted as flying, naked gods in human form, with red hair and without eyes. There were also chthonic powers: mountains, stones, tigers, snakes, monkeys, metals. Then there were the powerful exorcistic deities, like Zhao Gongming, who became the god of epidemics. Above all there were the Three Officials of Heaven, Earth, and Water. The higher gods rode on teams of clouds, were escorted by "jade maidens," and directed armies. The integration of the 24 gods of the body into this pantheon reveals yet another connection with the *weishu*, the Han apocryphal texts that gave the same names to these bodily gods who carried news of human misdeeds to Heaven (DZ 789, 4a; 1210, 15a). It was essential to know the names and appearances of the gods in order to have power over them and know how to command them. This is still the reason behind modern versions of these registers; they show the authority of a priest in the Celestial Masters church.

However, knowledge of the identity of the various spirits was not important only in exorcism. Several texts describe meditation techniques. By using some of these, the adept admits the general officers into his body in order to pacify it. In others he or she absorbs colored breaths, for example, the Three Cosmic Primordial Breaths melted into an egg of five colors that then turns yellow and enters the cinnabar field, the region of the abdomen below the navel (1294, 5b). Other comparable techniques involved absorbing the "ruling breath," that is to say, the breath of the current season according to the theory of the Five Agents, in order to admit it into the cinnabar field and then divert it to the *kunlun*, that is, up into the brain. We shall find these techniques in much more developed form in the "tradition of Ge Hong" (Chapter 4) and in the Shang-qing texts (Chapter 5).

The "Taipingjing"

Finally, we should take a look at the *Taipingjing* (*Book of Great Peace*), which dates in part from the first or second century A.D. Despite the revisions that it went through around the fourth century, it remains one of the most ancient extant Taoist texts and certainly reflects at least in part the thought of the Five Bushels of Rice movement. As is true of many Taoist texts, however, it is heavily influenced by classic ideas and beliefs from the Han period, not exclusively of Taoist inspiration.

A text with a similar title had been presented to the Emperor Cheng (32–7 B.C.) to encourage him to undertake reforms that would renew the decaying virtue of the Han dynasty. As pointed about above, we know that the Yellow Turban sect possessed a book by this title that may have been identical in part. Even though this sect was repudiated by the Celestial Masters, the latter certainly adopted the *Taipingjing*, which probably predated them. But a version of this work is also supposed to have been revealed to them, and at least one of the works emerging from the movement makes many allusions to it and quotes it (DZ 1301). The *Taipingjing* that we have today presents a teaching and a set of remedies emanating from the "divine men" or "celestial masters" sent by Heaven. It forecasts the end of humanity and provides a way to counteract the decadence of the period by proposing religious and cosmological remedies.

"Grand Peace" in the title of this work also means Great Equality. This term, which also designated the far east where the sun rises, is an ancient one. The *Taipingjing* associates it with another word, Dongji or Supreme Dong. *Dong*, literally "cave," is a word that evokes the void, communication, circulation. The Chinese often associate it with a homophone which means to undergo everything, in a universal way. The ancient ideal of Taiping is that of a utopian, communal state, which, as we have seen, is part of traditional Chinese thought and brings with it an idea of perfect harmony. The ideas of peace, circulation, and harmony are closely allied.

The *Taipingjing* is itself an emblem of harmony. The text is one of the talismans sent to the good ruler by Heaven, a cosmic entity somewhat anthropomorphized and deified, the first hypostasis of the Tao or of the Primordial Breath (Yuanqi), father and mother of humanity, a guide for human behavior who knows and supervises all things. This talisman is a sign of protection and favor for the sovereign who rules well, that is, one who has been able to establish happy accord among the people, Heaven, and himself, or among the Three Ways—Heaven, Earth, and Man. On another level, this accord can be seen as involving the Yang, Yin, and Central Harmony, with the last being the fruit of the interaction of the two first, and the source of all life. This tripartite dividing of the cosmos into Heaven, Earth, and Humanity was also part of the established Confucian ideology of the time. Growing out of the division into three of the Primordial Breath, it is repeated here in a triadic structure whose hierarchy rules the universe at every level in a series of closely controlled tripartite subdivisions. In the celestial vault, this organization involves the sun (Yang), the moon (Yin), and the stars (middle). On earth, we have mountains, rivers, and plains. In humans, the subdivision into three occurs again, whether it is in the family (father, mother, and child), in society (sovereign, minister, and people), or in moral matters (the Dao, the De, and the Confucian virtue of humaneness). The Prince is supposed to transmit the Celestial Breath downward—that is, to his minister, who in turn must send the Breath of the Earth up to his prince; the same is true of the people vis-à-vis the Breath of Central Harmony.

When communication had been established and the life powers were circulating among the three levels of the cosmos within a justly hierarchized collaboration, the celestial warrant, the *Taipingjing*, appeared. Conversely, the interruption of the celestial vital flow was marked by calamities. The *jinwen* ideology (or Han Confucianism) is operative here. But, taking up a more ancient Chinese theme, the book specifies that concord does not emanate only from on high. It must come from the people too, in the form of advice given by popular wisdom to the prince. This reveals an attempt to return to the people the power accorded them in the old tradition of Mencius that the Han literati had taken over to their own profit, setting themselves up as the only judges of imperial virtue and good government. To this end, a kind of mailbox was to be set up in huts where anyone could place suggestions. Similarly, all goods, whether spiritual or material, were supposed to circulate. It was a serious misdeed to stop this circulation by holding on to objects of value, wealth, vital physiological powers, recipes, or ideas.

Traditional morality and beliefs were rethought in an original fashion. Individual responsibility played a primary role, for it was only insofar as each person took his or her place in the group and acted correctly that the "non-intervention" of the ruler and the Great Peace could spread. Misdeeds were entered into the registers kept by the "longevity bureaus" and "offices of evil." These were the heavenly registers of life and the earthly registers of death; the first was stored in Heaven in the Palace of Light (Mingtang), and the second in the Great Yin. All misdeeds were punished by a shortening of the assigned life span. After death, the immortals rose to Heaven; all others went to the underworld. Repercussions from good as well as evil deeds would be felt by succeeding generations. Confucian virtues were valued, and filial piety consisted above all in finding ways to ensure long life for one's parents. The souls of the dead do not demand care or costly offerings. They are content to rest in peace under the earth, which they do if the earth is rich. They then return to "nourish" their descendants. Otherwise, they come back to trouble the living. It thus seems as though there is a communication in the flow of life between living and dead. In addition, the breaths of the dead are reincarnated after five generations, but not individually, it seems. Heaven is a father, and the Earth a mother. We should be as unwilling to dig in the Earth as we would be to cut into the body of our own mother. It was also forbidden to drill wells and to kill baby girls, a custom thus attested to by this text. They represent the Yin principle, which is necessary to life. Celibacy was condemned because it interrupts the flow of life.

In addition, the text presents precepts and techniques for achieving long life. The first condition for long life is to live morally and frugally. Medicinal plants can help by curing sicknesses. They are classified according to their efficacy into "celestial" plants, which work in a single day; "terrestrial" plants, whose effectiveness requires two days; and "human" plants (literally those of "human demons," or the souls of the dead), which work only at the end of three days. Acupuncture needles and moxibustion are also used. Of course, talismans and curses are also a significant resource. Finally, music has a therapeutic value, with each of the notes connected with a bodily organ that it could keep in good shape in line with the correspondences established by the Five Agents. One must eat seasonal foods and train oneself to eat little, finally reaching the point at which one's intake is limited to drugs and "non-material" foods, like breath, including the cosmic breaths of Yin and Yang. The text alludes to non-specific breathing techniques, in connection with which the "dark female" of Laozi is evoked in terms that presage the "embryonic breathing" of later texts. Interior visualization is recommended, and meditation techniques are described. One of them is called "preserving the One" and consists of visualizing colored breaths until one is as illuminated on the inside as on the outside. Another consists of seeing one's viscera taking on human forms and clothing of colors corresponding to the current season of the year.

Kou Qianzhi

The history of the Celestial Masters reached a turning point with Kou Qianzhi, who renewed the movement and gave it a time of glory at the court of the Northern Wei (in north China) between 424 and 448. This period is different in that this is not a popular movement but an elite one at the court, under the auspices of the emperor.

The Wei dynasty emerged from a barbarian tribe, the Tuoba, whose religion, a mixture of shamanism and animism, predisposed them to be receptive to the Taoist immortality techniques with their magico-religious cast. Some years earlier, a department consecrated to the immortals (in which Kou Qianzhi held office) and a laboratory for immortality drugs had been created. Furthermore, the court, in the person of the minister Cui Hao (381–450), appreciated suggestions favoring the installation of a new Chinese state in north China, which they found in the ideology of "chosen people" of the Celestial Masters and the conservative and counterrevolutionary tendencies of Kou Qianzhi.

Kou Qianzhi claimed to have received two texts, revealed to him in 415 and 423 by Lord Lao. By offering them to the court, he could be considered a celestial messenger who was bringing the young barbarian dynasty a warrant of confidence and support given it by Heaven in its mandate. Furthermore, as a member of the Chinese northern aristocracy, he brought the support of old families from that area who were already adherents of the Celestial Masters movement.

The new religious bent of Kou Qianzhi was influenced by many sources. His Confucianist taste for a hierarchical society organized by respect for rituals was mixed with the moral posture required by the Buddhists, among whom Kou Qianzhi had teachers. He was also influenced by considerations that had preoccupied the Chinese intelligentsia for nearly two centuries. These came in part from the School of Mystery (Xuanxue) and in part from the School of Names (Mingjiao). Such questions bore on the relationship between the personal life of the individual and that of society, between free, creative spontaneity and social obligations.[3] In addition, Kou Qianzhi wanted to channel and reduce the inherent tendency of Taoist communities to form a marginal society with revolutionary tendencies, as evidenced some years before by the revolt led by the Taoist Sun En (d. 402). In his desire to inaugurate an era of Great Peace rather than an egalitarian community, Kou Qianzhi dreamed of a well-ordered State, which agreed perfectly with the ideas of Cui Hao, who was his first promoter.

It was Cui Hao who supported him before the emperor and obtained for Kou Qianzhi the official title of Celestial Master. He also saw to it that Kou's new code, the *Laojun yinsong jiejing*, was promulgated throughout the empire. A Taoist altar was built in the southeastern quarter of the capital, and 120 Taoist priests were invited there to celebrate their cult. Kou then convinced the emperor to take as the reign name Perfect Sovereign of the Great Peace and to adopt the role implied by this title. This led to a solemn ceremony, during which Kou gave the emperor talismans and registers confirming his imperial virtue. Thus began a whole series of investiture ceremonies, which continued until 574, in which emperors received confirmation of their mandate from the Taoists.

The Taoist community in the capital had a hard time surviving the death of Kou Qianzhi in 448. Its dispersal was finally ordered in 548. This whole chapter is important in the history of Taoism, however, because it was the first time that the religion was instituted officially as a state religion.

The *Daozang* preserves for us the text by Kou Qianzhi that underlay his religious code, which was intended to purify the "false doctrine of the three Zhang" (the founding Celestial Masters). Religion was to be purged of sexual practices, the imposition of religious taxes on the faithful, the inheritance of religious titles, and the custom of banquets. In the text Kou also condemned messianic movements and called for the copying and psalmodic recitation of sacred texts, the *Daodejing* in particular. He instituted for his faithful certain rules of good behavior and regularized the rules that governed the written form of requests addressed to deities and the rites that governed the "entry into the pure chamber," to which the master withdrew while the faithful remained at the door, confessing their sins. Good people would become members of the "seed people" and have eternal life; the bad would go to hell and be reborn as insects or animals.

The influence of the Celestial Masters declined during the following centuries as new revelations and movements appeared. They came to rank on the lowest level of the hierarchy of Taoist schools. Apparently no text specifically from this school was produced under the Six Dynasties, but a large collection, the *Zhengyi fawen*, brought together the texts of the school at the end of this period and was added to during the Tang. Scattered later throughout several volumes, this collection has not come down to us as a whole.

Under the Tang, toward the end of the eighth century, there grew up a center and new line of Celestial Masters at Mount Longhu, but the religious districts disappeared. The activity of this center was essentially dedicated to the publishing and sale to the Inspectors of Merits (the heads of the liturgical organization) of registers of ordination that served as protective talismans. A cult grew up around these talismans. During the ninth century, associations and guilds patronized by local sages, wise men under the aegis of the Zhengyi church, developed. These became centers of local cults and survive to our day. This Taoist church then played an important role in the establishment, alongside the official administration, of networks of commercial and cultural exchange uniting villages and businessmen.[4]

The Zhengyi church revived greatly under the Song and was supported officially by the Ming emperors. Its priests were then promoted to the leadership of all the Taoist movements that had meanwhile been formed. Today, this sect is the most flourishing and active of all surviving Taoist movements.

4

Ge Hong and His Tradition

Ge Hong

Ge Hong (ca. 280–ca. 343) is a significant figure in a long tradition dating back to Han searchers for immortality. He is one of the links in the chain of those who continued and developed the line of correlative thought of the Five Agents school. The text he has left us, known from his pseudonym as the *Baopuzi* (*The Master Who Embraces Simplicity*, a quotation from Laozi), unfortunately is not a methodical presentation of the techniques he discusses and thus does not permit a systematic reconstruction of them. It does, however, give enough data to enable us to connect it to other writings that, although often abbreviated and changed, round it out. Thus we can get some idea of the beliefs and practices in effect at least from the beginning of the Han to Ge Hong's own time. We can also see the unity that, despite some evolution, exists among various currents of Taoist thought from the Han to the Chinese middle ages (fourth to sixth centuries A.D.). Ge Hong also became a reference point for many later writers who cited him or claimed his authority, signing their texts with his name (the custom in ancient China among those who considered themselves the spiritual descendants of a great master). Finally, he is the only author in the history of Taoism who left a personal point of view and the only practitioner of the ancient tradition of immortality techniques who placed them in the general Taoist context of the search for immortality, beyond simple hygienic or therapeutic techniques.

Ge Hong has often been presented as an alchemist. This is not completely false, but it is inaccurate as an overall judgment. Above all, he was a seeker after immortality. In this connection he made it clear that although this was his dominant concern, such a quest did not *define* Taoism. And although he became involved in al-chemical work, which he considered an indispensable and useful tool, he repeatedly insisted that many other conditions and prac-tices are no less indispensable. He reveals both his belief in im-mortality and the many requirements imposed by searching for it without imposing any systematic methodology or making an effort at synthesis. His work is a rich source of information, but it is of-ten cluttered and disorganized.

I begin by fixing Ge Hong in his tradition, reconstructing the lineage of masters and texts into which he fits. Then, after laying out the main lines of his thought, I shall try to give some insight into the various methods that he used (filling out his own state-ments with data from texts by other authors who describe them more fully and either are apparently contemporaneous with him or come from circles he claimed adherence to).

The Tradition Behind Ge Hong

Ge Hong belonged to an aristocratic family from south China, a region where the Celestial Masters movement had not yet spread widely and that still adhered to the tradition of the *fangshi* magi-cians. He represents a long line going back at least to the *fangshi* who surrounded Emperor Wu of the Han. The immortals or searchers for immortality he admires are those that Zhuangzi spoke of, along with those mentioned in the *Chuci* and the histo-ries of the preceding dynasties, as well as earlier hagiographies like the *Liexian zhuan* (*Biographies of Immortals*). Apart from these people, he constantly alluded to writings and methods whose number and diversity attest to the secular activity and speculations to which he was heir. Some of the methods that he described can be directly connected to knowledge going back to the Warring Kingdoms (at least to the third century B.C.). In addition, he compiled a catalogue of the library of his master; unfortunately practically all the works listed have disappeared, and their contents are unknown to us. Still, the fact that the library existed is yet another indication of the long history of the tradition and the antiquity of its roots.

The existence of this library underlines a fact that distinguishes Ge Hong's tradition sharply from that of the Celestial Masters. The revelation on which the latter school is based is not a text but simply a covenant (between Laojun and Zhang Daoling), and the transmission of knowledge and power from master to disciples is through "registers," an inventory of the cosmic or divine forces under the master's power. In the tradition that Ge Hong inherited, we are immediately faced with a *library*, and many references are made to specific texts.

Ge Hong says that his master was a disciple of Ge's great-uncle, Ge Xuan (164–244), who was himself a member of the school of Zuo Ci (155–220), a *fangshi* of the group around Cao Cao. From this line he received the *Lingbao wufujing* (*The Five Talismans from Lingbao*), which gave him entrance into the mountains, as well as the *Text of Cinnabar-Nine and the Golden Elixir*, whose origins seem to date at least to Li Shaojun, the court alchemist of Emperor Wu of the Han. He also announced his connection with his father-in-law, Baojing (230 or 260–330), a high official from a traditional Taoist family. Baojing received the transmission of a method of "freeing from the corpse" by means of a sword as well as two fundamental Taoist texts: the *Sanhuang wen* (*Text of the Three August Ones*), supposedly revealed to him in a cave, which allowed him to "command deities in the sky and spirits from the earth," and the "Diagram of the True Form of the Five Peaks," a work originally allied to cosmic diagrams that legend says had previously been revealed to Emperor Wu. This text is associated with the art of commanding the gods of days marked by the *jia* cyclical signs (the "Six *jia*") and with another text that contains the description of the isles of immortality. Ge Hong also possessed a method for "pacing out the Big Dipper" that permitted the adept to be pardoned for his transgressions and have his name inscribed in the heavens.

All these texts, with the exception of the alchemical treatise, were similar in type. They were associated with the Five Agents and the five directions corresponding to them. They were magical talismans that let their possessor dominate and win over spirits. In addition, all of them passed through the same hands: the people who had come from all corners of China to live at the courts of Emperor Wu and Cao Cao, where they had gathered in response to the interest of those two statesmen in magical practices and the search for immortality. These texts survive in the *Daozang*, and although they have been changed, edited, and shortened, it is possible to determine that at least in part they correspond to the texts that Ge Hong knew.

The text about the Six *jia* is a talisman that gives power over spirits and subjugates demons, allows the user to change his form and disappear, and to command the forces of nature: control the sun, bring thunder, call up wind and rain—all arts that the legendary Taoist saints excelled in. It also lets the user "summon the traveling kitchen" (*xingchu*), an expression connected to alchemical techniques like those of Li Shaojun, of whom it was said that he "summoned beings [gods] by sacrificing at the oven." The expression also reminds us of the "heavenly kitchens" or feasts where, during ritual ceremonies already known among the Celestial Masters, dishes were passed around (*xing*); at the same time, gods were summoned to participate in these agapes (see Chapter 3). The term "kitchen" goes back to the idea of cooking and to the viscera that "cook" foods. Thus we have closely connected ideas of spirit summoning, communal feasts, and meditation on the viscera.

The "Six *jia*" text, by providing the names and descriptions of the Six *jia*, gives one power over these deities, to which we shall return below. Similarly the *Text of the Three August Ones*, that of the *Five Talismans* (preserved in part in the *Daozang*), and that of the

"Five Peaks" were originally talismans that made visible both gods and those "plants of life" to which various texts had been grafted. The *Text of the Five Talismans* contains the names of deities of the human body, and the *Text of the Three August Ones* lets the user control evil spirits and invoke the gods of heaven (the All High—*Gaoshang*—or the High Heaven—*Gaotian*), the gods of heavenly bodies (sun, moon, and Big Dipper), or those of nature and the earth (the ancient earth and river gods).

Ge Hong's View of the Tao and Immortality

As was pointed out above, Ge Hong's sole concern was immortality, a fact that gives these texts and practices an undeniable unity in that all of them share this single goal, and their role and ranking are assigned with it in mind. In addition, Ge endowed his work with a more elevated inspiration than that detectable in the texts just mentioned. He placed it emblematically under the sign of what he refers to as the "Mystery" (*xuan*), as shown by the first lines of the *Baopuzi*:

> The Mystery is the first ancestor of the Spontaneous,
> the root of the many diversities.
> Unfathomable and murky in its depths, it is also called
>   imperceivable;
> stretching far into the distance, it is also called wonderful;
> so high that it covers the nine empyreans,
> so wide that it encompasses the eight cardinal points;
> shining beyond the sun and the moon,
> speedy beyond the rapid light;
> it both suddenly shines forth and disappears like a shadow.
> it both surges up in a whirlwind and streaks away like a comet;
> it is both stirred up by deep eddies and like a clear deep pool,
> it is both flaky and at the same time misty, rising up in clouds;
> it takes on form and gender, and it exists [*you*];
> it returns to darkness and solitude, and it is no more [*wu*];
> it plunges beyond, into the great darkness, and buries itself deep;
> it rises above the stars and floats on high;
> neither metal nor stone can equal its hardness,
> and the moist dew cannot attain its softness.
> Square without set-square, round without compasses,
> it comes and no one sees it,

it leaves and no one follows it;
through it, the sky is high and the earth low;
through it, the clouds rush by and the rain falls.
It carries within it the embryo of the Original One,
it forms and shapes the two Principles (Yin and Yang);
it exhales and absorbs the great Genesis,
it inspires and transforms the multitude of species,
it makes the constellations go round,
it shaped the primordial Darkness,
it guides the wonderful mainspring of the universe,
it exhales the four seasons,
it encloses the void and silence in darkness,
it frees and parcels out natural abundance,
it makes the heavy fall and the light rise up,
it makes the rivers Ho and Wei flow.
If one adds to it, it does not increase.
If one takes away from it, it does not grow less.
If something is given to it, it is not increased in glory.
If something is taken from it, it does not suffer.
Where the Mystery is present, joy is infinite;
where the Mystery has departed, efficacy is exhausted
    and the spirit disappears.

By thus beginning the *Baopuzi* with the subject of the Mystery—
another name for the Tao—Ge Hong associates his work with the
ineffable that supports and encloses all things and, more important for him, with the incomprehensible mystery and marvel of
life. This short segment is close to the way in which the Taoists
(Huainanzi, for example) describe the Tao (or the Sage; see Anna
Seidel's translation of the *Laozi bianhuajing*), which is the "basis,"
the "ancestor," the first unity that gives life and form to all the
multiple mutations. In this role, It encompasses all oppositions; It
can be both large and small, revealed and hidden, flexible and
rigid (the two poles of the universe in the *Book of Change*), wide
and deep, horizontal and vertical, present or absent. It gives each
thing its characteristic qualities: height to Heaven, lowness to
Earth, speed to clouds, wetness to rain, and so on; furthermore,
the Tao gives movement to the circle and stability to the square,
elevation to upward motion, and depth to downward motion. In
talking of the person who attains the Mystery, Ge Hong continues:

He is so high that no one can reach him,
so deep that no one can penetrate to his depth;
he rides the fluid light,
he whips space in the six directions,
he crosses the watery expanses,
he emerges beyond height,
he penetrates below depth,
he crosses the threshold of vastness,
he takes his pleasure in the distant, remote plains,
he splashes in the vague darkness,
he sails to the point of the indefinite,
he absorbs the nine efflorescences at the edge of the clouds,
he tastes the six breaths of the empyrean,
he goes here and there in the shadowy darkness,
he leaps into the thinnest minuteness.

"He who attains the Mystery" is described in terms that draw on those depicting the frolicking of the Sage in the *Zhuangzi* or the ecstatic wanderings of the poet in the *Chuci*. These terms had been adopted by the Han court poet Sima Xiangru (179–117 B.C.) to describe the celestial flight of the Great Man. The elements of this flight include light, space, darkness, clouds, and the empyrean, in which he disports himself, on which he feeds, and which he exhales. He crosses them, or he "rides" them or "walks on" them. The vocabulary used gives an impression of infinity and liberty so great as to verge on the ineffable. The author draws on the arsenal of "atmospheric" binomes in the Chinese language, using many terms borrowed from Zhuangzi and the *Chuci*—words that describe the movements of the wings of birds as they rise up and descend, turn, come and go, or else the obscurity of mystical darkness, free wandering, the empty vastness of space, going beyond all limits, both upward and outward.

In addition, to talk about the elusive nature of the Tao (chap. 9),[1] Ge Hong used the terms *you* and *wu* ("existence," or "being there," and its negation); this is an echo of Wang Bi, who, in his commentary on the *Daodejing*, wrote of the Ultimate Truth: "We would like to say it is *wu* [it does not exist], yet it accomplishes everything. We would like to say that it is *you* [existence, being there], yet we cannot see any form in it" (*Daodejing* 14). Ge Hong may have been influenced by this text when he wrote: "If one talks of its absence [*wu*], then, shadow and echo, it is as if it were present [*you*]; if one talks of its presence [*you*], then the ten thousand beings are like an absence [*wu*]" (Ware 9.1a). The fine end of an autumnal hair (than which there is nothing smaller) is too big for it, and the immensity of space is too little for it. In terms reminiscent of Laozi, Ge Hong says that the Tao has no name, the term "Tao" is a "borrowed name" (*Daodejing* 25), and, adds Ge, all the myriad namings, distinctions, and speculations on it are only aberrations. Then we seem to be hearing Zhuangzi again: "Maintain yourself in calm non-intervention, and there will be no need for exorcism or invocations; the Tao is here and not far away, and our fate lies in ourselves, not in the exterior world." The first part of this statement clearly shows Ge Hong's double position: he aligns himself in a way with the "philosophical Taoism" of Laozi and Zhuangzi, who teach that non-intervention alone is enough, and yet elsewhere he openly accuses them of not having transmitted any precise mode of action and dedicates a large part of his book to talking about this. The second part of the statement expresses a fundamental position of his, as well as that of many other authors who use the same formula. Contradicting the first half of the sentence, it justifies the need for effective methods: immortality actually lies in our own hands; it is not a matter of fate; it is the result of a long effort. For Ge Hong, big principles were not enough: Laozi and Zhuangzi fly too high above us and bring no aid to those who seek immortality. He states that Taoism is not limited to "nourishing life," but then dedicates the bulk of his book to methods for achieving immortality.

Ge Hong divided the *Baopuzi* into two parts, *wai* and *nei*—the exoteric *wai* devoted to Confucianism, and the esoteric *nei* devoted to Taoism. In terms of his conception of the nature of Taoism, the latter is a complement to the former. On the one hand is Confucianism, dedicated to organizing society and regulating human behavior, and, on the other, Taoism, which advocates the renunciation of honors, material possessions, knowledge, the exterior world, and personal desires. To the complex body of rules governing Confucian life, he opposed the silent teaching of Taoism and the simplicity of its commands. Each has its territory, according to Ge Hong, who claimed that Huangdi, the Yellow Emperor, was the only person who knew how to cultivate both Confucian wisdom and Taoist sanctity. This is his explanation of that ambiguous person, who was both wise sovereign and Taoist mystic. However, Ge did cite him as an exception to the fact that official life and the cares of government are incompatible with the quest for immortality. By now all the ancient political aims of Taoism have disappeared. Yet Ge Hong, in a formula that recurs frequently in Taoist texts, states that in Taoism "caring for oneself and ruling the Nation" go hand in hand—the principles governing these actions are identical. But the means were not the same as those of Confucianism, since the Taoist ruler brings order to everything according to natural harmony—by achieving his own inner rectitude and by simply placing himself in the direct line of the Tao, respecting it, and submitting himself to it. There is no need to set up rites or rules governing morality and behavior, nor any specifically prescribed means of government.[2]

The immortals do exist, even if they are not visible to the vulgar herd who do not believe in them. Ge Hong argued passionately against skepticism. He fully believed in the reality of the experiences he reported; hence the importance of the retelling of the miracles worked by the immortals and recorded in hagiographies and the official histories. There is no end to the marvels of this world, he proposed. How could one presume to know everything, and why should we deny the existence of miracles when we know almost nothing about what exists in Heaven and here on Earth? Why should we limit ourselves to what we have seen and heard? That is tantamount to cutting off a limb. Is it not pitiful to deny the existence of knowledge beyond reason and to limit ourselves to the conceivable and our mundane existence? Let us try, like the Sage, to transcend this world; Confucian wisdom, human in its kind, is easy to understand because it relies on primary evidence, but it is incomplete in comparison with Taoist saintliness, which deals with mystery, life, things difficult to understand. Taoist thought passes beyond mere evidence and has knowledge of longevity and immortality. The immortal is as real and as hidden as is the precious stone in its matrix; the fact that it is concealed does not mean that it does not exist. Change is part of the nature of the world. Metamorphoses happen constantly. Thus, what is there to prevent one from becoming an immortal? We are not, nor should we consider ourselves, unchangeable. However, this is a matter of faith, he concluded; people cannot be forced to believe this. Ge Hong claimed to be addressing only those who believe in extraordinary things, in marvels, about which the Confucian classics are silent; despite his stated opposition to skepticism, he maintained that it was fruitless to try to convince skeptics.

Ge Hong placed the immortals in the category of natural phenomena resulting from transformation. In order to support this belief, he used as an argument the metamorphoses that occur in nature, already obligingly described by the authors of antiquity—Zhuangzi, Huainanzi, and Liezi. These transformations testify to the existence of a cosmic continuum and a process of development. Still, when he compared natural metamorphoses to dyeing, in the same way that the *Huainanzi* compared these changes to the production of fabric from hemp fibers, he introduced an element of "human labor"; although natural, immortality is still a transformation and the result of deliberate action. It remains a natural phenomenon, although pushed a little farther. That it is inexplicable reflects only our inability to understand it. But there is more. For Ge Hong, death does not seem to be as natural a phenomenon as it at first appears. It is the result of contrary forces, miasmas of all sorts, sicknesses, aging. All these things can be combated.

We must distinguish between longevity and immortality; the first is only a single step toward, and a necessary condition for, the second. There are also three kinds of immortals. Ge Hong, like most Taoist writers, distinguished between those who live on earth (terrestrial immortals who enjoy supernatural powers), those who take up residence in Kunlun (the axis of the world), and those who dwell in the skies (Ware 4.7b). Elsewhere (8.2b) he put on the lowest level those who practice "freeing from the corpse" (see below). Above them are the "terrestrial immortals" (often confused with the former in Taoist texts), whose state is sometimes the result of a free choice on the part of those who do not want to renounce ordinary desires or to ascend into the void (3.8a). Then come the "divine immortals" who "go up into the sky in broad daylight." They have succeeded both in preserving their physical integrity and in making their bodies so pure and light that they can rise into Heaven in bodily form.

In any case, to Ge Hong immortality was physical. The idea of immortality would later undergo change, but it is clear that Ge Hong and most of the Taoists of his period saw it as something more than a state of consciousness. A great number of their practices had as their goal the purification and sublimation of the body; saintliness was achieved through this sublimation. However, even though immortals as Ge Hong envisaged them may have moved in infinite spheres, they do not seem to have the same cosmic qualities as the immortals we encounter in Zhuangzi—this despite a single strange, but apparently isolated remark (8.2a) that the Alchemical Elixir guarantees the immortality of the entire world and not just of a single individual.

Immortality was bodily and, in some ways, natural but still "godlike" and exceptional, achieved only after great effort. It could and should be cultivated. In this Ge Hong took his place in a long debate that occupied the Chinese both before and after his time: immortality and saintliness were possible—but did one have to work for them or were they innate? In the eyes of Ge Hong, immortality was the ultimate aim of all ritual practices, none of which could be complete in itself but each of which complemented all the others and had a usefulness and limits that had to be fully understood.

The first condition for achieving immortality was to believe in it. Ge Hong frequently insisted on the need for faith and firm purpose. Ascesis was long and hard, and if the will of the adept was not firmly founded, he was likely to abandon his efforts. This firm purpose, this faith, is a gift. It is part of the fate of each person, of the individual's innate vocation to consecrate himself to this effort, and this faith cannot be fabricated. "Vocation" is probably the appropriate word to use here, because Ge Hong explained that it depended on the star that presides over our birth (7.1a) and destines each individual to dedicate his life to a certain art or trade. Because of the need for this vocation, the first step toward the search for immortality had to be spontaneous. Thus it was obviously useless to undertake any form of proselytizing.

It was then necessary to find a competent master who not only transmitted secret texts but also rounded them out with necessary oral information. Such a master knew how to be a wise guide. But he would accept as a disciple only the person whose firmness and perseverance he had tested over a long period (see, e.g., 14.5a). Because the choice of a knowledgeable master was so necessary, Ge Hong spoke as harshly as did the Confucians against false masters, charlatans, and messiahs of all persuasions who mislead and abuse the people.

However, guidance from a master and help from the gods were merely necessary adjuncts: only the individual himself could preserve his own life and achieve longevity, which is, in the last resort, dependent on neither morality nor intelligence (7.2b–3a). Ge Hong roundly criticized those who expect the gods to give them good fortune and blame demons for all the evils that befall them instead of looking to their own behavior. He did not believe in the efficacy of sacrifices and prayers since they are often made by dissolute people and unrepentant sinners. "Our fate is in our own hands": what can the gods do if we insist on destroying our bodies by our own acts? Here we can hear the "technician" speaking.

Above all else one must lead a healthy life, both morally and physically. Morality is necessary because one must maintain the necessary serenity, untroubled by desires, whether for sex or for power and fame. The rules that Ge Hong recommended derived from contemporary morality. The only special quality is a kind of universal love that must be extended even to "crawling creatures" (6.5a–b and 3.8b). All the calls for concord within the village have disappeared, which should not be surprising given the social milieu Ge Hong lived in.

Punishment for transgression could fall on the members of a miscreant's family, an idea in line with the ancient Chinese penal system and the concept of family solidarity. One had to pay for a misdeed not only through the ritual means indicated by texts but also by a compensatory act along the lines of the misdeed committed. Thus, someone who had benefited from ill-gotten gains should give alms to beggars, and someone who had shifted blame onto an innocent party had to undertake to promote competent men to official positions.

Ge Hong's prescriptions for living a physically healthy life are sensible and can be found in almost identical form in other Taoist texts in this same spirit (DZ 821, 3b; 862, 9b and 13a). All excesses must be avoided: one should not remain seated, lying down, or standing too long; one should neither overtire oneself nor rest too much; one should not eat or drink too much; one should not abstain from sexual relations but neither should one overindulge in them; one should not bathe too often; one should not strain the eyes by trying to see too far, and so on (Ware 13.7b–8a). One also had to know how to avoid sicknesses and how to cure them. This was the goal of all the various physical practices, such as taking drugs, circulating the breath, exercising, and practicing techniques of visual meditation.

Of course, it was also important to know how to avoid perils, dangerous beasts, and political enemies. This is the true reason for the supernatural powers conferred by talismans or certain techniques that permit one to disappear, to change form, or even to become invulnerable. Some of these go back to the period of the Warring States and were among the arts of war.

Help from the gods is invaluable in keeping away evil. This is why one had to know techniques for controlling them. In addition, it was both good and necessary to stimulate the vital powers, either by using drugs or engaging in physical exercises, or by arousing the gods who reside within the body (6.3a).

We shall look more closely at some of these practices, but after this brief explanation of the overall way of thinking that, according to Ge Hong, should govern the use of methods intended to ensure immortality, let us take a look at the general view of the nature of the world and of humanity that underlies them. This can be reconstructed from a group of texts by writers from the same tradition as Ge Hong. Some date from before his time (like the *Huainanzi* and Heshang gong's commentary on the *Daodejing*, in addition to the works noted at the beginning of this chapter); others are contemporaneous with him. This view of the nature of the world and humankind persisted long after Ge Hong's time—in fact, down to our own days—as the basis of Taoist cosmology and anthropology. Of course, it has been elaborated along the way.

The Art of "Nourishing the Vital Principle"

Yangsheng (or *zhisheng*), the art of "nourishing the vital principle" (a phrase used by Zhuangzi), consists of adopting a way of life ruled by physico-mental hygienic principles. This is not specifically a Taoist art and derives from ancient Chinese practices; Taoism adopted, developed, and modified them by introducing the idea of the "primordial breath" (*yuanqi*) by associating them with the Taoist authorities and gods, as well as with certain more specifically religious practices, by giving them a cosmic dimension, and by adding the idea of purification and sublimation. Even when they seem to be eclipsed by new tendencies, the rules of this art remain a foundation of all Taoist practices in all eras—exorcism, therapy, liturgy, "interior alchemy"—and have never ceased to be the subject of many treatises during all epochs.

This art is traditionally compared with that of governing a country. It consists of controlling, and thus making more healthy (the two meanings of the word *zhi*, which is used to express the idea of "governing"), the vital forces, most prominently the breath (*qi*) and the semen (*jing*). Two basic principles govern the proper use of these: they are to be saved (one is to avoid all excessive and ill-considered expenditure), and they must circulate in a balanced fashion so as to make them harmoniously active. Any sickness or physical problem arises from a lack, an excess, or a blockage of these two fluids—this is one of the essential rules of both Chinese medicine and Chinese cosmology. The story of the Great Yu, one of the forefathers of Taoism, testifies to this fact. He was able to "cure" (*zhi*) China of its "great floods," not by building dams (as his father unsuccessfully tried to do) but by opening natural pathways along the lines of force in earthly geography to drain the water. Obviously one has to know the map of both the world and the body in order to know how to direct the vital forces and let them circulate.

Cosmology and Anthropology

Life and death. In the tradition established by Ge Hong, the concept of human life and death derives from two major inspirations: on the one hand, the very idea of life, which is defined mainly in terms of solidarity and harmony with Nature, and on the other, immortality, the main goal of the tradition. The idea of life as a form of harmony with Nature owes much to the principles of the Yin-Yang school and the Five Agents (see the Introduction). To these Ge added traditional ancient Chinese beliefs about phenomena that govern everything one does.

Life is "breath." Death occurs when the breath disappears. But the human body is also the abode of a number of different spirits who give it life. Life lasts only as long as these spirits are present in the body, and their departure marks death. In addition, the star that rules over the birth of each individual gives a set life span, which may, however, be shortened as a punishment for bad behavior. Some spirits, like the god of fate (Siming), the god of the hearth, and the "three worms" (or "three corpses"), already mentioned in the *weishu* (the esoteric apocrypha; see Chapter 2), watch over the acts of human beings and report regularly to Heaven, which responds severely to evildoing by shortening the life span originally allotted the transgressor. This is, of course, the worst punishment that can befall seekers after immortality. It was in this spirit that later editors drew up inventories of sins and good deeds, all of which determined one's life span, which was shortened or lengthened according to sins committed or good deeds performed. The oldest of these inventories dates to 1171; the number of them multiplied in later periods. By the seventeenth century, they had become personal guides to conduct among the adepts, within the framework of popular morality.

The celestial and terrestrial pantheons. The main divinities or spirits of concern here are, on the cosmic level, the Three-One, the star gods controlling time and the calendar, and the deities presiding over the four cardinal directions and the center. Most of them are very ancient.

The One, already exalted by Laozi and Zhuangzi who said that it was to be "embraced" or "kept," is either identified with the Tao or said to be engendered by It. In many interpretations, it is the Ultimate Truth or its first comprehensible form. It is reflected in the three levels of the universe. The principle of the triad, according to Laozi, gave birth to the world. It is the number Three, made up of the union between Heaven and Earth and their product, Humanity (or the Child), or of Yin and Yang and the product of their union, Harmony. These forms of the Three-One, because of their primordial nature, are also called the Three Originals (*sanyuan*). Here again we see beliefs expressed in the *weishu*.

The Six *jia* (*liujia*) are deities that the *weishu* placed on the same level as the cosmic entities, along with Heaven, Earth, and the four seasons. They are also tied to the calendrical speculations that govern the study of astral influences and played an important role in the knowledge, needed for all religious activities, of auspicious and unlucky days. According to Chinese calculation of such days, within the set of 60 cyclical signs that plays a large part in divination (Ngo Van Xuyet, p. 193), the Six *jia* control the first day of each decade or of each lunar cycle or year.[3] They are thus gods we could call "chronocrats," controlling the division of time. In addition, according to Du Guangting, the great ninth-century scholar of ritual, they participate in the shaping of the embryo, in the same way that the Nine Supreme Heavens do in the Shangqing texts.

These celestial deities have earthly counterparts, of which the main ones are simply ancient deifications of the four cardinal directions and the center. They take the form of heraldic animals (dragon for the east, red bird for the south, tiger for the west, turtle for the north) or of the Five Emperors living at the five points, which are marked by the Five Sacred Peaks of Taoism, the mountains that moor the earth and assure its stability, its primary characteristic. These mountains are the earthly analogues of the five planets. Such deities (whether heraldic animals or emperors) are thus charged with giving a shape to space (in this case, terrestrial) and with determining the center and protecting the adept.

At the terrestrial poles live spirits inherited from Chinese mythology. In the middle rises Kunlun, the axis of the world, whose summit touches the Polestar and whose base is rooted in the underworld (the Yellow Springs). An earthly double of the Big Dipper, it shares the same functions. It is the abode of the ancient Queen Mother of the West and the earthly immortals. The most ancient detailed description we have of Kunlun, in the *Huainanzi*, describes it as a paradisaical place of initiation surrounded by a moat of "weak water" on which not even a feather can float. Thus it can be reached only through the air.

The body. The oldest work describing Taoist physiology is the *Huangtingjing* (*The Book of the Yellow Court*), which describes it in cryptic terms. It is a reference work that has given rise to many commentaries and further elaborations.[4]

The body, on the pattern of the universe, is divided into three parts; each of these has a center (called the "cinnabar field") where the hypostases of the primordial One come to settle. Thus, in the lower belly, two or three inches below the navel, is the lower cinnabar field, which goes by many names, among them Gate of Fate (*ming*, "fate," is also used for the vital force). In the thorax, the middle cinnabar field lies in the heart, or Scarlet Palace. The upper cinnabar field, in the head, occupies a "palace" called the *niwan*. In these three cinnabar fields live the "three worms," the chthonic powers who bring destruction and death. Thus, these cinnabar fields are three special places, home simultaneously of health and death, Heavenly Originals, and worldly demons.

Whereas the three cinnabar fields correspond to the vertical axis of the world, the five *zang* (receptacles)—liver, heart, spleen, lungs, and kidneys—occupy special points in the relationship of human beings with the cosmos, since they are under the direction of the Five Agents, that is, in a horizontal plane. The Five Agents, through the *zang*, thus control the life and balance of each human being, each of them according to its own mode of action (this or that food, color, sound, according to the Agent concerned) and its time (hour of the day or season of the year). The *zang* correspond to the five planets and the Five Sacred Peaks. In addition, they hold the spiritual forces, which are, in order, the *hun* (Yang, heavenly souls), the spirit (*shen*), the will, the *po* (Yin, earthly souls), and seminal fluid (*jing*) (there is some variation in the textual sources). The body is also inhabited by 24 spirits of light, whom the Celestial Masters also recognize under other names. They correspond to the 24 solar divisions along the tropics, or the "breaths" of the year.

Basic Practices

On the basis of this general overview, we can now look at various kinds of Taoist practices mentioned by Ge Hong.

Purification. Before engaging in a practice, the Taoist must attain a prescribed state of moral and ritual purity. Participants need to achieve both physical purity, achieved by ritual washing and by fasting, and mental purity. The adept should withdraw from the world so as to avoid contact with all ordinary, impure, or skeptical people and live in a state of perfect calm. No ritual practice can be effective without the help of gods invited to participate in it by means of a preliminary religious ceremony. The gods will not come or will leave if any unbeliever or disturbing element is present. In addition, the spirits love peacefulness and will leave troubled places. Even if only to retain their interior gods, adepts need serenity. This is also why Taoists prefer to work in the mountains, but Ge Hong made clear that one should choose "big mountains" ruled by gods and not "little mountains" infested by spirits of a lower sort (spirits of trees and stones, vampires, and the like; Ware 4.16b–17a). (This indicates a perceived need to separate Taoism from suspect popular beliefs.) The need for tranquillity explains why Ge Hong thought that men burdened by official duties or overwhelmed with worries could not undertake the quest for immortality.

In addition to mountains, adepts retired to chapels called "purity chambers," which have their origin in the practices of the Celestial Masters. The building and furnishing of these chapels had to follow strict rules. In addition, as adepts began each period of meditation, they established symbolically a sacred, closed area by calling on the four heraldic animals to occupy the four corners of the space, thus enclosing and protecting it.

Time. Time is qualitative and cyclical, defined by the evolutions of Yin, Yang, and the Five Agents. Because the division of the day is set, on the model of the year, by the influences of Yin and Yang, it is wise to exert oneself only at moments of "living breath," that is, during the Yang hours that extend from midnight to noon.

In most of the practices Ge Hong reported, the season of the year determined the direction of prayer and the identity of the divinities or entities whose intervention was sought: emperors of the four cardinal directions, stars, colored breaths, and the like. Especially crucial were the "eight articulations" of the year, those times when the balance between Yin and Yang changes. These are the first days of each season (in the Chinese calendar, the first day of the first [spring], fourth [summer], seventh [autumn], and tenth [winter] months), the solstices, and the equinoxes—two times when either Yang or Yin is at a peak and two of balance between them. Many practices had to be carried out at these times. In the works of Ge Hong (as in later ones, like those of the Shangqing school, which derive from the same lineage), we find notes on auspicious and inauspicious days, part of the heritage bequeathed by the calendrists of the Warring States.[5]

Drugs. Among the lesser procedures, Ge Hong included the taking of drugs—both vegetable and mineral in origin. Contemporary Taoists in Ge Hong's tradition, unlike the Celestial Masters, were relatively unconcerned with herbalism and medicine. Beginning in Han times a medical specialization had grown up, and the medical tradition was largely separate from that of Taoism. But the split was never complete. Sun Simiao, the famous Tang doctor, wrote works on Taoist meditation. In addition, Taoists continued to prepare and use drugs, and several of them were called to imperial sickbeds. Many people were also cured by ritual or meditation, among them founders of schools, great figures in Taoism, and emperors.

However, the procedure Ge Hong discussed differed somewhat from this medical use of drugs. He made clear that the Taoists' vegetable drugs are something only they can use. They are not the same ones that the botanists list and name. The most special drugs are *zhi*, miraculous herbs with fantastic descriptions. (A section of chap. 11 of the *Baopuzi* is dedicated to them, as is a whole treatise preserved in the *Daozang*.) These herbs grow in the mountains and can be found only by initiates who have placated the gods by certain rites.

The minerals most used for compounding drugs were cinnabar, gold, realgar, malachite, sulfur, mica, saltpeter, and orpiment. Many of them were appreciated for symbolic reasons. For example, mica does not burn or rot and holds within it all the colors of the rainbow. The red of cinnabar (red, the color associated with Yang), the brilliance of gold and its stable nature, and the Chinese names of realgar ("male yellow," with yellow the color signifying the center) and of orpiment ("female yellow") account for, at least in part, the value attributed to them. Alchemical drugs, as Ge Hong pointed out, are different from those that doctors use. They are secret and expensive, for their purpose is not simply to cure but to bring long life. They are "distant," whereas medical drugs are "close." "Distant" (*yuan*) here is semantically associated with "heaven" (*tian*) and "mystery" (*xuan*). They cannot be obtained during times of trouble (16.5b-6a); once again emphasis is placed on serenity. The names given to ingredients, Ge Hong adds, "are sometimes the same as those of ordinary ingredients, but their true nature is different" (16.6b). One can also interpret this last phrase to mean "they are actually different." From the evidence, the reference is to some kind of secret code as well as to a different spirit governing the use of these various ingredients—all of which gives them a different meaning. Some processes seem to have an almost entirely symbolic nature, for example, feeding red meat and cinnabar to an unfledged young bird so that the feathers will be red when they appear. These feathers, along with the dried flesh of the bird, were then to be ground into a powder that would guarantee 500 years of life to anyone eating it.

This tradition comes in a direct line from the *weishu*, as proved by the direct quotation of passages in these works in the *Baopuzi* of Ge Hong.[6]

Sexual practices. Although Ge Hong discouraged chastity because it produces anxiety, careful control of sexuality is absolutely necessary, according to Ge, because such techniques permit one to have sexual relations without loss of vitality. By pressing on the base of the penis at the moment of ejaculation, the Taoists claim that they could make "the semen (*jing*) go back up into the brain." Women were supposed to concentrate on their hearts and make the breath descend to the kidneys and then travel up the spinal column to the brain. This procedure can be understood quite literally, and it often was. At other times it definitely had a symbolic meaning: certain texts use the same terms to designate practices that are strictly respiratory and visual (DZ 818, 17a-b).

Furthermore, just as one can "increase the breath" by breathing techniques, one can "increase the *jing*" (sexual energy) by stirring it up and moving it around in sexual relations that avoid actual ejaculation. After several acts of *coitus interruptus*, ejaculation would not result in loss of vital force. These practices are not strictly Taoist and have been described elsewhere.[7]

Avoiding cereals. Cereals are terrestrial in nature and thus heavy and solid in comparison with the celestial airy breath. They are to be avoided, but this prohibition is a secondary one and cannot of itself guarantee longevity. It is only one of the set of rules governing food and follows the idea, already laid out in detail in the *Huainanzi*, that we are what we eat. One who eats coarse food will become coarse; one who survives on breath or light will become breath or light. This is why the immortals of Zhuangzi and the *Chuci*, for example, eat in such an ethereal fashion.

Avoiding cereals constitutes a kind of fasting, which, unlike other fasts in which the adept survives on only breaths and magic talismans, does not cause a weakening of the body. It actually improves the health and makes one invulnerable to wind, cold, and poisons. As a result, one can drink large quantities of wine without getting drunk, one of the characteristics of the saint. Some texts express this by saying that by avoiding cereals, one also avoids nourishing the "three worms," so harmful to man, since their usual food is cereals. This practice also speeds up the effects of the absorption of the Great Alchemical Medicine. As one stops eating cereals, they are to be replaced by drugs derived from minerals.

Talismans and holy texts. Talismans have only an ancillary role, but a necessary one, and they play an important part in all Taoist religious practices from the earliest times down to our own day. The holy texts themselves act as talismans; they were, originally, spells that grew into texts, and they are often accompanied by complementary spells. The word used for these talismans evokes the talismanic treasures of rulers that show the divine protection they had received, as well as the ancient tesserae that sealed contracts between lords and their subjects. Throughout the history of Taoism, the writers of these talismans used a highly stylized form of pseudo-archaic script mimicking that used on the ancient bronzes. More and more such bronzes were discovered throughout the medieval period, and spiritual forces of good omen were attributed to them. The holy texts reveal the secret and "true" names (that is to say, the names that reveal their divine nature) of terrestrial and heavenly places, mountains and rivers, and their attendant spirits. They also describe the pathways and repositories of divine energies within the human body and, in the world, the topology and toponymy of the earthly and heavenly paradises, knowledge essential to those trying to reach them.

Revealed by gods who retained half the talismans and the original forms of the texts, they are the guarantee of the divine compact with human beings, who receive them from their masters in the course of a consecration rite accompanied by a sworn oath the gods are summoned to witness. The talismans and often the texts consist of incantatory sounds and pictures that must be written down and recited. They bring the adept the divine help he needs to carry out religious practices effectively.

Metamorphoses, Transmutations, and Circulation

As the preceding presentation should make clear, Ge Hong's discussions of the Taoist rituals in his tradition allow us to outline their general meaning. Now let us look more closely at a few matters Ge Hong mentions only briefly that other texts discuss in more detail or treat as more important or in a different manner.

Metamorphoses and Transmutations

The thousand transformations of the Breath give rise to the diversity of beings; the mechanism of life consists of mutations and evolutions, the *bianhua*, which make up the natural "tao" (or way), the spontaneous motions of Yin and Yang. According to the *Book of Change*, anyone who knows them also knows how the spirits operate, and according to Zhuangzi, the Sage acts in accordance with them and reveals himself through them. We have seen that Ge Hong considered the achievement of immortality a metamorphosis. From this to considering the Taoist as a master of the art of metamorphosis was only a small step.

Ge Hong mentioned a number of methods that allow the adept, by means of drugs or talismans, to achieve transformations. Thus one can make a river appear from a drop of water, a mountain from a pinch of dirt, a forest from a single seed. These lesser procedures tend to accelerate a natural process of transformation. By using wood, one obtains wood. With the help of stone, one gets stone. By imitating a woman, one becomes a woman. By drawing a river, one can make the water actually flow. The gift of ubiquity derives from an analogous process. It consists of reduplicating one's image, and meditation techniques that teach one how to concentrate on one's own body were recommended for this purpose. The ability to become invisible, a gift with which the hagiographies endow the Taoist saints, is of the same kind and is the flip side of the power to make divinities appear: "The human body is naturally visible," says Ge Hong, "and there are ways to make it invisible; spirits and demons are naturally invisible, and there are ways to make them visible" (Ware 16.2a). Herein lies the principle of metamorphosis, he adds. To become invisible is simply to change appearances. In other terms, there is no discontinuity between the invisible and the visible state; it is only a kind of shift.

Just as it is possible to make the fire of Heaven concrete by concentrating it on a solar mirror and to condense the water of the moon onto a lunar mirror, there are also mirrors that can reveal the "true form" of demons and reflect future events. They can make the invisible concrete. Conversely, the adept can disappear: he can either blend into his surroundings and so become invisible (becoming wood when he enters a forest, water when he enters water, an ordinary, unnoticeable man when he enters a crowd), or he can use magical methods that let him disappear completely, let him "dive into the earth in broad daylight." To dive into the earth in broad daylight, to enter the subterranean world whose abyss, in the Taoist cosmology, is connected with the highest point of the heavens, parallels the act of "rising into Heaven in broad daylight," the ultimate goal of the Taoists.

In the final analysis, these are methods of metamorphosis and thus natural, and they allow the adept to sublimate and purify his body, even to change into a winged immortal. The images used in the texts convey the conception of this transformation: the precious stone removed from its matrix, the insect emerging from the chrysalis—we have a transformation that is the accomplishment of an order, the "divine decree." This idea matches perfectly the principle that one becomes that which one eats: the interior shapes the exterior.

Such a transformation is, however, difficult and slow, and sometimes death intervenes before it has been completed. This is why the adept frequently resorts to the "escape from the corpse," a procedure by which he escapes from his body (or some part of it), still too fleshy, and flies up, leaving it behind in the coffin. The adept is then said to "give the appearance of death" or "transform his body," because he may leave his body behind in the form of a pair of sandals, a sword, or a staff—all emblems of the Taoist hermit. Clearly we have here a form of metamorphosis, like the others, that needs some kind of material support. It is written that "to escape from one's corpse" means "going away with the help of a material object." The main difference, however, between ordinary metamorphoses and the escape from the corpse is that the latter takes place only at the end of one's life. It is not a matter of a simple supernatural or magical power but a kind of escape, after which the adept is immortal and lives with the spirits, usually in the mountains or, according to some texts, underground. The corpse usually continues to purify after death, until it disappears at the end of a fixed number of years, sometimes centuries. The material object that may take its place is also eventually transformed and flies off: the sandals become birds, the sword or staff a dragon.

There are many methods for accomplishing this great change. The noblest of these escapes involves a sword—either an ordinary sword that the adept lays on his bed or (for a higher form of deliverance) a magical, divine sword forged according to a fixed ritual in a remote spot. Then the Supreme One appears and carries the adept off on his divine horse, while the sword, transformed into a corpse, takes his place in the coffin. The adept himself in turn takes on the appearance of the Supreme One, obviously identifying himself with this god.

Another form of transformation, but this time a complete one, is "going up to Heaven in broad daylight." To do this, the adept works at building for himself an immortal body. This must be done by means of fire: either the fire of laboratory alchemy or the fire that makes up the Yang "breath," which, like the fire of the alchemical furnace, "fuses souls." The binome that stands for these transformations, *bianhua*, is frequently associated with a term that means dissolution and shows clearly the transmutative nature of this immortal body. The term *lianhua* is also used, in which *lian* may be written with the metal radical and means "purify by fire" or with the silk radical, meaning here "practice," "work." The word *hua* means both "change" and "improve" or "cultivate," or even, in the binome *huohua*, "purify by fire." In Taoist ritual, *hua* is the word used to signify the burning of petitions addressed to Heaven; the prayers rise up with the smoke.

Thus we come to the "fusion of breaths" and the "fusion of the *jing*," which "dissolve the flesh and make the body light." But first, for convenience of presentation, let us look at the alchemy of the laboratory.

Laboratory Alchemy

Chinese alchemy roughly resembles Western alchemy. Alchemical endeavors are by nature religious. The "philosophical stone" or "elixir of immortality" is either of gold or of cinnabar, according to different texts, with cinnabar and gold representing the final result of a long process of transformation toward a perfect, achieved state. The gold that is sought is alchemical gold, artificial, made by man, and more valuable than natural gold. (Here we can see the vast distance between Ge Hong, who seeks immortality, and Zhuangzi, who sings of achieving consummate mastery.)

Two basic principles govern this alchemy. One arises from the idea of metamorphosis. Natural gold, the purest and most stable of metals, is the product of a slow metamorphosis, a long maturation that takes place within the earth. Alchemical gold is made by man but shares the same nature: it is simply the product of an induced transmutation. The other principle arises from analogical thought and is an application of the laws of correspondences that rule the world. Man is a microcosm whose structure is the same as that of the macrocosm, and the same is true in alchemical operations, in both space and time. The time of maturation needed to produce natural gold can thus be contracted in line with the dimensions of the microcosm and so accelerated (or, more exactly, reduced). The idea of the reduction of time is significant: acceleration is only the manifestation and result of the miniaturization of the whole, which brings with it an intensification.[8] The formation of natural cinnabar by the spontaneous transformation of "fluid mercury" combined with lead takes 4,320 years. On an alchemical scale, this process can be reduced to one year. Thus, the athanor, or alchemical furnace, is a miniaturization, a world made small. This fact is revealed in its shape, often suggesting the cosmic egg and usually having either three legs or three levels, for the three levels of the universe (heavenly, earthly, and human). The uppermost segment must be round like Heaven, and the lower squared like the earth. It must be hermetically sealed, in the image of the adept who must shut out the exterior world from his meditation. Its dimensions match symbolic numbers obeying cosmic laws.

Along with time and the alchemical vessel, the third important element is the ingredients. Among these, five are traditionally considered fundamental, with occasional variants: cinnabar, realgar, kalenite (or orpiment, or arselonite), malachite, and magnetite. These are seen as related to the Five Agents—of which they are potential representations—and the five planets, and they follow the same distribution. According to one text, realgar is on the left (wood), orpiment on the right (metal), cinnabar on top (fire), and malachite at the bottom (water). But there are many variations to these equations.

To this basic pattern is added a constant metaphorical dimension. Metamorphosis is actually a progressive purification. The elixir becomes perfect only after a great many reprocessings, each of them marking one more step in its sublimation, making it ever more efficacious, with the purest form capable of assuring immortality in a single day. Purification and cooking are carried out by fire or by water.

This is a simple account of alchemical procedures that the texts obviously portray as much more complex. Ingredients, as we have seen, are often chosen for symbolic reasons. Gold and mercury, two materials considered inalterable, play an important role. The first corresponds to the sun and the "ruler," the second to the moon and to the "minister." The dynamic that controls these ingredients is the same as that which rules the Five Agents: lead thus contains the "yellow germ" because Metal contains Earth, whose "breath" it receives. This is because, according to the law that controls the production of the Agents from one another, Earth gives rise to Metal, and so the son contains the mother because he has derived from her.

The same laws of alternance, concentration, transmutation, and reciprocal enclosure that govern the movements of Yin and Yang in nature hold here, too. The ingredients that the alchemist uses must be put through operations that will transmute, sublimate, and condense them, in turn, just as Yin and Yang transmute from one to the other each time they reach a point of extreme concentration.

But things are not this simple. There are often a great many ingredients, and it is sometimes hard to find the reason for their choice. Many of the minerals used to make alchemical elixirs are toxic, a fact well known to the Chinese. Although they used these ingredients carefully in medicine, they prescribed much stronger doses in the making of elixirs, with the proviso that certain vegetable drugs should be taken beforehand to "prepare" the body. Some recipes describe identifiable chemical preparations; others do not. They use a secret code and shifting metaphors to refer to ingredients and so require the help of a master for interpretation. Even when the recipes are formulated in apparently clear language, they do not seem to lead to any special results, except in a few cases.

In fact, no one has yet been able to answer the question of the extent to which this alchemy was supposed to be carried out physically. We know that it was to some extent, since it resulted in chemical discoveries. But the complexity of the physical operations, combined with that of the theoretical and symbolic speculations, produced a whole that is sometimes confused and governed by conflicting laws. Thus practice came to rely on theory, without always following it. It is clear, however, that certain chemical reactions were seen as significant only in terms of a network of symbolic meanings in which the problematics of the Yin-Yang school and the Five Agents played a role along with the language of the hexagrams of the *Book of Change*. Alchemy also became more and more interiorized, with an increasingly marked predominance of the symbolic element. The result is that in certain texts, from Tang times on, it is difficult if not impossible to know if the alchemy involves actual laboratory procedures or is a purely spiritual alchemy.

Breath and *jing* Practices

To recapitulate, the *qi* is the Vital Breath, the dynamic principle that is at the foundation of the world, existing before it existed and constantly present in all things. It is eternity, and it ensures the unity of the cosmos. In this sense it is the Original Breath, the Ultimate Truth, the equivalent of the Tao. The adept who seeks to become immortal tries to "feed" on it, to nourish it in himself, and to identify himself with it. This breath is the only eternal principle, since the present heaven and earth are destined to disappear in order to be replaced by others. As early as the third and fourth centuries of our era (contrary to the statements of Maspero), there are texts that talk of the absorption and circulation of the Primordial Breath (for example, DZ 820, 4b–5a).

In addition, this breath is our element: "Man exists in the *qi*, and the *qi* dwells inside man," writes Ge Hong. "From Heaven and Earth down to every created thing, there is nothing and no one who does not need *qi* in order to maintain life. Those who know how to circulate their *qi* preserve the integrity of self and ward off evil powers that could harm them" (Ware 5.5b). The natural process that leads to death is a loss of energy. To guard against this and ensure a long life, one must go back to the source of this energy, the Primordial Breath, and then channel and circulate it, guarding against its unnecessary expenditure.

The *qi* exists in different forms and in various states. The term thus assumes different meanings or values depending on the more or less specific form of the original to which it corresponds. In the human body, *qi* is the Yang energy, the air principle. As such, it is the corollary of the Yin energy of the body. When the Yin energy takes a solid form, *qi* then becomes the counterpart either of the material body as a whole or else of the "savors," foods, the solid element of nutrition, which are Yin and so in opposition to the air element, the Yang breath. When the Yin energy is represented by liquid elements, *qi* is opposed to the *jing*, the humors, or else the blood. In this case it stands for something much more general than the breath of breathing, which is only its most specialized corporeal form.

This term does not always carry a positive connotation, however, because the differentiation in the universe between pure and impure breaths is also found in the individual person, who consists of a combination of the two. Thus the division of humankind into those who are naturally good and those who tend toward evil is explained by an unequal distribution in them of pure and impure breaths. There are thus pernicious breaths that must be eliminated. To do this, one has to learn how to "spit out the old [breath] and breathe in the new," with everything "old" and worn out being considered as bad. This can be done by breathing gently, in through the nose (which corresponds to Heaven) and out through the mouth (the Earth). This procedure is called "harmonizing the breath," and purifies it, as well as increasing and intensifying it. To this end, one "nourishes one's breath" by keeping it "pent up" as long as possible. This is "embryonic breathing," comparable to that of the embryo in its mother's womb. Thus increased, breath gives extraordinary power. The greatest is that of inhibiting processes: the blood from flowing, fire from burning, boiling water from scalding, snakes from poisoning, and so on. The harmonized breath can also heal when one directs it into a diseased organ. Making it circulate throughout the body brings flexibility and health to the body and sharpness to the sensory organs. It is propelled by thought, and its path is made easier by gymnastic movements (known and attested since the fourth century B.C). These movements make the limbs flexible and are accompanied by massage.

But these practices do not belong to the Taoists alone. Physicians and Buddhists also used them, and they were secularized at an early date. The exercises take on a truly Taoist coloration and dimension when they involve the Primordial Breath and certain places in the body that have a special meaning in Taoism, like the cinnabar fields. Only then are we really in the area of Taoist practices, intended to organize the vision of the world, and thus of the body, as a function of the transcendence that will center and exalt them. Then it becomes a matter of the Primordial Breath that must circulate throughout the body and the entire world, insofar as that body is in harmony with the universe. This is achieved at certain places in the body that have specific connections to the world: the three cinnabar fields, connected by the vertebral column, and the five viscera. The adept thus guides the breath spiritually, either into the five viscera, in harmony with the current season of the year, blowing into them the "breath" that comes to him from the point in space bound to it, or along the vertical axis that goes from the lower cinnabar field to the upper one and then through the "three barriers" (three points in the back) and the middle cinnabar field. Knowing how to circulate one's breath means knowing the places through which it must pass—that is, not only the points to be visited but also their value, their meaning—while connecting them with the universal movement of life and with the whole of space.

Special mention should be made of the kidneys, which fulfill almost the same function as the lower cinnabar field and are for this reason often confused with it. With the lower cinnabar field and the navel they are located in a region holding the mysterious Source of Life, and whose various points have esoteric metaphorical names: Secret Doorway, Doorway of Life, Dark Gateway, Gate of Fate ("fate," *ming*, also refers to the vital force bestowed by Nature, or Heaven), Sea of the Breath, Palace Where Life is Received. The whole world is contained in it, along with its gods: the Queen Mother of the West and her companion, the Old Man King of the East, she carrying the moon and he, the sun, and the pair identified as the primordial couple formed by Fu Xi and Nü Gua, the founders of the ordered and civilized world. The right kidney is the Great Yin, and the left, the young Yang that is its product. From them arise the light from the north and the winter solstice, the place and the time of year with which they are closely associated. This is the Earth place, the chthonic region where the male seed is stored up, where the Yang conceals itself during the winter. It is the vast pathway of the Womb and the entrails and the beginning of life. It is the *Prima Materia* of the Taoist, the Mother of the Tao, the Primordial Chaos, whose names it carries: Great Genesis, Great Purity, Great Harmony. It is the source of embryonic breathing, of the Breath that goes through the whole body and rises into the brain, the Heaven of the human body.

The space between the kidneys, naturally, symbolizes the midpoint between Yin and Yang, the equivalent of the Supreme Pinnacle, the Center, and the highest point of the world that encloses Yin and Yang. It is both the primordial couple and the place of their union, and at the same time the child born of them. This is the source of the Breath, as well as its counterpart, the *jing*, the semen, or, in more general terms, the moist Yin principle of the body that forms a pair with the *qi*. Like *qi*, the word "jing" may refer to various levels of particularization of the Yin: the moist humors of the body, semen, even the saliva that makes up the Yin of the Yang, that is, the moist Yin element that is in the upper part of the body, in its Yang part, the counterpart of rain from the heavens. Inherited from the mother, as the *qi* comes from the father, the *jing* irrigates and makes the body fertile. Like the *qi*, and in a complementary fashion, it must circulate. The *qi* and the *jing* complement each other, intermingle, and change into each other. The adept makes his *qi* rise into his brain (just as the Yang rose up to form Heaven at the beginning of time). He must make his *jing* move downward (just as the Yin sank down to form the Earth), in the form of saliva. But he must also make his *qi* move downward, in the same way as the celestial influx descended on men and the Earth, and make his *jing* move upward, as the waters of the Earth rise in steam and clouds up to Heaven.

In fact, just as the breath can be seen either as something breathed in by the nose or as something that surges upward from a lower source, from the Sea of Breath, there are also an upper *jing*, the saliva, sometimes seen as arising from a transmutation of the breath, and a lower *jing*, the semen. The latter, which contains the lower *qi*, moves upward to "repair the brain." The *qi* and the *jing* also react to each other, intermingle, and unite to form the embryo of immortality, the "child," the germ of the subtle body that each adept grows inside his body. In this context, which is no longer exactly that of Ge Hong but follows a logical development recorded in the same tradition, "sexual practices" may be sublimated and completely subsumed into this form in the more general framework of the circulation of the breath. (In addition, as we saw above, Ge Hong used an expression generally reserved for sexual practices to apply to those of the breath.)

Saliva is a complementary replica both of the lower Yin and of the upper and lower *qi*, and it is very important. It is the "divine juice," the "golden liquor" (gold is Yang, and "liquor," or "elixir," is Yin; here we have the same terminology as in alchemy), the "jade juice" (jade is Yin), the "soft dew" (which, in Chinese mythology, is a sign of celestial favor). It performs two complementary functions. One is purification by water, in contrast to the *qi* purification by fire, and manifested when the adept ritually rinses his mouth. It is also, like the *qi*, a nourisher of immortality, the water of life. Like the *qi*, it makes the joints flexible, irrigates and harmonizes the five viscera, and sustains the spirits dwelling in the body. Gulps of saliva punctuate breathing exercises, and they are compared to pearls that one threads and sends down the throat. Thus the throat is to the saliva and its downward movement what the vertebral column is to the breath, providing an axis for vertical movement. Many texts from all epochs describe that the union of the saliva with the breath forms a little yellow pill with a taste like that of honey, the food of life.

All these practices (developed to a lesser or greater extent and with more or fewer variants), as well as the principles on which they are based, would continue as a substratum, sometimes unacknowledged or scarcely mentioned, in Shangqing practices. Sometimes they would, however, be the subject of expositions dedicated entirely to them, like that of Sima Chengzhen (647–735), or might be combined with other procedures and other symbolisms, as in interior alchemy. But they would always play a role.

The Body Made Cosmic and Divine

In the religious, firmly Taoist perspective that we are following, it is a given that, beyond ineffable transcendence, a paradoxically much more concrete divine element has a role to play. The body is actually a dwelling place for gods, who either live there permanently or are called there by various religious practices. As a result, the body is not only "cosmicized," it also becomes divine, or, at least, entirely occupied and animated by gods. These take up residence only if the body (along with the mind that is its inevitable partner) is pure, because, as mentioned above, they do not like disturbed places. In addition, the adept's knowledge of their names and their appearance gives him the power to summon them and keep them inside himself (*cun*, or "meditate," means in the first place "to cause to endure," "to retain").

This knowledge, this summoning, is a direct action, according to the principle that to name and depict something or someone gives power over that thing or person. This ancient principle is found in all civilizations and has been applied in China from antiquity. The world of the gods thus takes form in language and vision; the process of sanctification occurs through that knowledge of topology and toponymy at the core of many Taoist texts. It happens through speech and sight. Indeed, the character for "holy" in Chinese includes the elements used to write the words for "ear" and "mouth," and the holy man is a person with acute vision and hearing. He can see what is hidden. The adept must also become part of the invisible, tenuous, subtle world of gods and emanations, and to do this he must develop a special kind of vision that fixes and collects, that epiphanizes forces from the beyond, in a creative and imaginative activity directed toward an interior perception of the world of spirits, who are at the same time physical and celestial.

Meditation includes a significant visual component. The Taoist must direct his breath into different parts of his body; he must *see* his viscera and the spirits who live in them, turning his gaze inward, into his own body, and he must circulate his living breath in order to renew and refine his body. The contemplation of the viscera is ancient: it is mentioned in the *Taipingjing*. Their description is the subject of many texts, and in particular of a group of writings going back to the *Huangtingjing* (*Book of the Yellow Court*), which probably predates Ge Hong.

These practices take on the double aspect of closing and opening. There is a closing off not only of the exterior world of the senses but also of the interior world of the emotions and thought—with the latter being considered as having roots in the former. This is a separation from and a closing off of the immediate world of the ordinary man and personal individuality, and thus a concentration. But at the same time we see an opening to the universe, even if an imaginary and symbolic universe, the land of spirits, considered as based in the Origin, the Primordial Breath, and as opening to the infinite. Thus, even though we see constant reminders to "save up," to "hoard," one's vital forces, there is nothing selfish in this. Hoarding is a prerequisite of communication.

This can be seen clearly when the adept nourishes his viscera with each of the corresponding cosmic breaths, by introducing into each organ the breath of the appropriate pole and so infusing it with a cardinal dimension. It is also as an organism with macrocosmic correspondences that the adept can give rise to either the heraldic animals of the Five Agents or the emperors of the four cardinal points and the center. At dawn, when the "two breaths are not yet separated," the adept absorbs the "germs" of these poles by using a practice whose elements can be found in the extant fragments of the work known as the *Wufujing* (*Text of the Five Talismans*) and that were later much developed. The adept thus nourishes his viscera with "cloud germs," that is, the breaths of the five directions still in a tender state "comparable to the growing sprouts of plants," in order to "fix and strengthen his viscera and organs." In this way he "gathers from afar the essence of Heaven and of Earth [that is, the cosmic essence] and reassembles them close by, in his body." These "germs" are the "emanations of the extreme poles," full of the power of the ends of the earth. "Tender and like the growing sprouts of plants," they have all the strength of being in the state of being born, at a moment, dawn, which is equivalent to the embryonic state of the world, the state closest to the Primordial Unity. Young and supple, with a refined and pure essence, they sustain the viscera with the subtle emanations of the universe, far from the gross food consumed by ordinary humans.

The Tang dynasty text *Xuanmen dayi* (DZ 1124, 16b), which tries to coordinate these various practices and establish a hierarchy among them, states that whoever feeds on the "five germs" becomes germinal essence, whoever feeds on light becomes light, whoever feeds on the breaths of the Five Poles can travel in space and through the universe, whoever feeds on cosmic breaths makes his body one with the universe, and, finally, whoever undertakes embryonic breathing returns to the state of a newborn child and becomes one with the Tao. This is the application of the ancient principle—set out, for example, in the *Huainanzi*—by which beings acquire the nature of what they eat.

5

The Shangqing School

Ge Hong was the last great figure in the southern Chinese Taoist tradition before it began receiving a large admixture of new elements, mostly from the Celestial Masters tradition. By the end of the fourth century, only a few decades after Ge finished compiling the *Baopuzi*, the Shangqing (highest purity) movement had appeared. This new movement retained most of the elements of Ge Hong's tradition and borrowed certain individual features like the "purity chambers" from the Celestial Masters (see Chapter 4). At the same time, it added further, substantial elements from the Celestial Masters school, incorporated certain local cults, and, for the first time in Taoism, adapted Buddhist practices (these, however, were superficial additions). It also included traces of the debates over *wu* (absence, lack of existence) and *you* (presence, existence) that had engaged the Chinese intelligentsia of the third and fourth centuries.

All these elements were blended into a whole that was strongly colored by Chinese literary tradition—both in its elegant literary form and in the injection of myths surviving from antiquity. However, it remained largely true to the tradition of the individualistic Taoists from which it claimed to derive; adoptions of ritual from the Celestial Masters were limited almost entirely to practices surrounding entry into the chapel or purity chamber. The visual side of meditation still dominated, but the ancient immortality techniques preached by Ge Hong declined in importance. The Shangqing movement is the first clearly constituted *school*, solidly based on canonical texts that make up a coherent, articulated whole following strictly enforced rules of transmission.

History

The Shangqing movement developed on the basis of a group of texts revealed and dictated to a certain Yang Xi by gods and spirits who appeared to him at night from 364 to 370. Little is known of Yang Xi, except that he was a client of the Xu family, a family of southern aristocrats related through many generations with that of Ge Hong. The revelations were addressed to this family. Despite contrary claims, this revelation was not part of the crude system of "planchette" revelations used by mediums, who draw vague outlines while in a trance, drawings that a priest has to interpret before they can be understood. Proofs of the difference in the Shangqing revelation, if any is needed, lie in the handwriting of Yang Xi (his calligraphy was greatly admired by Tao Hongjing [456–536], the school's great theoretician); the high literary quality of the texts, which far surpasses that of earlier Taoist texts; and the coherence of the body of texts. The phenomenon should instead be compared to those visions of enlightenment accompanied by voices dictating texts well known in the wider history of religion, the most famous examples being the Apocalypse of Saint John, the Koran, and the visions of Emanuel Swedenborg.

Some of the spirits that appeared to Yang Xi were legendary immortals of the Han dynasty, bearing hagiographies telling of their exploits. Others were local saints, like the Mao brothers, who also lived under the Han and gave their name to Mao Shan (Mount Mao). This mountain south of Nanjing became the center of the Shangqing movement, and because of this the school is also called the Mao Shan movement. Others were gods or spirits unknown until that time, like the Lady Wei Huacun (251–334), main initiator of Yang Xi and first "patriarch" of the Shangqing movement. She had died 30 years earlier and had been a libation pourer, which implies membership in the hierarchical organization of the Celestial Masters. She is the source for a ritual that she dictated to Yang Xi, part of which is preserved in the Taoist Canon as one of the most ancient written records of the Celestial Masters liturgy.

The Shangqing revelations occurred at a time when the Celestial Masters adepts had launched a crusade, accompanied by the destruction of temples and altars, against popular beliefs and the ancient customs of the southern lands: songs and dances, drum beating, and animal sacrifices. The Celestial Masters had migrated from the north, fleeing from the barbarians along with the court. Their actions were part of a political and social takeover of these southern lands, by tradition separatist. The Celestial Masters were the ideological and religious arm of this takeover. The Xu family, whose members became part of the government faction, were received into the Celestial Masters faith.

But the Shangqing revelations—the revenge of the south on the north—claimed to be on a higher plane than its forerunners. It promised its adepts access to a higher heaven, the Shangqing Heaven, the Heaven of Highest Purity. It offered sacred texts and more polished methods. It relegated the old immortals (*xian*)— among them Ge Xuan, the great-uncle of Ge Hong—to a secondary position, below its own gods and "true men" (*zhenren*). It battled the Celestial Masters on two fronts: the revelatory gods of Shangqing competed against the Celestial Masters but it also co-opted the battle against local cults. This conflict did not prevent them, as was pointed out above, from surreptitiously absorbing elements of these cults.

The revelation spread in southern aristocratic circles. A group started to coalesce, bringing together people united by family connections. They found in the Shangqing revelation a new religious bond, given concrete form by the transmission of the sacred texts accompanied by sworn oaths. This group found its great theoretician in the person of Tao Hongjing, a member of a family related through many generations to the Xu and Ge families. Tao Hongjing was both a careful historian and a bibliographer. He gathered, authenticated, organized, and promoted the sacred texts. The facts that he reported in his annotations to the *Zhen-gao*, in which Yang Xi and the brothers Xu narrate the various circumstances surrounding the revelation made to them, show the wide diffusion of the Shangqing texts among the Chinese intelligentsia and their great popularity. This double-edged success resulted, throughout the fifth century, in all kinds of shady dealings: thefts of prestigious documents, fraudulent copies, plagiarization, and sale of texts for purely material gain. The positive side of the success led, toward the middle of the century, to the growth at Mao Shan of a group of the faithful who dedicated themselves to the study of the revealed texts. They are mentioned by the official histories as the outstanding hermits of their age, sometimes honored by official recognition from princes and emperors. The most famous was Gu Huan (ca. 420–ca. 483), who was the movement's first "historian" and bibliographer. His pioneering work was taken up and completed by Tao Hongjing.

These men, all endowed with high education and belonging to powerful clans, were bound by oath in a kind of religious brotherhood. Their possession of the highly esteemed Shangqing texts gave them great prestige within Taoism, and the religion began to take a new tack. They became its leaders, put new structures into place, and formed a new spiritual elite. Monasteries or communities, supported by donations, arose. These establishments included both men and women—married and unmarried, laypeople and others—and they were visited by pilgrims who came in great numbers during religious holidays. The Celestial Masters faded into the background, clearly going into a decline, as evidenced by a weakening of their credibility and loss of reputation.

Tao Hongjing was a many-sided genius, a knowledgeable herbalist, and a friend of the Buddhists. He spent many years compiling and authenticating the Shangqing texts, but he was also a friend of Emperor Wu of the Liang, a ruler with Buddhist leanings. For him he prepared alchemical concoctions, and this imperial favor protected his hermitage during the proscriptions against Taoism in 504 and 517. These attacks, which forced a number of Taoists to emigrate to the north, were ironically the immediate cause of the spread of the new school's teachings throughout China during the sixth century. The Taoist encyclopedia that appeared under the auspices of the Northern Zhou emperor Wu (r. 561-77) gave most space to the texts of this school and ranked them above all others. Still, the center of the movement remained in the south, where the disciples of Tao Hongjing continued to live. From the sixth to the tenth century, under the Six Dynasties and the Tang, the Shangqing was the most influential Taoist school. Wang Yuan-zhi (d. 635), the tenth Shangqing patriarch, also gained the favor of Taizu (founder of the Tang dynasty), whose legitimacy he confirmed through his religious support and whom he initiated into certain texts. The conversations of his successor, Pan Shizheng (587-684), with Emperor Gaozong (r. 650-83) revealed his knowledge of both the Shangqing texts and those of Buddhism. Sima Chengzhen, to whom we shall return below, was one of the greatest masters of his time and initiated Emperor Xuanzong (r. 713-55) and the poet Li Bo (701-62) into certain texts of the school. At his request, Xuanzong issued an edict in 721 that took control of the cult of sacred mountains away from local gods and gave it to the Shangqing deities. Sima Chengzhen later settled at Mount Tiantai (in modern Zhejiang), but he was recalled to the capital on several occasions by successive rulers who constructed temples in his honor.

Throughout the ninth century, the Shangqing texts aroused great interest in literary circles. Poets and prose writers drew so much inspiration from them that their writings, bristling with allusions to texts and hagiographies of the school, can be fully understood only in the light of these texts. This fact, unfortunately, is unrecognized by most historians of Chinese literature.[1]

The success of the school was long-lived: even in the eleventh century the patriarchs of the school continued to enjoy the support of emperors, to transmit their teachings and their "registers" to rulers and their families, and to erect temples thanks to imperial gifts.

The Shangqing texts, along with the school's meditation methods, were important in the evolution and shaping of Taoism. All early rankings of the various Taoist schools gave pre-eminence to the Shangqing school. The following centuries saw a great many Shangqing texts selected for codification and development, and the integration and elaboration of Shangqing ideas. The section dedicated to Taoism in the *Taiping yulan*, the great encyclopedia compiled on imperial orders and completed in 983, consisted mostly of Shangqing texts. They were also gathered into collections, sometimes along with major rituals that incorporated whole sections from them, like the Great Ritual of the Hall of Jade, which appeared in 1120. The texts also contributed to the liturgy both hymns and the form of the meditations into which the principal officiant enters during the ritual, as well as many practices and concepts, like the "untying of the knots" and representations of the sun and moon. During the thirteenth and fourteenth centuries, the Shangqing school lost power to the resurgent Celestial Masters, who once more gained ascendancy over the other schools. The Celestial Masters did, however, adopt the Shangqing ordination registers and value them above all others.

Over time the texts and spirit of the Shangqing school changed. The feature that had originally characterized it, the emphasis on visual meditation and personal practices, faded as the school became steadily more institutionalized. The texts were gradually codified and organized (with Tao Hongjing being the first to dedicate himself to this task) according to a scale of values that defined the rank of the adept in the hierarchy of the movement. This hierarchy was based on the possession, knowledge, and practice of certain texts, in a fashion analogous to the registers of the Celestial Masters. Collections of texts appeared that were intended to systematize the pantheon of the school and arrange its works into a logical order. Between the second half of the fourth century and the end of the sixth, the corpus of Shangqing scriptures changed considerably. New texts, diverse in contents and hard to date, were grafted onto the old ones or incorporated into them. These new contributions included elements from the Lingbao school (see Chapter 6) and from the Celestial Masters, along with more significant traces of Buddhism. The general tendency of these revisions was toward ritualization and institutionalization. The master took on more and more importance, as did codes for the transmission of texts. Precepts to be followed mixed Confucian and Buddhist virtues, and their moralizing vein increased as the emphasis on ritual purity declined. Procedures for visualization were simplified and the recitation of texts tended to assume more importance than acting them out. Lyricism disappeared. A ritual took shape, and ordination registers like those used by the Celestial Masters appeared. At the same time, the relationship between the faithful and the gods gradually took on the form it had among the Celestial Masters: requests to the gods increased, and the number of prayers in the form of poems declined. A Shangqing ritual appeared. Its basic premises had been established at the time of Tao Hongjing, but over time it incorporated elements from the Lingbao school, and new talismans and texts started to appear and became inextricably mixed with those from earlier times.

Then, under the Song, new revelations emanated from Mao Shan. This mountain was originally simply a local cult site, but after the Shangqing revelation it became a mountain studded with memorials, hermitages, and temples, venerated and celebrated throughout China. Every cavern charged with mystery, every peak and every stream was inventoried. (The forty-fifth patriarch of the School, Liu Dabin [fl. 1317–28], wrote a massive account of this mountain, which retraced its history and described its mythical and spiritual geography.) The new Mao Shan revelations, although different from earlier ones and oriented toward exorcism, borrowed much from the Shangqing school, from which they claimed to derive, both in the constitution of their pantheon and in the elaboration of certain practices, such as the absorption of starry effluvia and travel into the skies.

General Features and Innovations
of the Shangqing School

In the original form of Shangqing, that embodied in the revelation to Yang Xi, the basic principles of Shangqing religious practice are the same as those we have already seen in earlier contexts: topology and toponymy remain fundamental, the broad lines of cosmology and anthropology are almost unchanged, the rules for the transmission of knowledge are repeated but strongly emphasized, and a good number of ancient practices are retained, albeit in a more developed form. The main innovation lies in the relative value assigned to the various parts of the religion, reflecting a general change in orientation: a strong movement toward interiorization put special emphasis on meditation, primarily visual meditation. The Shangqing school ignored many legalistic aspects of the Celestial Masters school, de-emphasized physiological exercises and the use of drugs and herbs, and severely modified alchemical procedures. It gave a special place to myth and invention, stressed the deification and "cosmicization" of the adept, and emphasized the image and ecstatic wandering. The landscape had changed, the pantheon was quite different, and yet scarcely any element was truly new. Everything existed already, if only in a germinal state. But now the gods were invoked rather than summoned, the adept united with them instead of dominating them, and the relationship of Yang Xi with his celestial initiator, a daughter of the Queen Mother of the West, revived the suggestion of physical love found in the *Chuci*, even if chastity was expressly praised. Interior evocation and personal involvement in mental concentration had more force than ritual acts. The gods were intercessors and mediators, and salvation lay in knowing the "true form" of heavenly places and their inhabitants. Salvation resulted from a change in an adept's view of the world and his own person rather than from battles against the forces of evil. Relations based on power gave way to fusion and union, theurgy to mysticism. The gods became intercessors who deliver to the adept the keys of celestial kingdoms and nourish him with divine effluvia, sometimes mouth to mouth. The gods descend into the adept and take him up to the skies, hand in hand. Their forms are many and changing, like their names. This metamorphic variety is like that of the Tao.

This new relationship with the divine led the Shangqing school to become the first Taoist movement to produce a number of true hymns to the gods, blending bliss, exaltation, and mystical joy. Before this time, Ge Hong had been almost the only person to make a few comparable efforts to sing of the Xuan, the Mystery. Adepts now took part in the divine pastimes described by the texts, complete with music, celestial courts, floats and banners, feathered canopies, bands of dragons and singing phoenixes, and sky-blue carriages. They visited paradises like those described in the *Chuci* and the *Huainanzi.* Such paradises would later become a fundamental part of Taoism. The image of the Sage is central to Shangqing: it remained close to that given in ancient texts and in the popular hagiographies and mythologies of the Han. Constantly present, either in the promises made by the texts to the assiduous adept or in the vows that they formulated themselves, this image is the central motif of the adept's quest and illustrates its ultimate goal.

Centered mainly on mental visualization, the practices taught in the Shangqing texts fall halfway between physical techniques and mental speculations. They form a visionary mysticism that rounds out the speculative and that brings into play what Mircea Eliade has called "creative imagination" and Alain Corbin "active imagination"—what Paracelsus called quite simply the "Imagination." Everything happens in the world of Images, where "spirits take physical form and bodies take spiritual form." This world is a kind of intermediary between the world of tangible realities and that of ineffable realities, the world of *xiang* (images or symbols) that figured in the *Book of Change* and was explained by Wang Bi as intermediary between that of ideas and that of words. To sum up, the Taoists, and especially those of the Shangqing school, as they work through images, which are themselves words, are only making systematic something that is a general feature of Chinese thought: words that are themselves graphs (like Tao, Taiji, Yin, Yang, Qi, the numbers) are more images than concepts. They fall halfway between abstraction and concrete things and, like images, carry an active force that takes the place of the concept. Just as the world undergoes continuous creation, so do words and images: the force latent in them grows as they take over the person who handles them. Thought is based on analogy and works through symbols and signs. The great metaphysical and ontological questions—the relationship of the Self to the Other, of the One to the multiplicity, the origin of the world—are tackled through images. Visual meditation brings to life for the adept in a plastic and scenic form the things that metaphysics expresses through dialectic and discourse. The Shangqing texts are particularly exemplary in this respect; it is in them that this tendency is the most developed. But we shall see it in action again in interior alchemy (see Chapter 8).

A second characteristic of Shangqing, a corollary of this emphasis on forming images, is a strong orientation toward interiorization. Priority is given visual meditation by oneself in one's room. "Private contemplation," insists Yang Xi's initiator, is "the root and the origin of spiritual immortality." With Shangqing, ritual practice becomes more flexible. Absorption of effluvia from the sun and moon can take place indoors if the weather is bad. Only the imaginative vision counts. Similarly it is not necessary to withdraw into the mountains to practice rituals. It can be done within one's heart, for "there is no difference between one's body and the holy mountains." Exercises can be performed on days other than those specified if there is a compelling reason. Invocations are no longer simple magical formulas but true prayers addressing praises to the gods in a poetic form. The confession of sins is also completely private. Sicknesses and death are considered internal in origin. Sexual practices are formally condemned (they are, however, replaced by private contemplation of the same god invoked by the Celestial Masters adepts during their sexual practices, but it is made clear that one is no longer required to carry out the ancient practices). The gods mock the holy man who travels around the world to seek the truth, for it is within himself that he will find it at the end of his journeying. A passage from one text sums up this attitude: "One is schooled in immortality through the heart. If the heart is sincere, one attains the path of immortality. The path of immortality is a private quest; if one retires within oneself, the Tao will come."

This process is, however, carefully regulated. Meditation is practiced according to precise rules. These are dictated by the texts, which describe in detail the visions that the adept should cultivate within himself. They define the stage sets of meditations that constitute miniature "psychodramas," as well as the program they are to follow. These accounts, organized like a narrative, distinguish three stages: competence (worthiness of the adept, an idea to which we shall return), performance (the carrying out of the process of meditation), and sanction (revealed by the transformation of the devotee into an immortal). The adept is obviously quite different in kind from a mere medium or possessed individual. He summons up images, organized in a structured and well-articulated pattern that enable him to cause the gods to descend. These activities often end in ecstatic states of luminous exaltation in which the adept can no longer distinguish one thing from another, where the distinction between up and down, inside and outside, disappears. But a line is drawn clearly between such states and the state of ordinary consciousness, to avoid any danger of confusion. This distinction is marked by rites of passage (such as massages), by a clearly defined physical location (the purity chamber) and mental location (within the framework of the four heraldic animals of the four directions), and by clearly marked times (precise hours and dates)—all aspects of meditation are even more precisely delimited than in earlier traditions. The "short" time of the meditation practice is matched by the "long" time of the progressive journey of the adept through his initiation into the texts of the school, in an order leading the devotee gradually toward sainthood.

The Shangqing school thus organizes and to a certain extent codifies the relations between human beings and gods. It falls between the solitary path of the inspired hermits and the social organization of spiritual aspirations. As in the tradition of the seekers after immortality, but unlike the hierarchized church of the Celestial Masters, the adepts are their own priests. They have personal, direct access to the sacred. But this access is open to them only through a set of codified texts, whose transmission is subject to precise rules and whose possession indicates membership in a defined group of people.

The Text

The Shangqing school had as its foundation the text. It is in this school that we see the development in grand fashion of the theory of sacred writing that characterizes all of Taoism, is replicated even in ritual, and is based on a conception of the constraining force and fundamental significance of writing and depiction that is deeply rooted in Chinese antiquity. The power of writing is shown in the legends of the Great Yu, who gained power over beings and made the world inhabitable for humans by representing all things on the sacred tripods. This power is also shown in ancient legal customs; the written text is the only form of witnessing. Writing as an interpretation of this world has both a sacred origin—it was born in China from divination—and a cosmic value. It represents the form of beings and transcribes the outline of the designs that the stars draw in the sky and the mountains and rivers on earth. Writing makes the world intelligible, and thus lets us orient ourselves and control the world. It unveils the "true form" of beings and things, their secret form, which results from contemplation by God on High. Knowledge of their secret forms gives one influence over beings.

One of the first questions Yang Xi asked his celestial visitors dealt with the origin of the *jing*, the texts. This is a fundamental question about the nature of the teachings they convey. The *jing*, he was told, are the condensed form of the Primordial Breath. Born spontaneously from the Void, they existed before the start of the world. They appeared first in the form of invisible light rays and "solidified" as they descended, taking on an ever more solid form. Beginning as light, they became "cloud seals," still nebulous but as if congealing into a more permanent form. Then they were written down by the gods in non-human characters, in jade on tablets of gold, and stored in the Celestial Palaces or in the sacred mountains. Their transcription into human writing happened only later, when Heaven "sent down the tokens." The sacred texts that men possess are the manifestation of Heaven's grace, but they are only a "token," a solid imprint, the impression of a celestial prototype that remains in the heavens. Still, they are the sign that leads and releads us back to the heavenly counterparts. One of the meanings of the word *jing* is that of "guide," a synonym of "way."

The sacred text is at the beginning of the world; it is the trail one can follow to understand the world's structure and rediscover its primordial nature. It is a treasure comparable to the dynastic talismans possessed by the ruling and princely families that testify to the protection these families have received from Heaven. Like royal talismans, and just like the Primordial Breath and the vital power of which they are the incarnation and the receptacle, the texts must be preserved as treasures. They bring divine protection. They are the sign of a connection with celestial forces, and they testify to the spiritual genealogy that joins the adept to the gods in the skies.

The texts reach the adept after having been transmitted from god to god over thousands of cosmic eras and then, after being revealed to humankind, from master to disciple over generations—a long line that connects the adept with the Origin of the World. Furthermore, by unveiling the "names," the "sounds," and the forms of divine figures and places, and in this way the means of salvation, they are the visible token of the protection offered by the gods. By voluntarily giving these "treasures" to humanity, the gods at the same time contract to respond to them.

Beyond being simply writing, the texts also embody sounds. Writing and sound, the visible and the audible, reflect each other and round each other out. The texts appeared as letters of light in the void and were written down in golden letters by gods in the heavens. To copy them is a pious act. During rituals they must be present in written form, open on the altar, and the adept must hold them in his hands during meditation. All spells must be written down. They were, after all, revealed to humankind through dictation. But these texts must also be recited. The emphasis on recitation is greater in the Shangqing tradition than among the Celestial Masters. Every mistake in recitation must be followed by an act of contrition. Furthermore, the texts are sung by the gods in the heavens, echoing terrestrial recitation. The "true form" along with the "esoteric sound" have a joint effectiveness.

As the role of the sacred books was thus developed and amplified, the Shangqing school began to stress the rules for transmitting the *jing* much more than had been the case in the past. Henceforth these rules would be developed and made even more precise. The school would set great store by the establishment of these texts, in place of the earlier "registers," which were of a very different nature. Texts were transmitted from master to disciple, one by one, after a fast of several days; the two parties swore a contract, following a ritual inspired by ancient rites of consecration, bonding, and feudal ties, which, through invocations and imprecatory formulas, the gods and infernal powers were called to witness. This transmission was accompanied by gifts from the disciple to the master. This practice recalls ancient myths of the civilizing rulers to whom Heaven sent talismans or sacred books in return for devotion and sacrifice. Such "payments," tokens of sincerity, were called "pledges" (*xin*). Rings and seals were broken in two, with master and disciple each retaining a half, thus reproducing the ancient tesserae used in contracts.

Above all else, the disciple swore never to reveal the text without good cause. The text could be transmitted only to those worthy to receive it, those whose names were inscribed in the celestial registers and who possessed "jade bones," made of the incorruptible and precious substance that forms the body of the immortal. In short, the texts could be passed only to those predestined by nature for immortality. Obviously anyone who received a *jing* received as well the revelation and assurance of his predestination and proof of his qualification for immortality. Obtaining a sacred text improperly amounted to "stealing a treasure from Heaven" and nullified its power, which exists only insofar as the disciple is fitting. This worthiness constitutes the second half of the power inherent in the text. A sacred book transmitted or acquired improperly will spontaneously fly up to heaven or catch fire. To transmit it frivolously is referred to by a term that suggests water escaping through a crack. The sin is of the same order as that of letting one's vital juices escape. This is the most serious sin that a disciple can commit, and by committing it he ensures that he will never attain immortality. On the other hand, the legitimate possession of a book brings with it divine protection in the form of jade boys and girls who watch over the book and its guardian. It also implies duties, because the human side of the contract must be carried out: the adept must pay homage to it, praising it in song and practicing the methods that it holds.

The role of the master in the Shangqing tradition is thus more one of transmitting the *jing* than of guiding disciples. It is the text itself that plays the role of the guide and brings knowledge. This can be seen in the fact that "oral formulas," the parts of the teaching transmitted personally "from mouth to mouth," were often subsequently written down and added to the text. Thus we move from a semi-oral tradition to one that is almost totally written and codified. Revelation is completed and is totally contained in the corpus of Shangqing texts. This is the most characteristic feature of the school. The master is now nothing more than a guarantor of the legitimacy of the transmission. The texts characterize the bond between him and the disciple as like that of parent and child, and that between disciples as like that between siblings. (In the Shangqing tradition, these roles of "master" and disciples could also be filled by women.) The master does not officiate in any way, and the method he transmitted does not bear his or her name, as was often the case in the tradition of seekers after immortality. The master is no more than a simple link in the chain that connects the gods and a line of human beings, but, as the guarantor of the legitimate transmission of the book, the master is the guarantor of its power.

Thus it is the book, or the whole collection of scriptures, that is at the center of the Shangqing school. A spiritual hierarchy, culminating in the person of its patriarch, replaces the earlier church organization. Levels in the hierarchy of initiation are measured in terms of texts received and put into practice.

The Ideas of Salvation and Immortality

The compilers of the Shangqing texts had to reconcile various ideas about salvation and sought answers to two fundamental questions. First, who is to be saved? The answer to this question is shaped by the basic idea of the nature of the human individual.

Second, what is salvation? The Shangqing answer to the first question reconciles three different concepts into a clear, coherent whole. The answer to the second is more mixed and problematic.

The first basic factor determining who is to be saved is retribution. The salvation of an individual is tied to the behavior of his ancestors going back seven or nine generations. The sins of the ancestors are visited upon the individual, and similarly that person's sins are visited on his or her descendants in turn, just as in the *Taipingjing*. This concept derives from the traditional Chinese idea that the individual can never be completely separated from the family and always retains a certain collective identity. Here we see the influence of the ancestor cult, an influence found in a completely analogous form in the legal system: punishments extend to the family of the guilty party.

But this concept of retribution is tied logically to the notion that, as we shall see below, purification can be achieved even after death. An adept can guarantee the salvation of his ancestors by asking pardon for his own faults and for theirs; his practices benefit the ancestors as well. The salvation of individuals is not separable from that of their ancestors. All the Shangqing texts promise the adept that the ancestors will be saved at the moment he or she achieves salvation. The individual's efforts at salvation extend to the ancestors; ontologically they cannot be separated.

Superimposed on this basic idea is a completely different image: that of the Sage, "unique" and cosmic, a central image with roots in Zhuangzi, Liezi, and the *Huainanzi*, one that gives rise to the search for immortality. This search is tricked out with fantastic details springing from popular imagery. The prayers of the adept and the promises made in the texts repeatedly mention the same images. The adept will wear the traditional robe of feathers that allies him with the birds. He will ride the light and mount the stars or float in the void. He will have the wind and the light as carriages, with dragons to pull them along. His bones will become jade, his face will shine, a halo will surround his head, and his whole body will emit a supernatural radiance and will be as incandescent as the sun and moon. He will know the future, can travel a thousand *li* in a single day, plunge into water without getting wet, enter fire without being burned, and cannot be harmed by wild beasts or weapons. He will control natural forces and spirits. He will be able to achieve all his desires and enjoy eternal youth. He will be the equal of Heaven and Earth, of the sun and the moon. The final vision of the Shangqing believer is both cosmic and mystical, comprising both mystical participation in the cosmos and union with the supreme truth or the Tao. He pledges himself to melting into the universe, to becoming one with the great forces of the world, the Yin and the Yang, the mysterious Mother, the Three Originals.

The third panel of this complex triptych derives from the tradition of the seekers after immortality: salvation is a personal matter. Unlike the Celestial Masters, the Shangqing school emphasizes technical and mystical practices carried out on an individual basis. The participation of the adept in salvation is completely private, direct, and active, without the intervention or mediation of any other human being. Freedom for the adept suffering from the consequences of ancestral sins lies within, and it is the adept who must do the job: "one's salvation is in one's own hands." Here we see the tradition of the *fangshi.*

Thus the adept must take on a triple role, whose various parts fit together fairly well: that of a social human being tied to his or her lineage, that of the Cosmic Man, and that of the private individual. The idea of what constitutes salvation is much more complex, however.

First, the predestination implied by success in acquiring a sacred text legitimately (to have "jade bones" and get one's name inscribed in the heavenly registers) seems to be in contradiction with the obligation to carry out certain duties, an obligation required even of divine figures. The state of being a cosmic, total, and unique immortal is absolute; it should not permit degrees. Yet there exist a hierarchy of celestial officials and a precise gradation among subterranean, earthly, and heavenly immortals. Furthermore, this gradation is a continuum; even after death the believer can continue his efforts at perfecting himself and rise from the state of an "underworld governor" (*dixiazhu*) to that of a heavenly immortal. The Shangqing tradition maintains side by side two points of view—instant salvation and gradualism, to use Buddhist terminology. We have here another example of the eternal problem of grace and works faced by every mystic.

Becoming an immortal is the goal proposed by and reflected in the texts at every turn; no longer is the goal to become a celestial official. Only rarely does one see, as in earlier texts, the adept seeking a rank in the celestial hierarchy, even if the latter continues to exist. The believer desires above all else to reach the state of an immortal, the same state described by Zhuangzi and Ge Hong, with a few variations. In the Shangqing texts, the Sage is no longer a figure of legend. His image is interiorized and forms the model with which every adept identifies. The same expressions and the same images are used. However, the cosmic and extra-cosmic dimensions of immortality are stressed. The adept asks to "become the equal of the Three Luminaries," to "be born in the Breath of Spontaneity," "to reach up to the heavenly immortals and down to the abysses," "to take his pleasure far away, where there is no round or square, deeply quiet beyond phenomena, the *you* [existence] and the *wu* [lack of existence] blended in the Darkness." Without rising above the level of simple, concrete wonders, this final vision guiding the adherent to the Shangqing tradition at times takes on a truly mystical color, for example, when he wishes "to dwell forever on the summits of the Great Void, in the Chamber of the Precious Palace; in the morning to take his pleasure with the Jade Emperor and in the evening to rest with the Mysterious Mother; when thirsty, to drink his fill among the jade plants of the Immense Spring of Lang Well" on the cosmic Mount Kunlun.

We have here a universal form of salvation, but its expression and representation are completely different from those of Buddhism. Certain indications suggest going beyond fusion with the cosmos. "May I be born with the Void," he cries out, "and may I die with the Void; may I die and be reborn." It is true that for these adepts, "Long Life is to be found in the mystical glance; the Tao is to be found in the essential minuteness; the essential minuteness gives a body peace and sublime serenity, floods the spirit with the True Breath, and puts the heart at rest in the Mysterious Source [of the World]." Some of the terms used clearly indicate a transcendence of the alternatives of life and death, as in Zhuangzi, when there is mention of "neither dying nor being born any more," of "ridding oneself of life and death," or of "equalizing and dividing life-death." This mode of talking, completely absent from earlier texts, is an innovation in Taoist texts. Furthermore, grafted to this is a new idea of the nature of rebirth, an idea to which we shall return below.

Practices

The *Dadong zhenjing*

The most important Shangqing text and one of the most significant Taoist texts is the *Dadong zhenjing* (*The True Text of the Great Dong*). The word *dong* has many meanings—"cave," "hollow," "depth," "to go across," "to communicate." Caves play a great role in Taoism, especially beginning with the Shangqing school when they were first inventoried and described. Nestled into the mountain hollows where hermits set up their retreats, they constitute earthly paradises, coiled labyrinths in the bowels of the earth. They conceal the treasures of life, holy texts and protective talismans, and are so connected that travel from one cave-heaven to another by underground passages is possible. They are miniature worlds, difficult of access through their hidden, narrow entrances. Sometimes they contain three levels. Each such world has its own sun and moon and provides a passageway to the heavens on high. "That which is called a 'void' in the skies is called a 'cave' in the mountains and a 'chamber' [for deities] in the body; they are all forms of the same thing," says one text. Moreover, the three main sections of the Taoist Canon are called "caves." As for the Dadong, commentators explain the term by saying that it means "Supreme Void" or the "Great Boundless Mystery."

Reciting this text, as we shall see, is enough to activate it and so ensure immortality; such recitation makes the alchemical methods unnecessary. The text is constructed on two levels, a heavenly one and a bodily one (the body must be preserved from death). Before reciting it, the adept must call up a number of gods whose intercession and protection he seeks. Each of them must take his or her place in the meditation chamber. Then the adept must visualize himself in glory, seated on lions, dressed in sacred insignia—the feather robe, the "jade star" headdress—and flanked by the emblematic animals of the east and the west, the green dragon and the white tiger. Thus rendered sacred and exalted, in an oratory filled with a crowd of attending gods and heavenly tinted clouds and supernatural scents, he chants the *Dadong zhenjing*.

The recitation of each section of the text is accompanied by the visualization of the gods of the body. These gods descend from the brain toward one of the "gates of death," which are precise points in the body through which a fatal breath can be inhaled. They keep these apertures hermetically closed and make the adept's body into both the abode of heavenly spirits and the material for the refining process to which he is consecrating himself. Only when this has been done does the adept intone the verses addressed to the great gods in Heaven, celebrating their divine revels.

Strangely enough, these great gods do not play a large role in the Shangqing texts; in fact, they appear only rarely. Rather, it is the gods of the body who are most often involved in the exercises set out in these texts. But they do not serve only as the guardians against fatal breaches: they represent essential life forces and establish the otherwise undetectable features of the immaterial, non-corporeal body. The list of these gods is long—in fact there are 39 of them. We do not need to go into detail about them here; I have analyzed them at greater length elsewhere.[2]

The recitation and the visualization-cum-animation that accompanies it are meant to join the spirits and the body that is their home. They are also intended to effect the fusion and union of the spirits of the body with the gods in Heaven. The reading of each stanza addressed to the gods on high is associated with the visualization of the gods of the body, to the point where the text's description of the revels of the gods can be applied both to the heavenly gods and to those of the body. The human body, sanctified by the presence of gods, ends up becoming a kind of terrestrial heaven. Furthermore, each of the "bodily" gods also has a heavenly dwelling that reproduces his bodily home.

The ultimate goal is to arrive at Oneness through the diversity and the multiplicity of forms of the life that animates our body. The human being is conceived as a plurality that must be harmonized, a totality that must be overcome, a oneness that must be constructed while retaining complexity. The "hundred spirits," as the *Dadong zhenjing* says repeatedly, must fuse and achieve Oneness. The Dadong method is defined as that of "uniting fusion" and "returning to the Origin."

The fusing power is the Whirling Wind, a "divine wind" that cuts through impediments and is exhaled by the Imperial One. The adept, after having recited the *jing*, sees this wind in the form of a "white breath" (the color of light), born of the union of the "hundred spirits," entering his mouth, traveling through his whole body, re-emerging, surrounding him, and illuminating him, turning purple (color of the Center as projected into Heaven), and "knotting" itself to form the Imperial One of the Dadong. The latter in turn exhales another Whirling Wind that lights everything up like a "white sun." This wind is none other than the Primordial Breath (found in the slightly later Lingbao school under the name Universal Wind). In its circular movement outward, "turning like a wheel," it animates one after another the ends of the world and activates the Five Agents, uniting Oneness with multiplicity. It is a close relative of the wind that Liezi rode, a violent, mad wind that rises up "like a ram's horn," a bird-wind, the great phoenix of Zhuangzi, at once the means of flight and the one who flies, both the divine chariot and the spirit who rides in it. All this we are told in a preface to the *Dadong zhenjing*.

Complex Oneness

The Oneness that must be achieved and preserved is a complex oneness, not simply that of the Formless Origin but also the reciprocal Oneness that includes and enfolds multiplicity. Thus it is seen as tri-form or three times tri-form (giving the number nine, the final number before the return to One).

Among the many bodily gods, and always within the context of the unification of the individual, three gods play an especially important role: the by now familiar Three Originals (*sanyuan*). But the Shangqing texts, apparently adopting and adapting earlier texts, develop and elaborate above all else meditation on the idea of the three in one. Three gods, the Three Originals, control the 24 breaths of the body and live in the three cinnabar fields. They become the focus of meditation exercises during which the adept, accompanied by them and by their acolytes, rises into the Big Dipper, the symbol of the center and of Oneness projected onto the vault of Heaven.

But the brain, the Kunlun of the human body and seat of the Highest Original, receives special attention. Its mystical geography becomes even more complex in the Shangqing texts. It is seen as containing nine compartments, interconnected palaces sheltering gods and aligned on two levels. In addition, the *niwan*, the upper cinnabar field that is part of the brain, connects to the throat and thence to the whole body. The contemplation of the gods who live in these palaces is in itself enough to bring immortality. These gods are divided into two groups: male and female. Meditations on the gods of the "Male-One" and on those of the "Female-One"—the latter rank higher than the former—complement each other and culminate in the visualization of the True Lord of the Supreme One (the Taiyi of antiquity); the process ends with the flight of the adept and the Taiyi up to the Big Dipper. Thus Supreme One completes the triad of the Three in One along with the Male One and the Female One, who are in turn of multiple nature. The Supreme One achieves the union of the two Ones.

In the Shangqing texts, the Taiyi rules over all the gods of the body. He is called "the essence of the embryo, the master of transformations," a title that reveals he is both the original source and the principle of evolution and thus of multiplicity, that he is life as transformation, the oneness that develops. This is why his names and the places he is supposed to occupy are multiple. He is everywhere and many-formed. The adept visualizes him in his own form and identifies with him.

Embryonic Knots, Death, and Rebirth

The Taiyi is in motion. The term *Dadong*, another Shangqing name for the Tao, brings to mind the idea of communication. Life is transformation. The breath must circulate. Conversely, death is stasis. The Shangqing tradition added a new symbol to ancient ones such as the three worms: the "embryonic knots" that must be untied in order to obtain immortality. At the moment of conception, while the embryo is still in the womb where it receives the "breaths of the Nine Heavens" that give it life, twelve knots and nodules form, the "mortal roots of the womb" that "keep the five interiors [the viscera] in a state of tight twisting" and cause sicknesses. Even before birth, each person carries within the germs of death in the form of impediments to the free influx of the vital current. In order to untie these knots, the adept must relive his embryonic life on a divine and cosmic scale. Once again he lives through the development of the embryo by receiving the Breaths of the Nine Primordial Heavens, one each month, at the same time invoking the Original Celestial Father and the Mysterious (*xuan*) Earthly Mother and bringing down into his body the Kings of the Nine Heavens, who, one by one according to their role, refine and transmute one of his organs. Thus he creates for himself an immortal body of gold and jade. These are the "nine transmutations" or the "cinnabar nine," a completely interior version of the alchemy of Ge Hong, from whom this term derives.

In the course of other exercises also intended to untie these knots, it is the 24 spirits of the body who undo the knots of red thread in their charge and then burn the threads in a great fire 7that consumes the entire body of the adept and reduces it to ashes. These spirits are points of light sent down in three groups of eight by the deities of the Female One into the three cinnabar fields.

Although the proper carrying out of these practices "resides in the excellence of the heart and requires more than a heavenly name on white tablets," to achieve immortality one's name must, as in earlier traditions, be written in the heavenly registers. The gods regularly make a tour of inspection around the world and update the registers of life and death. They meet in great solemn assemblies, the sublimated, heavenly counterpart to those earthly assemblies with the same purpose among the Celestial Masters. These divine assemblies happen on precise dates when the faithful try to erase all trace of sin by meditating on the untying of the knots. The "five spirits of the registers" who have the special responsibility of overseeing human beings play the main roles in these assemblies. This group, led by the Taiyi in the brain, consists of the gods who live in the liver, the lungs, the heart, and the navel; thus they correspond, with some variants, to the "five viscera." The spleen, the organ corresponding to the center, is replaced by the brain, a projection of the center upward, and the kidneys by the navel, which is located in a part of the body with the same symbolic role. Once the knots are untied, the adept should see, in a kind of psychodrama, the five spirits solemnly writing his name on the tablets of the registers of life. This is the basic schema of this exercise, which exists in several variants.

The existence of these knots shows that the germs of death have an ontological nature in human beings since they already exist in the embryo. This implies a concept of death quite different from that in the works of Ge Hong. In order to undo the knots, one must live through life again, go through the entire period of gestation, pass through a new birth by "returning to the embryonic state," an expression not found in Ge Hong but one that foreshadows the "embryo of immortality" of interior alchemy. Here we encounter a great truth: those who give life are not one's fleshly parents but the Original cosmic and infinite Father and Mother or else the Nine Primordial Breaths, one for each month of gestation. The result is not only the refined body that Ge Hong tried to achieve. It is a "spiritual body," to use the precise term used by Tao Hongjing.

Rebirth is an idea that does not appear in earlier texts. It takes shape in various meditation techniques. As taken up by the Shangqing tradition, the idea of *shijie* (freeing from the corpse) undergoes a meaningful evolution that is revealed in the description of the "purification by the supreme Yin," one of the forms of *shijie*. In this case, thanks to help from the gods that have watched over it, at the end of 100 years and sometimes even after having rotted away, the body rises up again in the supreme Yin. The *Xiang'er*, the commentary on the *Daodejing* attributed to Zhang Lu, calls the supreme Yin the "palace of purification of the body," a sort of crucible or womb that prepares for a new birth. "After death," says a quotation from the *Dengzhen yinjue* (*Taiping yulan* 664.14) on the subject of the *shijie*, "the spirit can progress, while the body cannot go away."

This example of "liberation from the body" means that, if the purification is incomplete, a kind of partial death takes place, with an afterlife in an intermediary place while it awaits a more complete purification and ultimate salvation. In fact, *shijie* so conceived is a step in Taoist ascesis, a procedure of salvation after death. It is not a "ritual suicide," an interpretation that has grown up without any supporting evidence.

The adept can also be reborn in the Palace of Red Fire or in the Court of Liquid Fire, paradises located in the extreme south, where he undergoes a purification by fire and is reborn—not as a man, as in Buddhism, but as an immortal. This is a pathway to salvation that is completely opposite to that of Buddhist reincarnation.

In addition, after death those who go down into hell can, if they can prove their purity, rise up through the precisely calibrated hierarchy of subterranean officials and ultimately ascend to the Heavens. The progression is uninterrupted, and there is a direct communication between hell and heaven.

Ecstatic Wanderings

Earthly paradises. The Shangqing adept is able to travel in his own mind, without ever leaving his chamber. As he does this, he is mimicking the ancient wanderings of the Sage of Zhuangzi and Huainanzi, wanderings that took the Sage to the ends of the universe and beyond the four seas. He also commemorates the expeditions of those ancient monarchs who traveled around their world in order to control its spaces and to bring to it their royal efficacy, only to return to the capital with their special virtues concentrated in their own persons.[3] The adept wanders like a traveling shaman, as did Huangdi and the Great Yu, and as the patron saints of his own school did when, impelled by their quest, legend says that they traveled on foot through the mountains and the Polar Seas. In these mental wanderings, he puts into effect the adage of Laozi: "Without going outside his door, he knows the universe."

He travels to distant frontiers, to foreign, unpacified countries, into wild territories, the lands of barbarians and monsters, of marvels and the extraordinary, rich in untapped powers, as described in the *Shanhai jing* (*Book of Mountains and Seas*).[4] But, contrary to the descriptions in this work and in the *Chuci*, for whom these lands are dangerous and peopled with monsters, they are in the Shangqing tradition full of benefits for the adept. There he meets the famous spirits of Chinese mythology—the four corner posts of the world, the four emperors, or the "five old men" (including the one in the center)—and receives from them the food of immortality. He conjures them to enter his prayer room and even his viscera, and he feeds on their secretions. He dares to go as far as to the famous "isles of immortality," where emperors once sent their agents. He even goes to Kunlun or its companion sacred mountains, the axes of the world or "marchmounts," the sacred peaks of Taoism. These landmarks anchor the world; they are earthly counterparts of the planets in the skies and the five viscera in man and perform the same functions. They are also abodes of the immortals, as well as of the Five Emperors, and provide storage places for the sacred texts. The "Picture of the True Form of the Five Peaks" from the southern Taoist tradition, the result of the "mysterious contemplation" of Lord Lao, reveals "the configuration of their contorted and labyrinthine summits." Like the description of the isles of the immortals, it is supposed to have been given to men by Dongfang Shuo, the fallen immortal and the banished companion of the Queen Mother of the West who lived among the courtiers of Emperor Wu of the Han. This schema, which exists in several versions, includes labyrinthine maps and talismans that give access to the mountains (as well as to the whole world) to those who possess them. The mountains are places imbued with magic, rich in Yang power.

Another Shangqing work that describes the "outer regions" is also attributed to Dongfang Shuo, a sort of inspired jester, a divine ne'er-do-well, also called the Azure Lad. The adept travels into the regions described in this book and sings of the six names of the four cardinal directions, the zenith, and the nadir, onto which are superimposed, according to the traditional division by nine, 36 underground kingdoms and 36 (four times nine) heavens ranged in levels in a pyramid upward.

These voyages to distant places can be undertaken only with the help of guides, maps, and talismans. Also needed is a knowledge of the esoteric, divine sounds in the names of the gods to be visited and the gates to be passed—names that are also passwords revealed by divine powers. The adept travels by looking inward and trying to acquire the sharp vision characteristic of the Sage, in order to see clearly as far as the end of the earth, with its flora and fauna, its people and its gods. At the same time, he tries to make these come to him, in a double movement in which his room and his body contain the world that he wanders from end to end.

Planets, sun, and moon. Such voyages are not restricted to the earthly domain. They culminate in a flight to the planets and the stars, sun, moon, and the Dipper. They become celestial wanderings, nourished by light. The stars play a major role in Shangqing practices. They are both temporal and cosmic destinations, both the agents and the regulators of the process of transformation to which the adept devotes himself and over which they preside.

The relationship between the adept and the deities of the planets, which with the sun and the moon form a triad corresponding to that of the cinnabar fields, is almost the same as the relationship that binds him to the Five Emperors of the Poles. The heavenly bodies are in direct connection with the terrestrial marchmounts, as well as with the spirits that preside over the four corners of the world. The configuration is the same, raised by a degree, in the celestial vault.

The sun and moon, heavenly manifestations of Yang and Yin, have a special role. As Marcel Granet so clearly showed,[5] in ancient Chinese myths, the sun makes a voyage across the sky—either of a day or of a year—that starts from the Eastern Valley, where it bathes its rays, up the solar Mulberry Tree, passing through one constellation after another, stopping at various points, and finally disappearing into the Tree of the Sunset. Eventually the mythical kings would be seen as making a similar journey. The *Huangqi yangjing jing* (*Book of the Yellow Breath* [that of the moon] *and of the Yang Essence* [that of the sun]) is a Shangqing work that develops these elements and applies them also to the moon. At the eight articulations of the year—the solstices, the equinoxes, and the first day of each season—the adept accompanies the stars to each of their stations. These, also located at the Poles, are further lands of immortality; in the tree of life that grows there nest the birds whose golden plumes are used to make the fabric for the robes of immortality worn by the faithful. The tree bears fruit that confers immortality on those who eat it. At the foot of the tree is a water source, a spring or pool, where the stars, the inhabitants of this earth, and the adept who has come to visit them can purify themselves. The lords of these happy lands are none other than the guardian spirits, the regulators of the "happy virtues" that ancient Chinese mythology saw as living at the poles.

At each station of one of the stars in one of these lands, the adept must draw a talisman; he throws this talisman into water, which he later uses to perform his purifying ablutions, a memory of the apotropaic and therapeutic rites of the Celestial Masters. Then he rises on light from the star to the palace corresponding to the station. There he receives fruits of immortality from the hands of the local sovereign. Then he swallows the talisman he has drawn.

These exercises have several meanings. On the one hand, the adept feeds on light, admitting it to the part of the body that corresponds to the current season and to the rhythm of the passage of the stars (or, alternatively, the planet on which he is meditating), and becomes light himself. "The purple breath [of the sun]," says the *Huangqi yangjing jing*, "accumulates and drops down to cover the body [of the adept]. He thinks that he is within the light of the sun. The light of the sun envelops his body, and he rises into the Palace of Universal Yang [the solar station of high noon, which corresponds to the summer solstice]." Then, "all is light, within and without." Everyone who follows these practices acquires a "vermilion face" and a "bright and glowing" body; he "glows with an extraordinary light; the nape of his neck wears a round burst of light, and he illuminates the six directions." Like the sun and the moon, he has rejoined the Sage of Zhuangzi and the *Huainanzi*.

He also meditates on the alternating and parallel, opposed and complementary, movements of the Yin and the Yang, the moon and the sun, which intersect each other and meet. All these movements are explained by a complicated system of hierogamic exchanges of attributes. (Both the sun and moon, for example, are composed of fire and water.)

This is not a solar or star cult. The accent is on the concerted action of the two principles, on the merger, the contrast, and the harmony in their movements. The sun and the moon are inseparable here. Like the five planets and the five peaks on another level, they represent the world and that which measures it and the four directions and that which joins them in pairs. In themselves, in their double progress, they represent the fundamental bipolarity that the Primordial Unity quarters (as a shield in heraldry) and the *coincidentia oppositorum* announces. The adept is the third term, the center, in the sky on par with the sun and the moon, as he was the fifth term when the four emblems of the terrestrial poles surrounded him. In addition, reliving again the development of the universe through his practices, he brings the three worlds into harmony: the exterior world through which the sun and moon move, the symbolic world inhabited by the gods, and his own interior world that holds the first two because it is at once physical and symbolic.

The Dipper (Ursa Major). The sun and the moon are actually located halfway between Heaven and Earth, since they visit the terrestrial polar regions. A true vertical dimension is lacking: the sun and the moon correspond to the east and the west, not to the north and the south. Up and down are absent. It is the Dipper's role to represent, in a symbol at the same time single and double, the fundamental Oneness of the two principles of Yin and Yang.

The Dipper also forms a triad, of which it is the center, with the Yang-sun and the Yin-moon. Its magico-religious prestige is ancient: it appears in the *Chuci*, it was the object of a cult headed by Emperor Wu of the Han, and it is mentioned in the *Huainanzi*. We need do no more than call to mind the deeply religious meanings of astro-calendrical calculations in ancient China in order to understand the importance assumed by the Dipper in Taoism, the direct product of this milieu. At the center of the sky, it takes the place of the Polestar, which, close to the Dipper but not part of it, rarely plays any significant role in Taoism. Through the apparent movement of its "handle," the Dipper directs and indicates the natural rhythms that allow us to determine the proper orientation for carrying out religious acts in accord with the symbolic and divine proceedings that must be part of the act in order to ensure its effectiveness. The Dipper thus provides a ritual area and gives entry to it, and it dictates the time and the form of the actions to be carried out.[6] As the director of the auspicious aspect of the world, it is also a protector charged with apotropaic powers. As the Center, it is the abode of the Supreme One, the Taiyi.

Whereas the sun-moon / Yang-Yin pair reveals the dualism inherent in the entire universe, the Dipper is the single, central Pole of the world. But its unity is complex, because it comprises nine stars (nine being the figure of totality, of the completion of the series of numbers, of multiplicity returning to unity). Two of them are invisible, capable of being seen only by those worthy of this honor, and seeing them brings several centuries of life. This figure nine fits perfectly with the Dipper's status as the abode of the Taiyi, since in Han speculations this god built the Nine Palaces of Heaven (just as the Great Yu made the nine regions of the earth) and gave them the configuration of single, articulated totality. To do this, he divided Heaven into several sectors that he coordinated by his single, moving presence, going from one to the other in turn and joining them together regularly at the center when he paused there.

In the Shangqing texts, each star in the Dipper contains a paradise constructed on the same pattern as those of the moon and the sun. The Dipper itself is surrounded by "black stars," which are *po* souls, where female gods live, the wives of the lords of the stars of the Dipper, on which they shed a "dark light." Here we are truly in the celestial world, the inverted world, where Yang and light are within, and darkness, souls, and Yin are outside. In the human body, these gods live in the brain, and the male gods of the stars of the Dipper live in the heart.

The Shangqing texts taught several kinds of activities involving the Dipper. Because of its apotropaic role (which expanded considerably during later centuries), the adept can invoke the Dipper simply as it is or can cover himself with the protective mantle of its stars. He can also, however, rise up toward it, to "lodge in the Dipper," or "pace the Dipper," a practice attested as early as the first century A.D. Traces of this practice are found in texts in the Celestial Masters tradition and perhaps also in Ge Hong. The Shangqing tradition, however, developed the first detailed forms of the practice and used it extensively in liturgy.

This pacing follows the Step of Yu, the same step that, for Ge Hong, gave access to the mountains. As applied to pacing the stars, this step reproduces the union of Yin and Yang. It is "the essence of flight into the heavens, the spirit of walking on earth, the truth of man's movement," explain later texts. Thus, it is the quintessence of all movement—whether heavenly, earthly, or human—the dance that joins Heaven, Earth, and Humanity. The formula "three steps, nine footprints," sometimes used to describe it, connects it with the Three Originals and the nine stars of the Dipper. This pacing of the Dipper is called "pacing the network" or "pacing the void." It gave rise to famous religious hymns and was a theme that inspired many poets.[7]

The practice of "pacing out time," that is, writing it in space, originated in the pacing of the Taiyi god, who, by his progress, divided the Breath and distributed it in parts, each carrying its own particular virtues, among various sectors of space in a temporal sequence. This is the role of the god, a role reproduced by ancient sovereigns in the Palace of Light (Mingtang), the adept in his prayer chamber, and then, later, the priest in the ritual area. The role is that of the organizer who unifies and mediates between Heaven (the celestial movements of the stars) and Earth (to which the organizer transfers the same movements, using the same landmarks, transposed from one plane to another). *Bugang*, "pacing the network," also means "walking on the firm surface" (*gang*, written with a similar character with the same pronunciation; the two characters are, in fact, regarded as interchangeable), the continuous, the One Yang. It is a division of Unity.

This division begins at the Heavenly Center and "moves downward" from Heaven to Earth, or upward to the One-Center, going up from Earth to Heaven, depending on whether the adept moves from the first star of the Dipper to the last or vice versa. The two movements alternate, both in Shangqing practices and in ritual. The "descent" from the One to the multiple is followed by the "ascent," here that of the adept to Heaven. One version of this exercise has "three ways": one "straight ahead" (from the first star to the last), the next "backward" (in the opposite direction), and the third, the "return," in which the adept goes back up to Heaven after having descended to Earth.

In the Shangqing texts, where this practice has not yet reached the great complexity that it would acquire later, the adept draws the stars of Ursa Major on a silk ribbon, and, after constructing a sacred enclosure by commanding the planets to take their places around him, he "clothes himself" in the stars of the Dipper and then rises into the constellation. First, he walks around the outer circle of "dark stars," invoking the goddesses who live in them. Only then can he proceed to the male gods of the Dipper, making the resident god appear as he steps on each star in turn, following a strict order.

The symbolic implications of the Dipper, inherited from the Han, are many. Although it is the center, the Dipper also stands for the north, and consequently the Origin, the location of the cyclical signs associated with the embryo, the pole that symbolizes water, the Great Yin that engenders the Yang, the place where all things begin. Its seven stars open the seven orifices of the embryo and give it life. The Dipper's nine stars connect it with everything counted by nine, as stated on the first page of the *Winged Text of the Flying Stars and the Nine True Things*, which is dedicated to it.

Through One, it is the place of Origin; through Nine, that of Return. The days of the "return to the Origin" (*huiyuan*) are consecrated to it and are days of renewal. The titles borne by its goddesses suggest phenomena of change and imply that their function is to protect the embryo. Birth, return, turning—all together it is the manifested form, in the process of becoming, of the Taiyi, the Supreme One, who in his hidden form, enclosed upon itself, is represented by the Polestar.

The Dipper is the most concentrated representation in the skies of the ordered unrolling of the world centered on the One. The *Winged Text* assigns to each star in the Dipper functions of government, supervision, and rule in both heavenly and terrestrial domains. It orients and orders things; in addition, it divides the good from the bad and then punishes and rewards. Many of the practices that invoke the Dipper are dedicated to asking pardon for sins and getting one's name erased from the register of the dead. As the judge of good and evil, the Dipper is also connected with the various hells. This is why one of the Shangqing texts dedicated to it, the *Kaitian santu jing* (*Text of the Three Diagrams That Open the Sky*), contains a "method for entering life and guaranteeing immortality." In this procedure, the adept, turning with the Dipper in the sky, is carried by its stars to the three celestial gates. This text also lists the names of the Six Infernal Courts (six being the number of hells) of the city of Feng, which are paired with the three Heavenly Passes, just as the Celestial Masters contrast the Six Demon Heavens with the Three Heavens. In this city located in the northeast, which has the same name as an ancient Zhou capital, sit the infernal judges, under the orders of the Lord of the Dipper. They include ancient emperors or legendary heroes, as well as the "underworld commanders," the *dixiazhu* of the Han *weishu*, who must from time to time adjust the accounts of the dead with the living.

The Dipper, says one text, is "a twisted, sinuous network," a multiple unity, which both moors and orders things at the same time as it puts them into motion and makes them evolve. A chariot that can carry one away, the Dipper is closely associated with the idea of passage. Its seven stars "allow passage." The expression "the seven passages" recalls the act of walking on the Dipper. Its last star is called "Heavenly Gate" and sometimes gives its name to the entire constellation, which is called "hinge between disjunction and junction." To have this door opened, the adept must present a religious identity card drawn up according to prescribed forms.

The Shangqing adept first travels to the four corners of the world. Following the track of the sun and the moon, he marks the four corners of the earth and measures its four sectors. Then he ascends the central axis, which has two facets, for the center is double in that it both gathers and disperses and both conceals the up and the down and makes them manifest: a disjunction between up and down, Heaven and Earth, and/or conjunction within the Dipper and Yin and Yang, a disjunction/conjunction seen also in the relations between humans and the gods. The adept rises up to the gods, and they come down to him, an assumption and incarnation that can never be separated. Here we see both the duality of the vertical poles and the duality of the adept's relation to the divine. From the sun-moon pair to the constellation of the Dipper, evolution proceeds in the direction of increased intensity. The Dipper is a concentration into a single constellation of what is represented by the two great lights and their wide sweep around the earth. It gathers into a single unit the space measured out by the sun and the moon. The same relationship is seen in the adept's practices, which may take as long as a month or a year for those dedicated to the sun-moon pair or only a single ritual act for those invoking the Dipper.

Returning now to the procedures of laboratory alchemy, we can see the connection between this kind of alchemy, the astral practices of Shangqing, and the interior alchemy, which developed later. The few alchemical recipes given in the Shangqing texts are distinctive in that the names of some drugs connect them with astral practices. For example, orpiment and realgar are respectively called "*hun* soul of the sun" and "flower of the moon." One elixir has the name that is given to the lunar essence that the adept absorbs during meditation. Another has the name of an immortality drink that the Shangqing gods introduce into the mouth of the meditating adept. Alchemy takes on astral colors. Conversely the sun is compared with a furnace: it must "liquefy the organs"; it is the "light of cinnabar"; and, as fire, it is one of the agents of purification along with the water of the moon. The term used to refer to the cosmic rotations into which the adept is pulled, *zhuan*, also refers to alchemical transmutations. In alchemy, there is a displacement and evolution toward the absorption of lunar and solar essences, the drugs of immortality. The immortality drinks that the gods bring to the meditating adept have names borrowed from traditional alchemical techniques, such as Golden Liquor, or Liquid Gold (*jinyi*).

If we examine how, in certain recipes, Ge Hong obtained the waters of the moon and sun in order to make elixirs and then absorb them, we can see the inward turn of procedures in developments leading to the Shangqing tradition. This interiorizing is still under way in the practice of incorporating, month after month, the breaths of the Nine Great Primordial Heavens in order to regenerate the body. The procedure is called, significantly, the method of the "nine cinnabars" (*jiudan*), a reflection of the fact that such regeneration of the body, achieved according to the same plan, month after month, organ by organ, was reported as being attained by ingesting drugs in the *Wufujing* (*Text of the Five Talismans*), a most important writing in Ge Hong's tradition.

Certain Shangqing methods are thus clearly sublimated and interiorized versions of alchemical procedures. The gestation of the spiritual body must be achieved by meditation and takes the form of a union of complementary cosmic principles (the moon and the sun, original Father and Mother), in repeated motions of ascent and precipitation, of sublimation and condensation, which foreshadow in a striking fashion the principles and formulations of the practice of interior alchemy.

6

The Lingbao School

By the end of the fourth century, the Shangqing school had already reached a culmination—in both its methods and the spirit of its seekers after immortality—that permitted no further innovations, only refinements. Renewal could come only from outside, from a new direction in Taoism that emerged as a direct result of the Shangqing texts but drew inspiration from other sources, particuarly the Celestial Masters school (for rituals) and Buddhism. To these were added certain Confucian elements (primarily respect for Confucian virtues) that had had some small influence in earlier schools (in the *Taipingjing*, for example) but would now become a permanent part of all Taoism. The result is known as the Lingbao school.

The compound *lingbao*, usually translated into English as "sacred jewel," is an earlier name applied to sorceresses. The rich connotations of the word *bao* (treasure) were explained earlier (see Chapter 1); the word *ling*, which may be translated "sacred, spirit," functions in this compound as a noun modifier. The *ling* element signifies the deity associated with the *bao*, the treasure, an object or a human being (magician or medium) who serves as a container for the divine spirit and permits it to be incarnated.

Both parts of the term carry sexual connotations: the masculine Heaven (in *ling*) is related to the feminine Earth (in *bao*), the cosmic pair whose coupling and separation are fundamental to the existence of life.

The Lingbao school is important for two reasons: this group has, down to modern times, determined the essential form of Taoist ritual, and with this school we find the first true infiltration of Buddhism into Taoism. (Buddhism had little influence on the development of the Shangqing school.) The form of Buddhism involved had, however, already been greatly sinicized.

The emergence of the Lingbao scriptures is a direct result of the success of the Shangqing texts. All are based on the text called the *Wufujing* (*Text of the Five Talismans*), fragments of which survive in the Taoist Canon. This text was connected with the apocryphal *weishu* texts "Hetu" ("[Yellow] River Chart") and "Luoshu" ("Luo [River] Writings"). The *Five Talismans* is the most ancient of the Lingbao texts and supplied the framework for most of the Lingbao canon, a structure based on the five directionally oriented divisions of space and time. This explains how people came to believe that all the other texts, with their connection to this one work, had been revealed to Ge Xuan, the great-uncle of Ge Hong and the actual owner of the *Five Talismans* scripture. He supposedly transmitted the Lingbao texts to his disciple Zheng Siyuan and, via him, to Ge Hong. But he is also supposed to have passed them on to a Buddhist monk, Falan, known to have lived around 241 A.D., and to Sun Quan (185–252), founder of the Kingdom of Wu (with its capital at Nanjing).

The claim that the texts derive from Ge Xuan was, however, simply a way of legitimizing them by exaggerating their antiquity. Actually they were put together between 397 and 402 by Ge Chaofu, about whom we know practically nothing except that he belonged to the family of Ge Xuan and Ge Hong and undoubtedly had access to their library as he compiled the texts. Certainly he also knew the Shangqing texts, which inspired him and from which he also sought legitimization. Within a decade, the Lingbao texts had become so successful that, during the time of Tao

Hongjing, monasteries sheltering adherents to this school had been set up on Mao Shan near those of the Shangqing group. The heart of this body of scriptures is the *Chi shu wutian* (*Red Book of the Five Writings*, DZ 22) and the *Durenjing* (*Book of Human Salvation*). The whole corpus in part grew out of the *Five Talismans*. At times we find a relatively coherent synthesis, and at others a crude mishmash of the source material. The texts mix features of the Celestial Masters school (some ritual, and along with it a part of the pantheon) and some elements inherited from the Shangqing school (the idea of a sacred text of cosmic dimensions, hymns, some cosmological data, a few visualization methods). To these are added borrowings from ancient texts known to Ge Hong (such as the *Sanhuang wen* [*Text of the Three August Ones*]) and Buddhist elements (a distinctive idea of salvation along with some cosmological data). These elements are organized around a vision of the world that is drawn in large part from the *Five Talismans*, with its division into five sectors dominated by the Five Agents, whose function, as we have seen, is to ensure the coordination of a group of world reference points, on various levels and with close correspondences among them—all this makes possible, through rituals and invocations, the driving away of demons and the prevention of disasters. Many of these texts are called "red texts," a claim to a form of purification by the "red fire" of the south, or extreme Yang. In fact this color is primarily an indicator of a connection with the tradition that the *Five Talismans* and the "River Chart" were originally written in red characters.

In addition to its greater emphasis, thanks to Buddhism, on the idea of salvation, now extended to all creatures, the major contribution of the Lingbao movement to the growth of Taoism lies in its more complex and systematized development of Celestial Masters ritual. The school is the true source of Taoist liturgy.

Established Taoist liturgy may be said to begin with the important figure of Lu Xiujing (406–77), who was above all else a ritualist. He compiled the first Taoist bibliographic catalog, in an attempt to order the extant corpus of Taoist texts. To do this, he relied on indications in the Lingbao texts and established a hierarchy among Taoist texts, dividing them into three "grottoes," along the pattern of the Buddhist Tripitaka (three baskets). He always extolled the Shangqing texts as the most significant, but in his actual codification of ritual he relied mostly on the Lingbao scriptures. He also established a ritual for the transmission of the Lingbao Canon on the basis of ancient principles: the exchange of texts for sworn "pledges of good faith." This new ritual was much more solemn than its antecedents, however, and occurred in the course of a ceremony comparable to the later great Lingbao rites.

Over time all these rituals underwent an evolution. They became both more complex and more numerous. Unlike the practices of the Celestial Masters, from which they derive, the participation of the general public was constantly reduced and the role of priests grew, to the point that today there are ceremonies in which the lay public no longer participates except through the mediation of a few representatives.

This evolution in the Lingbao tradition means that we should look at the school in two stages: first, the patterns of thought in what is called "ancient Lingbao," which date from the end of the fourth century; and then the later ritual to which it gave birth.

Ancient Lingbao

In brief, we can say that, with a few variations, this movement maintained ancient values but subsumed them to the cause of "compassion" (*ci*). Lingbao practices were scarcely new: the ritual of the Celestial Masters was revived, but considerably developed, amplified, and dominated by the Five Agents system. The visualizations typical of Shangqing faded into the background but did continue. The ultimate goal was still to "ascend into Heaven in broad daylight," but it was modified by an idea, new to Taoism, of universal salvation. Apart from the *Five Talismans*, the earlier texts that were adopted and preached were the *Daodejing* (linking the school to the Celestial Masters), the *Texts of the Three August Ones* (connected with the tradition of Ge Hong), and the Shangqing texts (especially the *Dadong zhenjing*). On the other hand, as in the Shangqing school, gymnastic practices, the "nourishing of the vital principles," the taking of drugs, and laboratory alchemy were demoted to a lower rank (DZ 32, 14a; 671, 1.7a, 1.9b, 2.2b). Liturgical practices, primarily the recitation of texts, took precedence; the solitary meditating adept disappeared almost entirely. Once again, the master became an important figure. Along with the Tao and the text, he made up the Three Treasures, a pattern derived from Buddhism. Laojun, the deified form of Laozi, was his prototype. Meditations on the masters were incorporated into the ritual of entering a ritual space.

The Influence of Buddhism and Universal Salvation

Most of the Lingbao borrowings from Buddhism were superficial and clumsy. They did not derive from a scholarly form of Buddhism and, in fact, reveal a lack of knowledge of the religion. Sacred texts were no longer always written by the gods in the heavens but were often, like the sutras, put forward by a supreme deity before an assembly of gods from which a disciple sometimes emerged to ask questions. The Lingbao adherents had a habit of giving their heavens names copied from Buddhism and based on phonetic transcriptions of Sanskrit. (This was sometimes done in the Shangqing school, but in a less systematic fashion.) Ancient cosmological ideas were plastered over with Buddhist notions, as we shall see below. Terms were borrowed, but often given different meanings. Some expressions derived from Buddhism refer to punishments in hell, an idea absent from Taoism up to that time, and the idea of reincarnation here on earth made a tentative first appearance.

The only truly significant contribution from Buddhism is the idea of salvation, which began to replace that of immortality and developed into the notion of a universal salvation. This is clearly far from the goals of the seekers after immortality. But this idea of salvation in turn took two forms, both shaped by Buddhism.

As many have noted, this influence is obvious in the fact that for the Lingbao school individual salvation comes only through

salvation for all, "in uncountable numbers," as the then new, frequently used expression has it. The earliest Lingbao texts stop
there. But those that appeared a little later sometimes make use
of a formula closer to the spirit of Mahayana Buddhism: "Save
humanity before saving oneself" (DZ 361, 2.13b). This would become a constant refrain in certain Tang texts. There are also formulaic statements that all the saints had sworn to seek, over
hundreds of thousands of cosmic eras, to relieve suffering and
save sinners. Monks entering the religion took the oath to do
likewise.

This is completely contradictory to the ancient Chinese principle, Confucian as well as Taoist, that one must take command of
oneself before one can do anything for the world, a concept more
in harmony with Hinayana Buddhism. In fact the two attitudes
can be reconciled if one considers, in a very Mahayanistic way,
that the two forms of salvation constitute a pair of comparable
worth, and that the difference is only one of methodology. This
is, in fact, the position adopted readily by Taoists at a slightly
later period. They were not at all bothered by what could be seen,
at different times, either as an unconscious, superficial logical
contradiction in their beliefs or as an evolution.

This conception of salvation easily absorbed purely Chinese
elements, which became very important and appeared in many
forms in Lingbao texts. First, universal salvation specifically includes the salvation of the dead, especially ancestors. This fact
underlies the subsequent development of Taoist funeral rites.
Furthermore, salvation is also understood in terms of ancient
Chinese belief: the human being—and in antiquity the ruler—is
an integrating agent in the cosmos, and his well-being reflects
that of the universe (a legacy of Five Agents theory). Thus, the
human salvation of an individual or of a group depends on the
salvation of the universe, and vice versa. All liturgy, like that of
the ancient kings, is intended to bring about this balance.

Proof of this interpretation can be found in the supplications
of the faithful or the officiating master. Some could be prayers
formulated by emperors of earlier times and have nothing Buddhist about them. They ask that the earth remain vast and broad,

that it be neither flooded nor swallowed up, that the sun and the moon should not be eclipsed, that the four seasons should revolve in their proper order (see, e.g., DZ 330, 3a–5a). Other prayers are directed at controlling spirits, stabilizing the Sacred Mountains, preserving the length of months and years, controlling the path of the Three Luminaries, bringing the Great Peace, ensuring the wealth and happiness of the people, and saving all beings (DZ 330, 7a, 9b). Several levels are present here: the cosmic order, the state, the world of living beings, and that of the dead (DZ 457, 1a–2b; 369; 344, 15a; 352, 1a; 348, 1a).

The image of the Sage is present in all these petitions. Except at scattered, almost tangential points—especially in the hymns borrowed from the Shangqing school or inspired by them—the adept no longer aspires to identify with heavenly bodies or connect himself with their motions. A cosmo-political point of view has taken over. We are closer to the concept of the Sage in the *Book of Change*. The wish to save one's ancestors, regularly expressed by the adept in his petitions or by the officiating priest in the liturgy, signals the lack of consistency already noted in the Lingbao tradition. If all living and dead beings are to be saved, why make a special case of ancestors? Thus we find superimposed three different concepts of salvation deriving from the ancestor cult (the individual as part of a family), from the ritual and magical role of the Sage as a ruler ordering the cosmos, and from Buddhism.

Life and Death

In a typically Taoist fashion—that is, in a deeply Chinese way—the Lingbao tradition is a compromise rather than a synthesis. As Stephen Bokenkamp has shown, in the Lingbao tradition the purely Chinese and Taoist beliefs about survival after death are clumsily equated with the Buddhist expression *miedu* (literally, "to fade and go beyond"), which designates deliverance. A person's *hun* soul is held underground (recalling Han popular beliefs) by infernal powers, the Three Officers of the Celestial Masters, but it can be rescued by means of injunctions issued by an officiating priest on the basis of virtuous acts accomplished during the individual's lifetime. The soul is then transferred to the Southern Palace. The body, which remains in the ancient Palace of the Great Yin, in the extreme north, is taken over by the spirit or deity who presides over the sector of the world (there are five such sectors) where the dead person lived as well as over the time period of the deceased's date of birth. In this palace the body undergoes a purification process that will allow it to return to life. A rebirth is envisaged, in which the soul and the body are reunited. This progressive purification, ensured by Lingbao practices, takes place over nine steps, or, according to different texts, whatever number of rebirths may be necessary for the adept to accumulate enough merit to be ready, both physically and spiritually, to ascend to an eternal dwelling in the heavens (see, e.g., DZ 97, 2.18b). This sequence of rebirths happens here on earth, in Buddhist fashion, rather than in the heavens, as in the Shangqing tradition.

Parts of Shangqing teaching were retained, however. The parents who give birth to us are not our "true" parents, nor is our body our own (DZ 456, 33b). It is only a temporary abode (a reminder of Zhuangzi). Whoever attains the Tao no longer has a shape or body, which is the source of all trouble (reminiscent of Laozi), and his ego (*wo*) or person (*shen*, which also means "body") is now one with his spirit and forms with it his "true *shen*." He then returns to his true, original parents and never dies again. When he is thus delivered, *miedu*, his body no longer decays. On the other hand, the evildoer returns to his temporal, this-worldly parents, and his bad karma continues. When the spirit within one is delivered, it fuses with the light, and one is then reborn as a human, but of a finer sort, and the body and spirit are no longer separated.

This slightly confused formulation may be summarized as follows. The union between the body and the person is not fixed. Anyone doomed to evil by karma is reborn of parents who are not his "true" parents, and the instability continues. We see here the idea of "original" parents from the Shangqing tradition and of "true" in the sense of "holy." However, anyone who attains the

Tao no longer has an ordinary body (*xing*). His self and his *shen* (here the word probably suggests incarnate personality) are now one. He no longer dies, but returns to his "true" parents, that is, to his Origin. In the *Taishang jingjie* (DZ 787, 4a), written a few decades later, this union of body and spirit is achieved through meditation and the conservation of the breath and the *jing*. Another text (DZ 369) describes a way to help the dead rise on the pathway to salvation: texts are transmitted to them by being buried in their grave.

The Lingbao school continued the careful recording in registers of the number of years to be lived, with life spans a function of good and bad acts. In addition to the five Shangqing gods of the registers, the ancient hearth gods, and the "three corpses," almost all the gods now take part in this accounting—those of Heaven, Earth, the body, and the underworld. As in the Shangqing tradition, majestic assemblies of the gods are held regularly to reveal the registers; these assembly days became days of fasting and purification.

Hells have almost no place in the Shangqing texts, which mention only a city that is at the same time a place of judgment and an administrative center for the underworld. The Lingbao texts (especially DZ 456) provide many more details about this administration, drawn up on the basis of earlier accounts by the Celestial Masters. The fundamental structure, once again triadic, is based on the three judgment courts: the one on the left, deriving from the Great Yang and Fire, hears cases concerning life; the one on the right, connected with the Great Yin and Water, hears cases connected with death; the court in the center judges matters concerning both—it is called "knife wind," after the wind that cuts through the joints at death, somewhat in the tradition of the Divine Wind of Shangqing, which frees one from all ties, and the idea of deliverance from the corpse, *shijie*, in which the syllable *jie* includes the idea of dismemberment. Here we have deliverance, but also a distribution between right and left, death and life. Each of these three categories of court is repeated three times, for the three Originals—those of Heaven, Earth, and Water—with each of these domains being ruled by the Green Maiden and dealing with matters that concern, respectively, the celestial, terrestrial, and aquatic domains. Each court has twelve offices, administered by 1,200 officials. (This is reminiscent of the *sanguan* of the Celestial Masters.) These hells are thus, as in the Shangqing tradition, places of judgment and administration, dealing with matters of life and death, not places of suffering and punishment.

Pantheon and Cosmology

The only obvious reliance of the Lingbao school on the pantheon of the Celestial Masters appears in the petitions offered up by the officiating priest during rituals. Some of the Shangqing deities survived, along with the ancient gods connected with the calendar. In addition, gods specific to the Lingbao school itself started to appear, among whom the greatest are the higher gods of today's Taoist liturgy. The supreme god is the Yuanshi tianzun, the Celestial Venerable One of the Original Beginning, a Buddhicized version of the Yuanshi tianwang (with *wang* "king" substituted for *zun* "venerable one") of the Shangqing tradition, replacing the ancient Taiyi. Laojun, the deified Laozi, is next in importance. The Five Emperors, called the Five Old Men, as in the Shangqing tradition, the Demon Kings, and the dragon kings also play important roles. The Northern Dipper acquired four counterparts corresponding to the four cardinal points in space in order to fit the fundamental cosmological model of the *Five Talismans*. Ge Xuan naturally became one of the most important saints.

Perhaps it is in cosmology that the Lingbao tradition is the most innovative, in spite of its adoption of the traditional division of the world into five sectors. This division alternates with another, drawn from Buddhism, dividing the world into ten regions: eight for the eight directions on the wind rose, plus up and down. The latter was a new development, since in the Shangqing as well as the Chinese tradition as a whole one finds only divisions into four, five, six (four plus up and down), eight, or nine (eight and the center).

There were no longer 36 heavens, but rather 32, distributed

horizontally on the periphery of the celestial disk, with eight heavens for each of the four sectors. Their names are different from those in the Shangqing tradition and they are divided into "three worlds," as in Buddhism: the worlds of desire, form, and formlessness. On the other hand, the descriptions of heavens and paradises follow the Shangqing descriptions.

The traditional idea of the origin of the world from the Single Breath, which divided into Heaven and Earth, is retained. But this is also connected, although not in any truly coherent fashion, with that of the three original breaths—*xuan, yuan,* and *shi*—of the Celestial Masters.

The *Jiutian shengshen zhangjing (Commentary on the Stanzaic Scripture on the Generation of Divine Spirit Within the Nine Heavens,* DZ 187), one of the most important works of the Lingbao school, reveals a vast prelude to the appearance of the world. In this work the three Breaths are fundamentally only one and are shown to correspond to three deities, the three Lords (*jun*) of the Celestial Treasure (*tianbao*), of the Sacred Treasure (*lingbao*), and of the Divine Treasure (*shenbao*)—three terms that mean almost the same thing. In the course of the three successive cosmic eras and in three distinct heavens that would become the three great heavens of Taoism (*Yuqing,* or Jade Purity; *Shangqing,* or Highest Purity; and *Taiqing,* or Great Purity), these lords introduced three different teachings: that of the Dadong (Great Grotto), of the Dongxuan (Mysterious Grotto), and of the Dongshen (Divine Grotto). We have here the beginnings of the later classification of the texts of the *Daozang,* the Daoist Canon.

The most innovative aspect of the Lingbao school lay in fully developing certain ancient Chinese apocalyptic notions that had already started to reappear in some Shangqing texts. The ancient terrors engendered by natural disasters and carried to an extreme in fears of the end of the world were now expressed much more systematically. The compilers of Shangqing texts had touched on these subjects, using descriptions and terminology borrowed from the Han official history. In the Lingbao movement these ideas reappear, perhaps under the influence of the Buddhist idea of cosmic eras, but are structured according to schemas dictated by the theory of Yin and Yang and the Five Agents. In this school the apocalyptic tendency was to be long lived: texts dating from long after the original kernel of "ancient Lingbao" scriptures display apocalyptic concerns again and again (e.g., DZ 320, 321, 322).

Eschatological elements in Shangqing texts mingled two themes. First, there were cosmic speculations on the Yin and the Yang: this world would end either because of the exhaustion of supplies of Yin and Yang, or because of a dramatic and paroxysmal breakdown of the necessary balance and connection between these two forces, which would bring about the destruction of all things. This theme had already appeared under the Han, and there are suggestions of it in the *Hanshu* (*History of the Han*, by Ban Gu, completed about 82 A.D.), in a chapter dedicated to calendrical calculation. According to the *Santian zhenfa jing* (*Scripture of the Orthodox Law of the Three Heavens*), a lost text of the Shangqing tradition that survives only in fragments quoted in other works, the Yang is exhausted after 3,600 celestial revolutions, and the Yin after 3,300 terrestrial revolutions. This is the end of a small cycle. The great cycles come to an end after 9,900 celestial revolutions and 9,300 terrestrial revolutions. Then the world and its laws are overthrown, and, as at the beginning of the world and at the time of the appearance of a text that signals the dawn of a new era, the stars halt and change their paths.

Onto this eschatology, the Shangqing school grafted the ideas of the Founding Book of the World and of the Invulnerable Sage, immortal and of extra-cosmic dimensions. Just as the Book establishes the world and the Sage gives it order, at the apocalypse the sacred texts and the immortals overcome the cycles of Yin and Yang and their vicissitudes and survive the cosmic catastrophes by taking refuge on the *axis mundi*, Mount Kunlun.

Certain elements of ancient mythology also appear in the mention of mysterious beings who intervene to judge human beings: the Water Mother, the Heavenly or Metal (or Gold) Horse, and the Great Bird, which is probably a phoenix. In addition, one of the Shangqing texts mentions the descent of a Sage of a Later Age (*housheng*), that is, of the age after the formation of Heaven and

Earth (*houtian*) as opposed to the age preceding this formation (*xiantian*), a title that belongs to the highest ranking saints in the Shangqing celestial hierarchy.

Those who will be saved bear the "marks of holiness"— physical signs such as sunlight in the eyes, green teeth, white blood, a square mouth, and purple emanations from the belly and the mouth. All these signs are listed in great detail in the *Housheng lie ji* (*Annals of the Latter-day Sages*, DZ 198). The specific features manifested by adepts identify their connection with specific celestial palaces. The texts thus classify the faithful and promise them the supreme reward—survival at the end of the world.

Many Lingbao texts continued this line of thought, with variations. Sometimes the cosmic eras are correlated with heavenly revolutions connected with those of the Dipper. At other times, cosmic cycles succeed each other in accordance with a rhythm set by numbers and points corresponding to each of the Five Agents or "breaths." At the end of the reign of each of these, the emperor of the color associated with the Agent concerned descends to the appropriate earthly mountain to bring a teaching that will save a fixed number of men corresponding to the number of the Breath involved. In addition, there are short and long eras. Each ends in an excess of Yang (general conflagration) or of Yin (flooding). At the end of a short era, the Mother of Waters (the moon) produces a flood, the mountains are eroded away, the Five Emperors of the five sectors of the world gather in the Mysterious Capital of the highest heaven, the Nine Breaths of the universe are renewed, and the ten thousand emperors change their ranking. At the end of a great era, the Yang-nine is exhausted, as is the Yin-six, and evil creatures are unleashed, Heaven and Earth are turned upside down, metals and stones melt together, and the six directions of space merge into one.

This apocalyptic vision includes features we have already seen in the Shangqing tradition. At the end of the world, the gods, especially the Queen Mother of the West (a reminder of the Han millenarian movement with this deity as its focus), gather up the virtuous, "seed people," and transfer them to the "lands of bliss" or to cosmic mountains that the apocalyptic catastrophes cannot reach (thus giving occasion for a new description of Mount Kunlun). Also preserved there are sacred texts awaiting revelation. Those who possess these texts will be saved: at this desperate time the texts fulfill their fundamental purpose as talismans conferring life and salvation. The disappearance of the old world is followed by the appearance of a new, pure world. Dates for the end of the world were calculated on the basis of cyclical signs that could be interpreted in many different ways, but that were believed to designate the years 382 or 442. This belief was so strong that on several occasions groups of the faithful awaited in agony the expected cataclysms (Lagerwey, *Wushang pi-yao*, pp. 81, 86–87; DZ 352, 1.22b, 15b, 20a, 19b; 330, 1a; 22, 2.4b–8a).

Messianic Movements

This millenarian eschatology was accompanied in certain Taoist milieus by a form of messianism that seems to have been strongest during the fifth century. Its ultimate source lay in the theme of Laozi's reincarnations, a theme that took shape during the Han. The Sage of the Later Age of the Shangqing school is called Li Hongyuan. This name is close to Li Hong, the name of various false prophets who appeared at different times in the history of China. Some of them laid claim to the throne, as did the Li Hong who was executed in 324 for proclaiming he was destined to be king. Others, like one at the end of the fourth century who headed a rebel group, took the title "holy king of the Tao." At the beginning of the fifth century, Kou Qianzhi expressed vehement opposition to such messianic figures, a fact suggesting that the phenomenon was already widespread. According to the *Laojun bianhua wuji jing* (*Scripture of the Limitless Transformation of Lord Lao*, DZ 875), Li Hong was the name that Laozi intended to take after he had converted the western barbarians and returned to Sichuan. One of the Lingbao texts we have already discussed mentions a Li Hong who became a member of this school (DZ 322, 4b). Messiahs calling themselves Li Hong would continue to arise within Taoism at least until the Song.

An anonymous work, the *Book of Divine Incantations of the Abyssal Depths* (DZ 335), is dedicated to this theme. It comes from a sect that established liturgical communities to the south of the Yangzi River at the beginning of the fifth century. This group had its own clergy and rituals and was marked by extremely active proselytizing. With the exception of this last feature, highly unusual in Taoism, the overall message of the text is not especially distinctive. It is typical of this kind of literature and, with its many references to fundamental precepts of Taoism, can be seen as completely within this religious tradition. The text acts as a talisman and assures salvation. It announces an imminent end to the world, preceded by human and cosmic afflictions—epidemics, floods, wars, banditry, oppression by government power, famine, destitution, and the like—caused by armies of demons and the surrounding moral decay. Once again, the "seed people," those who possess this text, will be saved. The coming of a Li Hong who will save humankind completes the picture. Here, once again, the old fear of epidemics reappears, with renewed strength, and an emphasis on the prophylactic value of the text as well as an obsession with attacks from demons that must be fought off.

Practices and Conditions for Salvation

Whether used to escape from these cataclysms or to ensure personal salvation, the salvation of the dead, or that of all living creatures, the means were almost always the same: prayers, injunctions, the use of talismans, and the chanting of texts. These assumed more importance than they had in the Shangqing tradition, to the detriment of the few surviving techniques of visual meditation. The hierarchy of criteria to be met in order to be saved remained almost the same as that in the Shangqing tradition. The one Lingbao addition was that the seeker for salvation must be male—an influence from Buddhism. Otherwise the sequence remained the same: first, one practices the virtues, a criterion that is as much Confucian as Buddhist, and ancient methods (these two practices being assigned to the same level); then, one comes into legitimate possession of a text and chants it; finally, one implements the methods indicated by the text.

Doing good consists in the usual mixture of trends inherited from the Celestial Masters and Shangqing. Orders to respect nature go hand in hand with admonitions against unauthorized transmission of a text. To these were added more precise warnings against lack of respect for the master, completely in line with Lingbao practice, as more importance was given to ritual and a comparable importance was accorded the officiating priest.

The chanting of texts, also ritualistic in nature, was even more important than it was in the Shangqing tradition. Because the names of the heavens were "celestial sounds," their recitation acquired supernatural qualities. In line with a practice that had already begun to appear in the Shangqing tradition, these names were given a pseudo-Sanskrit form. They are the "secret words of the Great Brahman" and have an efficacy comparable to that of mantras. The essential purpose of the *Durenjing* is to reveal the names of the heavens and their inhabitants. Originally, before time began, it was recited by the Yuanshi tianzun (the Celestial Venerable One of the Original Beginning) and men, as they chant it, are re-enacting this first recitation that accompanied the formation of the world and took place inside a mystic pearl suspended in the void, the initial point of the cosmos, where all the gods were gathered together. Each of the repeated recitations of this text by the supreme god, one in each direction in space, was the source of life and renewal. The blind regained their sight, the deaf their hearing, the aged their youth, women their fertility, the dead their life. The recitation of the texts "flattened" the earth ("flat" earth is the equivalent of the Great Peace or Great Equality; *ping* means "spread, flat surface, plain," as well as "peace"). It also warded off cosmic disasters, wars, epidemics, imbalances in Yin and Yang or the course of the seasons, and the darkening of stars. The greater the number of recitations, the greater their power—which might even extend to communication with the gods and flights to heaven. We see once more the contribution of the Lingbao movement to this form of recitation, whose roots run deep in China: in certain texts, it also takes on a Buddhist coloring that certainly does not detract from it. Sometimes the Yuan-shi tianzun, moved to compassion by the suffering of human-kind, spreads his teaching by means of a light emerging from his mouth and flooding the world.

It is in Lingbao texts that we find the origins of the "casting dragons" ritual. This famous ritual was carried out on imperial orders from the seventh to the fourteenth centuries. It consisted of throwing prayers inscribed on metal or stone plaques into caverns, ravines, or springs. To the plaques were attached gold dragons that were to carry the prayers to the abode of the Three Originals. The dragon casting was done after a liturgical ceremony, usually carried out in a mountainous setting. This rite has its roots in expiation rites carried out by the kings of mythical antiquity.[1] This interpretation is supported by the fact that many details of the practice are explained in just this way in surviving texts. In addition to the golden dragons, the plaques were also accompanied by a jade ring and gold beads that took the place of the blood with which the lips were rubbed when oaths of allegiance were sworn. The silken threads tying the dragons, pieces of jade, and gold beads to the plaques symbolized hair cut off as an offering to the deity present as a witness to the oath. The rite was thus a symbolic transposition of the rites of personal sacrifice made by the rulers to ensure the well-being of the kingdom and their people, a fact that accounts for imperial involvement in these rites.

According to a text dating a few decades later than those of the "ancient Lingbao" (DZ 361, especially 1.1b), these plaques were supposedly sent to the 180 seas located in the 32 heavens and in the 32 watery abysses beneath the mountains, where the dragon kings frolicked. These dragon kings (the Buddhist *naga*s) were the greatest of the eight majestic and terrible animals (*bawei*) of the stars and the eight "gates" of the world (standing for the eight directions on the wind rose). They are poisonous to the evil beasts conquered by the Yuanshi tianzun and ward off all evils, especially wild beasts. The dragon kings also judge which beings can be saved and save the faithful at the end of the world.

Ritual

Structure

The Lingbao liturgy is a ritual of salvation and renewal. Along with the ecclesiastical organization derived from the Celestial Masters, it became one of the established aspects of Taoism. The importance that ritual acquired in Taoism goes hand in hand with the religion's evolution toward community organization and domination by priests, who form an institutionally established body. At first rites were carried out in isolation, as in the Shang-qing tradition, but gradually group services became the norm. During the fifth and sixth centuries such rites were sometimes carried out by small groups; very soon thereafter they brought together an extended family or a village, and then became official ceremonies on an imperial scale. Today Taoist ritual is maintained in rural settings and among the people, whose cults it has absorbed, and it is associated with local feasts, thus cementing regional structures.[2]

Current liturgy is largely based on the Lingbao revelation, which in turn incorporates elements from the Celestial Masters ritual. Codified by Lu Xiujing, it was reformulated in the eighth century by Zhang Wanfu, and again by Du Guangting (850–933), who became an authority on it. Variations arose at later dates, under the guise of new revelations, but the general structure of the liturgy remains that of the Lingbao school. A large number of variants were incorporated into the great collections of rituals, of which the most significant date from the twelfth and thirteenth centuries.

These rituals bring into play and illustrate most of the elements that we have already encountered. All the symbolic procedures that the adept had experienced internally during meditation were now presented on stage, in spectacular fashion— sometimes, especially nowadays, with an almost theatrical, dramatic quality. In fact, one of the sources of Chinese theater is Taoist ritual. The connection between this liturgy and the basic elements of earlier forms of meditation is so fundamental that the origin and deep meaning of the ritual cannot be understood unless we also understand the underlying principles, themes, and development of the various kinds of Taoist meditation that the ritual, for its part, illustrates and puts into practice. However, certain liturgical features were sometimes enriched and further developed, as with the cosmological and calendrical theories derived from Han thought that run throughout Taoism.

Several general distinguishing features of Lingbao liturgy can be discerned, but it should be remembered that some of them belong to the whole body of Taoist tradition. First, there is the theatrical, staged quality of ritual, which is accompanied by music, banners, chants, dances, and sometimes pantomime. Another feature is redundancy; each part of the ritual forms a whole encapsulating other rites, one within the other. The rites also have a multidimensional quality and are carried out on many levels at the same time. Both the pantheon involved and the prayers and confessions offered by the priest in the name of the congregation are generally impersonal in form, even if these ceremonies sometimes take on a local and popular nature. The ritual always involves three levels—Heaven and the stars, Earth and its mountains, and Man and his internal organs—all of which derive from the heavenly, divine domain toward which they converge and which in turn unifies them. These three levels manifest themselves in two ways. First, the exterior ceremony made up of physical actions is repeated in the interior meditation of the priest. Second, the actions have a symbolic value: when the priest, for example, sprinkles his sword with water, it is understood that we are to see here the water of the heavenly One and the demon-quelling sword of Zhang Daoling. The water is that which springs from the sacred central mountain, that is, from the Heart of the True Man, who is the transfigured officiant.

Many kinds and varieties of rituals have existed over time and still exist today. According to a rough traditional schema, they fall into three categories. The heavenly Golden Register of rituals is carried out to avoid natural disasters; it was originally dedicated to the rulers, and under the Tang was mainly celebrated in honor of the imperial family. The earthly Yellow Register is intended to ensure the repose of the dead, but under the Song it could also be carried out on behalf of the living. The human Jade Register was originally dedicated to princes and ensures the salvation of mankind. Today only the Yellow Register, called "dark," and the Golden Register, termed "pure," have survived. The Golden Register is supposed to ensure the salvation of all humankind. The structure of the two registers is essentially identical, but they differ in specific instruments used, as well as in some variations that have entered the ritual of the Yellow Register.

We need not dwell in detail on the progressive changes in the ritual, its evolution, and its various forms. Here I shall simply provide an overall sketch, on the basis of an examination of *Daozang* texts along with various studies on this subject.

Stages in the Ritual

In its essential form, which has not changed since the Six Dynasties, each ritual may be divided into three parts. The "vesper announcement," which takes place in the evening, re-creates the sacred world on the site of the ritual. The completion of the sacrifice itself, which takes place the following morning, is divided into two parts: the "fast" (*zhai*) and the "offering" (*jiao*). The fast consists of a pacing out of the miniature world represented by the sacred area, an action said to have been inspired by the Buddhist rite of perambulation. We cannot but be reminded, however, of its intimate connection with all the traditional Chinese "wanderings"—cosmo-theological, imperial, and ecstatic. The second is a test of competence in which the priest presents the powers of his "register" in order to verify its effectiveness, testify to it, and thus increase it. He re-establishes the bond between humankind and the gods and punctuates the procedure with an offering of food, derived ultimately from the ancient "kitchens." The ritual is crowned by the "proclamation of merits," that is, the proclamation of the result of the sacrifice, and the "sanction" that takes place the next day, ending with the ceremony in which one "dismisses" the gods, breaks up the altar, and burns the texts.

Preparation and "vesper announcement." The main parties to the ritual are, on the one hand, the gods and, on the other, all of humankind. Acting as intermediaries between them are the actual participants and instruments—physical, mental, and human—in the ritual. The ritual is played out before the entire celestial court. The assembled gods make up, with variants, a mixed pantheon in which gods from the ancient rites of the Celestial Masters find themselves alongside certain Shangqing deities (star gods in particular), in addition to local gods or legendary heroes and finally the Lingbao gods. There is a discernible hierarchy within the group, with two main levels. The higher level consists of major gods or authorities, some of which derive from our world and others from the world beyond; most of them take the abstract form of cosmic principles or forces: the Yuanshi tianzun, the Three Pure Ones, the Three August Ones, the Five Emperors, the Three Officials (*sanguan*), Laojun, the stars, thunder, and so on. The second level is made up of messenger deities, most of Celestial Masters origin, either "civil" ones, like the gods of the body (of the master) or those of the four directions, or else "warriors," like the "demon kings" or all sorts of armed and terrifying beings. In dealing with this second group, the master's technique derives from the fact that "by means of the True Breath of the Celestial Tao, he commands the 'correct' [i.e., orthodox, in the sense of being tamed and not wild] breaths of the three Cinnabar Fields and the five viscera, gives them the function of sacred deities," and knows how to make them "emerge" from his body in order to transform (*hua*) them into messengers that can ensure communication with Heaven. Between these two types of deities there is a fundamental distinction, and we can see the master as both the point of contact between them and their actual physical location. Before the first group he presents himself as a humble vassal, vastly below them in status; for the second group, he is the master, a general leading his troops. The whole group functions as a kind of celestial chancellery. This bureaucratic tendency supersedes the note of compassion contributed by Buddhism and the luminous radiance that dominated the Shangqing school. Still, these traits do not disappear completely.

The ritual is carried out on behalf of humankind: formerly it was performed for the emperor, but now it is most often done for members of a community, family, village, or guild. They are entitled, as believers, to ask for this ceremony, as long as they respect the prohibitions and commandments of their faith. This criterion explains the solemn proclamation of commandments and proscriptions made in the course of the ceremony, as well as the frequent repetition of the rites of purification and remission of sins during the ceremony.

The participants in the ritual are of two kinds: the material and "scenic" ones, and the human actors. First, the place consists of a sacred area and altar, not usually inside a temple but in the open air, often originally on a mountainside. Such settings are prepared specifically for the occasion. The sacred area is one of those "miniature worlds" in which Taoism operates, organized and oriented in line with traditional reference points, which determine, by giving them a precise location, the directions toward which the priest directs himself and turns in the course of the ritual. The whole ritual derives its meaning from the structure of this sacred area, a setting that provides the basis for everything else, with its four corners, its heaven and hell, all marked by placards, hangings, or inscriptions, like a theater set, or else by bushels of rice that recall the ancient customs of the Celestial Masters. One striking fact that has not, as far as I know, been noted up to now, is that the schematic structure of this world is exactly the same as that found in the divination tablets of the Han: its "four gates" are connected, as we shall see, with Man (or the moon), with the demons (or the sun), with Heaven, and with the Earth; the layout of the trigrams, constellations, and various numerical systems, along with their variants, is connected with the four directions, and so on. This ritual can thus be seen as drawing directly from the calendrical computations and speculations of the Han.

Several plans for the layout of the sacred area have survived and can be consulted. The one called the *Sanhuang zhai*, the *zhai* of the Three August Ones, for example, is constructed on the pattern of the Mingtang, the Hall of Light, the microcosm that served as a framework for the ritual government of the rulers of antiquity. This ritual area consists of a square divided into nine compartments, with four "doors" at the four corners; three tables set up with offerings for Heaven, Earth, and Man, and another table in the middle of the altar with an incense burner (Lagerwey, *Wushang piyao*, p. 152). Another ritual area is built in three "stories," three concentric squares outlined on the ground and corresponding, as one goes from the outermost to the innermost, to the three domains of the Bureaucrats: that of Water (the hells) surrounded by trigrams; that of the Earth, bounded by four doors; and that of Heaven, with ten directions of which two are in the middle and make up a double center that joins up and down (Lagerwey, pp. 163-64). Today this triple area is bounded at its outermost limit by 24 lamps that represent the 24 breaths of the year and the 24 stars of the Chinese zodiac that correspond to them. The inner area is defined by four gates and eight trigrams. The four gates are those of Heaven in the northwest, Earth in the southeast, the moon or humankind in the southwest, and the sun or demons in the northeast. This arrangement is matched by an arrangement of trigrams, in a pattern attributed to King Wen. Each cardinal point is associated with a number, according to the system called *nayin*, used by the Shangqing sect, designed in such a way that adding the numbers for north and west, and those for south and east gives, in both cases, the number twelve (with a grand total of 24 for the 24 breaths and stars); in addition, a division between the Yang numbers and Yin numbers is made along a northeast-southwest axis, which is that of the cosmic system "prior to Heaven," that is, before the formation of the world. On the altars are laid out talismans of the Five Directions, along with "tokens of faith" and offerings—varying according to the occasion and the time period, these could be wine, dried meat, incense, or gruel—making up the "banquet" (the "kitchen") offered to the gods. The main altar is likened to a "grotto," as well as to a mountain; it is called the "nine provinces," from the term that designated the entire known universe. Yet it is also located "beyond the three worlds," that is, in the highest heaven.

The visible altar is reproduced in an "internal" altar con-

structed by the priest in his meditations; he calls on the four heraldic animals to emerge from his body, as in the meditation exercises, and occupy the four sides of the sacred area to ward off
evil influences. The priest also calls on other exorcistic powers,
like that of the Dipper (with which he covers himself), the sword
that fends off demons, and purifying water. Thus the miniature
world is closed off, purified, and made sacred, "sealed" and
"forbidden," according to the vocabulary used. Finally, the very
body of the master himself is also a three-level altar, bounded by
the traditional reference points of Taoism.

The two kinds of musical instruments used, strings and per-
cussion, are matched by the bodily "instruments" of the master:
as he grinds his teeth, he is playing on a bell or sounding stone,
the bell being Yang and heavenly, and the stone Yin and earthly.
The incense burner is an instrument of purification; it seems to
have been introduced by the Shangqing school and revives once
again the ancient Chinese tradition of sacrificial vapors that had
become an important means of purification under the Han.[3]

The number of participants has changed over the centuries.
They have various functions: chanting texts, leading the ceremony, burning incense, and so forth. The principal chanter is the
most important of the acolytes. He pronounces the formulas of
invocation and consecration and recites the confessional texts.
But he is only the active counterpart of the master, who plays the
main role, mostly in silence; it is he who has the power to communicate with the gods. He proclaims solemnly that this power
comes to him from his "register," that is, from the document that
testifies to his enthronement as master and consists of the list of
spirits that he will use as messengers to Heaven, his intermediaries. In fact, his power to sanctify the altar and carry out the
ceremony by bringing the gods to this place comes from his powers of concentration, which derive from his own vital forces—
those of his five viscera or his four limbs, which match the heraldic animals mentioned above—added to those powers given to
him by his register. All this is the fruition of the transmission of
books and talismans he has received, his training, and finally the
personal meditation he has undertaken.

The stated object of the ceremony is the presentation of a petition to Heaven on behalf of the community. This petition is composed according to prescribed forms, following rules inherited from the Celestial Masters. But, as we shall see, what actually takes place is a reshaping of the world; the "return" of the officiant from Heaven to Earth is the token of this. The ritual purifies the community by expelling the "old," that is, the evil spirits, and welcoming the "new."

Here again written texts play a role. All the ritual is written down, and the sacred texts must be present on the altar. In the same way, talismans must be written out, following ritual rules. But sound also plays an important role: the petition is read aloud. This gives rise to the often-stressed insistence on correct expression: pronunciation, rhythm, and intonation. The petition announces the purpose of the ceremony: the consecration of a temple, a request for rain, a cure for sickness, the capture of a bandit, or the expulsion of a demon possessing one of the faithful. The petition can also constitute a thanksgiving for a birth (sometimes of an heir to the throne) or for the granting of a request. The priest also presents the desires of the community in a very general, standardized form, comparable to the prayers in the ancient Lingbao texts summarized above. To this petition is added the recitation of sacred texts, like the *Durenjing*, itself an incantation ensuring the protective presence of the gods. But the real aim underlying the stated object of the ceremony is in fact the renewing of the bond between men and gods, more specifically and concretely the bond between the officiating master and the deities in his register, because without this bond, which must constantly be reconfirmed, no petition can reach the celestial Golden Door.

Carrying out the ritual. The second act of the ceremony is its heart, toward which the two that frame it converge. It is called the "site of the Tao," that is, the universe made sacred by the Tao. It is the completion of the mystery, the ascent of the messengers and the priest himself to the sky, where they "seek audience" with and render homage to the Tao as they present petitions.

This ceremony has changed considerably over the centuries through repeated performances.

It takes place on several levels that are, in reality, only one: a microcosm consisting of the sacred area; the macrocosm represented by the trigrams; and the sky, especially the stars of the Dipper. What the participants in the ceremony see is the movements of the priest. He moves to and fro, advancing, twisting, and turning as he dances the Step of Yu; he brandishes the sword that fends off demons; and he moves his fingers to follow the pattern of his feet and imitate their pacing on the Dipper. He is surrounded by acolytes who burn incense, chant the text, and play musical instruments.

The priest paces out the world thus reproduced on its various levels to bring order to it, by distributing unity throughout. Following the example of the emperors in their Mingtang (Halls of Light), he measures out its width, length, depth, and height, just as Yu did throughout the whole empire, or as the Taiyi god of the *fangshi* did in the Nine Palaces or in Heaven on the stars of the Dipper. This journey fulfills a double function: the priest brings calm to the world, and he sanctifies it by commanding (as in Shangqing meditations) the presence of the various deities, coming from all directions, that preside over it. From within himself he produces divine powers, beginning with those of the lowest rank, those of the Celestial Masters, and then he brings them back down onto the altar, beginning this time with the higher powers, those of the Shangqing.

Several methods are used to symbolize externally the ascent to the heavens. They vary according to the construction of the altar. Thus, the master may enter either through the gate to the northeast, the gate of the demons and gateway to the capital of hell, or through that of the Earth, to the southeast. If he begins from the gate of hell, the realm of demons (*gui*) and the place to which everything returns (*gui*) and collects preparatory to leaving again,[4] the place where men are held in dark prisons, he makes his way toward the gate of the Earth, located at the "gate of men," and then toward that of Heaven. There, like the emperor, he turns to the south, the direction of the sky. Another method is to use the Step of Yu, "to pace out the Dipper," the heavenly ladder, or to step on trigrams, by moving toward the one that symbolizes Heaven (the trigram *qian*, the first one).

But, just as "deliverance from the corpse" (*shijie*) can be achieved within the Supreme Yin (Taiyin), the priest can, by beginning from Heaven and ending up on Earth, the Supreme Yin, set in motion a labyrinthine process patterned after an ancient technique of metamorphosis (*dunjia*) intended to result in invisibility. This technique dates from the Han and is closely connected with "pacing out the Dipper." It was recommended by Ge Hong as a way of "entering the mountain." Here we no longer see the intervention of the Six *jia* deities, mentioned above, but rather their Yin partners, the Six *ding* (the spirits of the six *ding* days that are related to the Yin just as the *jia* days are to the Yang). They emulate the Yin deities who surround the Dipper and preside over transformations and rebirth, as we saw above. For the Yin, as *wu* (non-being), can transform and change. Representing duality, it is itself double: it can "be *wu* and *you* [being], emerge into life and return into death; it can embrace both the invisible and the manifest," says one text (DZ 852, 2.2b); unfixed, it is the agent of transition; "it is without form," adds this text, which considers it inexhaustible, unlike the Yang, whose capacity is measurable. "I enter into the region of darkness," the priest then sings, "and I see forever."[5]

These external procedures accompany other, internal ones, such as the one that consists of visualizing the emergence of a fetus from the kidneys (considered as the north of the body, the hells). It climbs toward the brain, along the spinal column, the celestial bridge, and grows until it becomes the True Man, dressed in red, the color of the south and of cinnabar. Thus, one section of the ritual is carried out while the priest meditates silently, an influence of the Shangqing school. The new element contributed by the Lingbao school lies in the fact that this internal, visual meditation, here carried on in a communal setting, is no longer used to ensure the well-being of only the master and his family but that of the entire world.

This internal ascent is also a transformation. The Master

changes into the True Man, that is, into the Cosmic Man, into Laojun. As he ascends, he "repairs his brain," an ancient expression that designates the ascent of the essence toward the head. He lifts the Yang that had been in the Yin (the north, the hells), in the kidneys, and raises it up into the brain, the south. As he does this, he moves from one of the two arrangements of the trigrams, that of the system of the "latter heavens," which is the one of the world made manifest, the world of movement, to the other arrangement, that of the system "prior to Heaven," which represents both the world in its virtual state, the Origin, and the world in its achieved state, the end. He mutates and even disappears. The obvious aim is to present the petition to the gods and thus to renew the bond between men and gods by the intercession of the Master, marked by the offerings laid on the altar, a celestial banquet made up of dried foods and wine.

The ratification. The ceremony closes with the third act, the "proclamation of merits" (*gongde*), which takes place on the following day. The master then turns his back on the Gate of Heaven and faces the faithful. He has returned from Heaven to the abode of men.

This part of the ritual, although given a Buddhist name, corresponds to an ancient form of mental representation going back to the old earth god and later adopted by Taoism. The term "merit" is semantically and historically the equivalent of the word *fu*, "happiness" in the meaning of "celestial blessing," of the kind sought and obtained at the ancient "kitchens" in their function as rites of pardon liberating the faithful from their sins.[6]

The petition has been delivered. The master has returned from the celestial spheres. He has reintegrated within himself the deities he used as messengers. They return to him more powerful than before, as a result of having ascended to heaven and of having used once more their power of intercession to reconfirm the bond. The body of the master is glorified and made godlike by this process. The master asks these divine, or rather deified, forces that he has been able to unleash to "hold tight onto his body and surround his bones, to direct and combine his veins, to move throughout his body and his substance, to adjust him totally to Heaven and Earth, to enter below into the cinnabar field and to ascend into his *niwan* [the upper cinnabar field]." The True Man, whom he has made ascend inside himself to his sinciput, has redescended. But just as this latter, who emerged as a fetus, now returns as an Old Man after having for a time taken the form of the True Man, the master himself also returns proclaiming aloud the renewal of his "merits," that is, his power. He has brought together the states of virtual-origin and completion. By exteriorizing his deified vital forces, he has made them pass from the virtual state, "prior to Heaven," to the state of external manifestation, "after Heaven," in order finally to reintegrate them, in the perfected state achieved through their exteriorization. By transmitting the messages of the faithful to the God of the Origin, the Yuanshi tianzun, he has also reconnected the external world to its Origin and so revitalized it. The blind can see, the dead come back to life, the entire world is saved. As a result of all this, he has advanced one step up the ladder of merits and in the spiritual hierarchy. In an immense purifying holocaust, all the writings, sacred texts, talismans, and placards used in the ceremony are then burned so that they will disappear from the ordinary world.

Evolution of the ritual. During the Song many new rites appeared in revelations usually presented as superior to earlier ones. Each new revelation, however, had to be shown to derive from an ancient and respectable tradition and used this claim to authority in order to win an audience. Ritualists established these relationships by drawing up a mythical genealogy and borrowing from ancient traditions. These extremely varied connections might take the form of talismans. Thus we have the "fire bell" (*huoling*), the "five talismans" (*wufu*), the "eastern well" (*dongjing,* a station of the sun and moon), and special names given to the sun and moon (Yuyi and Jielin), among others.

Whether the revelations were found in caverns, like the ancient *Sanhuang wen,* or were dictated, as were the Shangqing texts, they generally claimed to date back to an ancient origin and relied on the authority of Zhang Daoling or the Shangqing school. These revelations were often associated with battles for influence on the political scene, and as a result their success depended on shifts in imperial favor, which gave supremacy to one group or another at various times.

Great collections of rituals began to be compiled during the reign of the Song emperor Huizong (1100–1125), who was so interested in Taoism and its rituals that he even composed hymns. These "encyclopedias" were revised and expanded in later centuries, especially when the empire was racked by social or political troubles. This may be explained by the largely exorcistic nature of the rituals: the Taoist ceremonies were a means of pacifying spirits and could readily be used to end a drought or an epidemic or to rid a region of bandits. The local magistrate took part in the ceremonies and sometimes even led them. Emperors ordered their celebration on various occasions—for example, in 875, on the occasion of a drought and during an epidemic. Taoist liturgy and state ritual were at times closely connected, as is attested in the person of Du Guangting, the dominant figure in Taoism during the ninth century and director of liturgical functions in the ancestral temple of the Tang emperors. Thus, Taoist rituals came to have more than a strictly religious purpose and, just as is the case with Buddhism, became a means of restoring order and health, a form of social as well as individual therapy. Accounts of the circumstances surrounding the various revelations show that a good proportion of the recipients of revelations had been cured of a serious illness by the revelation.

The major characteristic of the subsequent evolution of ritual is the incorporation of local cults. Such cults had expanded and multiplied during the division of the empire in the ninth century and had endured. Deities multiplied. Some had historical or legendary origins, emerging from popular cults dedicated to dead people other than ancestors—a practice completely opposed by Taoism in its original forms. A cult might grow up around a man who died on the battlefield, for example, and then became a dangerous and vindictive demon when revived by a cult whose members worshiped him without being able to subjugate him. Such a figure could, however, be dominated and used by the Taoist master.

In most of the new rites, increased importance was given to charms and talismans, sometimes considered central to the ritual and so multiplying freely. Particularly noticeable are rites involving the stars (generally the sun, the moon, and the Dipper) and the hells (which we should remember are connected to the Dipper), along with the cult of the Northern Emperor (Zhenwu, the "dark warrior") and the god Tianpeng, a star of the Dipper. The cult of the popular "dark warrior" flourished under the Song and grew even more widespread under the Ming, whose founder considered this spirit his protector. An exorcist with sparse hair, bare feet, and a sword in his hand, he is accompanied by the Black Exterminator and is associated with the god Tianpeng. The principal source for Tianpeng, as well as for the Three Luminaries, was the Shangqing school, which had a certain influence on these innovations.

Compared with these two major strains, developments based on the Five Agents are limited. The unavoidable conclusion is that they had moved into the background, although they were always present insofar as the Lingbao ritual continued to provide the basis for all new rituals. This shift in emphasis can be illustrated by the fact that purification—as one of the authors of the period notes—is more often achieved through the absorption of effluvia from the sun and moon than through the Water and Fire issuing from Metal and Wood—that is, more through the stars than through the Five Agents.

Tantric Buddhism also had an influence on the development of ritual, as evidenced by the use of "seals," that is, of "mudrâs," patterns of moving the fingers. One can, for example, pace out the Dipper, with the fingers. Sincerity in carrying out the ritual and in writing out spells is emphasized as well. Only sincerity can bring the desired effect, and it is expressly compared to the way of knowing practiced by the Confucianists, the *gewu* (DZ 224, 1.3b; see also 223, 25.5b, and 222, 1.2a), or "investigation of things," which can "bring the ancestors" (according to the etymology provided by the neo-Confucianist Cheng Yi) and leads to knowledge of the principle of things.

Many traces of the influence of interior alchemy can also be found, especially in the Qingwei rituals (see, e.g., DZ 222, 1.2a–b; 223, 25.3b–5a). Interior alchemy and ritual are closely connected. Bo Yuchan, for example, one of the greatest masters of interior alchemy, was also a renowned ritualist specializing in thunder rituals, and his successors followed him in this path.

Many schools grew up, sometimes differing very little. A single master could equally well practice the rites of various schools, combining techniques from several of them as he thought most effective.

One of the first of the great new revelations was that received by Li Lingsu (1076–1120), who enjoyed extraordinary favor from Huizong after 1116. He placed the *Durenjing* at the head of the Taoist Canon, adding 95 chapters to it, and instituted the rite called Shenxiao, the Divine Empyrean, from the name of a heavenly region that, according to him, lay above all those known up to that time. He presented this rite as the crowning of the Shangqing revelation. Huizong, considered the older brother of the Jade Emperor come down to earth to save humankind, received the title Great Emperor of Long Life. Deified in this way, not only was he placed at the head of this newly revealed order, thus becoming the object of a cult, but he also became responsible for the salvation of his subjects.

The style of this movement was essentially liturgical. A complete cycle of recitations ensures the salvation of humankind, equivalent to a Return to the Origin. It breaks the circle of life and death and permits rebirth in the Taiping heaven. An important place is reserved for the cosmic and apotropaic power of thunder and lightning, which the master must interiorize in order to make use of its power, along with the spell of the "fire bell" (*huoling*), which derives from the Shangqing school and plays a prominent role in exorcisms.

In 1119 Li Lingsu was expelled from the court, and he died

mysteriously the following year. His work was continued, however, by his disciple Wang Wenqing (1093–1153). When barbarians occupied north China and forced the court to flee to the
south, the Shenxiao movement, which had enjoyed a great success, was accused of responsibility for the defeat. (This was only
just, since the Taoist ritual claimed to guarantee the peace of the
empire!) After that time the movement fell from favor at the
court, but it continued to be followed in the coastal regions of
the south. It was adopted by the Celestial Masters and survived in
the form of the Shenxiao ritual of the Five Thunders. Later developments in ritual borrowed a great deal from it.

The Tianxin (Heart of the sky) rite appeared at the same time
and was also favored by Huizong. Its revelation is claimed to date
to the ninth century, but it was really formulated only in texts
from the twelfth and thirteenth centuries. Tianxin, identified as
the Dipper, is a term borrowed from the *dunjia* practice mentioned above, a practice that permitted "escape" and invisibility. It
is seen as connected with the North, with the cyclical sign *zi*, the
beginning of all life (see, e.g., DZ 1005, 2.2a), and with the *Book of
Change* hexagram Return (that is, the return of the Yang after the
Great Yin has taken place). Although thunder plays a role in the
rite, it is based primarily on the use of three main talismans that
are considered to derive from Zhang Daoling: that of the Three
Luminaries (sun, moon, and stars), that of the Dipper, and that of
the Northern Emperor, the Dark Warrior. It gives prime place to
the presentation of petitions by means of pacing out the Dipper,
which accompanies interior transformation and cures sickness.
The effectiveness of the talismans is due to the breathing techniques and meditations that let the priest, when he is writing
them, incorporate the cosmic powers that he has to bring into
play in his ministry. This ritual's aim is to help the state and save
people, down to the most humble villagers. It was especially
marked by an exorcistic and therapeutic tendency and specialized in curing cases of possession. For this reason, it spread
widely, especially beginning in the second half of the twelfth century, and many novels, like the *Shuihu zhuan* (*The Water Margin*),

were inspired by it. The rite spread particularly into southern China, and traces of it can still be found among the Yao of Thailand.

The ritual of the Jade Hall, Yutang, revealed in 1120 by Lu Shizhong, a famous exorcist, is close to that of Tianxin, and its practitioners claim it is the esoteric form of Tianxin. They also claim that it goes back to Zhang Daoling. Its pantheon and its spells are much like those of Tianxin. Features borrowed from Shangqing, especially long segments of text, are much more common in this ritual, even though they are mingled with exorcism techniques and elements of the salvation ritual of Lingbao. Terms designating the sun and the moon (Yuyi and Jielin) in Shangqing texts are here attached to the True Water and True Fire of the interior alchemy tradition.

Shangqing is also the source of the Tongchu (Birth of youth) rites, named after a Shangqing heaven reserved for men. Revealed to Yang Xizhen in 1121, they take from this tradition the famous invocation to Tianpeng, the ninth star of the Dipper and the first among the Four Holy Ones, of whom the fourth is the Dark Warrior mentioned above.

There are a great many thunder rites, in which the priest must incorporate the power of the thunder, fruit of the union between Yin and Yang (DZ 263, 97.10b), a manifestation of the dynamism of the Tao in its majestic and terrifying aspect (DZ 263, 45.14a), the secret moving force of the world. These rites underwent intensive development after the Ming and represent a more popular form of these rituals. In some ways, these thunder rites are a resurgence of the ancient cult of the powerful thunder god whom certain groups confused with the cosmic egg, the Original Chaos. They show up first among the Qingwei (Pure tenuity) rituals, which are supposed to have been established by a woman, Zu Shu (ca. 889–904), and are known from a text of the thirteenth century. One of the founders of this movement was Mo Qiyan (1226–94). Their practitioners bring together the traditions of the Celestial Masters (including the *Daodejing*), Lingbao, and Shangqing, and they incorporate into their pantheon the most powerful authorities and individuals from the preceding traditions. From

Guangxi, the land of their founding mother, these rituals spread as far as Mount Wudang in Hubei, and were adopted by the Celestial Masters.

However, as could be expected, the proliferation of more and more complex rituals also gave rise to a reaction toward greater simplicity. This was the case with Jin Yunzhong (fl. 1224–25), the author of the vast *Shangqing lingbao dafa* (DZ 1213). Reacting to what he considered distortions, especially those in the rituals adopted at Mount Tiantai, he proclaimed that the only valid rites were those inspired by interior alchemy. He also reduced considerably the number of spells used. In the same vein, Zheng Sixiao (1241–1318), adopting the tendency of interior alchemy that leaned toward a synthesis of the "three teachings" (Taoism, Buddhism, and Confucianism), wrote a ritual in which he preached and defended the primacy of meditation and of silent recitation carried on "in the heart," in a state of deep concentration. His work, which is actually on the borderline between a ritual and a treatise, is a good example of the incorporation of the techniques and vocabulary of interior alchemy into the part of the liturgy devoted to meditation.

7

The Tang Period

The Status of Taoism

The Tang dynasty (618–907) witnessed a movement toward the consolidation of Taoism and a true integration of Buddhist contributions. Imperial favor certainly helped this development. Taoism went through a great period of expansion, largely because the family name of the rulers was Li, the surname the *Shiji* gives for Laozi. They claimed Laozi as an ancestor and showed Taoism unprecedented favor.

Despite the religion's tendency to oppose imperial bureaucracy and power and the dominance of Confucian morality, it held a trump card that often won it the patronage of emperors. As we have seen, Taoism was a precious repository of Chinese culture. In addition, its rites and ideology were rooted in the idea of the Saintly Sage, a figure close to that of the wise sovereign and often identified with him. Both of these factors made Taoism an impetus toward ideological unity; it could provide a new dynasty a ritual validation whose roots drew on the imperial cult of the Han. Taoism's stated purpose was the establishment of a Great Peace throughout the empire. (In this it was like Confucianism, for which the promise of stability formed the very raison d'être.) Taoism thus had everything needed to strengthen the establishment of the new rulers, endowing them with an authority going back centuries.

It is true that revolts were often instigated under the inspiration of Taoist precepts or under the leadership of Taoist adepts, but they were always started in the name of Great Peace. They were launched to restore an order that had been compromised by a failing dynasty or emperor from whom the mandate of Heaven had been withdrawn. The position adopted by the leaders of such revolts was thus often comparable to that of a newly established dynasty.

The founding of the Tang dynasty is a clear example of this process. The Shangqing patriarch Wang Yuanzhi (d. 635) secretly assured the founder of the dynasty, Tang Gaozu (r. 618–26), that he had received the mandate of Heaven and provided him with religious confirmation of the establishment of the new dynasty even before he came to power. It is probably not just coincidence that many appearances of Laozi, especially on Mount Yangjiao, in southern Shanxi, were reported during this period.

Gaozong (r. 649–83) demonstrated his favor toward Taoism in a striking fashion. He gave Laozi a new title that proclaimed him an incarnation of the Primordial Chaos, he had Taoist temples built in every province, he included the *Daodejing* among the texts on which official examinations were based, he ordered (in 675) copies of all existing Taoist texts, he gave Taoist priests a rank just below that of prince (*wang*), he officially protected Pan Shizheng (585–682), Wang Yuanzhi's successor as head of the Shangqing school, and he asked Pan to explain certain doctrinal matters in terms that reveal both his knowledge of and his interest in the material. He made into a center of official worship the abbey of Louguan, which had been built at the spot where, according to legend, Laozi had left for the west to convert the barbarians and where he gave the *Daodejing* as a testament to the "guardian of the pass," Yin Xi. Its abbot, Yi Wencao (d. 688), compiled on imperial orders the voluminous *Annals of the Sage*. This work is no longer extant, but it provided the model for other such works under the Song. The *An-*

nals gathered, under the aegis of the god Laozi, the whole history of Taoism to that time. Under the guise of multiple incarnations, his high authority unified all the successive revelations over the centuries.

Xuanzong (r. 712–55) was initiated into the Shangqing school by the patriarch Li Hanguang (683–769). This emperor, known for his delight in the wonders worked by the Taoists and Tantrists summoned to his court, seems to have had the idea of making Taoism the official religion and tried to give it a position at least equal to that enjoyed by Buddhism, which was both richer and better established than Taoism at that time. In 741 he gave Taoism the status of an official teaching by establishing Taoist schools and official examinations on Taoist texts, whose study could thenceforth open the door to official appointment. Furthermore, he ordered that each household possess a copy of the *Daodejing*, which would thenceforth replace the *Classic of History* and the "teachings" of Confucius. He placed the Taoist clergy under the jurisdiction of the office charged with matters concerning the imperial family, on the grounds that Laozi was one of his ancestors. In this way both Taoist and Confucian rites became bound up with the cult offered to the imperial ancestors. A temple to Laozi was constructed in both capital cities and in each prefecture, and the temple at the birthplace of the god was restored and enlarged.

These essentially political moves were also dictated by the emperors' clear personal interest in Taoism. This is attested by the prefaces and commentaries that Xuanzong wrote to Taoist texts, such as his commentaries on the *Daodejing*. He apparently wanted to use Taoism to unite the various religious rites under the aegis of a single god, Laozi, recognized by his family and by the state, a universal figure at the same time public and private. Taoism by this time had learned from Buddhism some of the techniques of proselytizing—recitation of sacred texts, the telling of wonderful, edifying tales—and had done this so well that Taoist temples and festivals had become places and occasions for large gatherings. By integrating these centers into the mechanism of the state, Xuanzong could count on their influence in spreading the cult of Laozi.

Prestigious Taoists began to rise to prominence in official circles and to play an important role at the court. In addition to those mentioned above, their ranks included Ye Fashang, Cheng Xuanying, Li Rong, and Du Guangting, among many others. Strengthened by the support of the Taoist liturgy, Du Guangting in particular played a political role, setting himself up as the defender first of the Tang house during its decline and then, following the demise of the Tang, of the Wang family, founders of the short-lived Former Shu dynasty. The first Taoist Canon was compiled in 748 and was followed by others, none of which survives today. Furthermore, in 690 the emperor ordered all Taoist texts to be copied and revised for distribution to the principal temples. Still, even at the time of its greatest development and imperial protection, Taoism remained far behind Buddhism in its influence; in Chang'an, the Tang capital, there were sixteen Taoist establishments in 722 as opposed to 91 Buddhist ones.

This period also witnessed closer relations with Buddhism and Confucianism and efforts to harmonize the Three Teachings. The emperors themselves were involved in this. Xuanzong, for example, wrote commentaries not only on the *Daodejing* but also on the Buddhist *Vajracchedikā* (the *Diamond Sutra*) and the Confucian *Classic of Filial Piety*. There existed a long tradition of mutual interest and exchanges between Confucianism and Taoism. Under the Han it was difficult to draw the line between the Taoistic *fangshi* and the "Confucian literati," and during the Six Dynasties, as we have seen, a significant number of the intelligentsia dedicated themselves either to the study of Laozi and Zhuangzi or to longevity practices, and a thinker like Ge Hong could divide his work into two parts, one on Confucianism and the other on Taoism. For its part, Taoism had from its beginnings adopted the Confucian virtues, both among the Celestial Masters (as early as the *Taipingjing*) and, even more clearly, with Kou Qianzhi and the Lingbao school. Under the Tang this tradition became stronger with the appearance of movements like that of the Path of Filial Piety (Xiaodao), which was placed under the patronage of a popular local saint named Xu Sun. He is supposed to have lived in the third century, and from this movement derives the school of Jingming zhongxiao (the school "of purity and light, of loyalty and filial piety"). It was only under the Song that neo-Confucianism, by cutting itself off from Taoism (from which it had borrowed so much), created a rift that came into being, as we shall see, solely as a result of this action. Earlier, Taoism had been part of the culture of a great many educated people, and many Taoists had been trained from their youth in the Confucian classics and, as early as the Tang, supported actively the unity of the Three Teachings. (This is much earlier than is usually claimed by historians.)

Relations with Buddhism were more ambiguous and sometimes even stormy. Buddhism had made its way into China between the second and fourth centuries under the cover of Taoism. The Taoists at first thought they were dealing with a new pattern of thought that had risen in their own ranks. They were struck by certain fundamental resemblances, backed up by formal similarities: Did not the Buddhists, like them, use healing talismans and magical procedures, as well as meditation techniques somewhat like their own? The first Buddhists in China benefited from this misunderstanding. Many of them were also familiar with the Taoist classics and read their own texts in the light of Taoist ideas right up to the time when they started stressing their separateness in order to affirm their own, autonomous identity. The Buddhist religion was much more inclined to proselytizing, and it spread and became more widely established than did Taoism, which always had fewer temples, monasteries, and treasures even during its most prosperous periods.

The famous dispute of the *Huahujing* (*Book of the Conversion of the Barbarians* [by Laozi]) erupted, first in the fourth and sixth centuries and then again under the Tang in the seventh century. This book was written by Wangfu at the beginning of the fourth century but reflected a legend well known a century earlier. It claimed that the Buddha was only one incarnation of Laozi, who had gone off to evangelize the Indian barbarians, and thus Buddhism was only a coarser form of Taoism. It would take too long to examine the resulting hostilities, often acerbated by alternations of imperial favor and disfavor.[1] The continuing *Huahujing* conflict was damaging to the Taoists in that it regularly stirred up Buddhist rancor, and each time the Taoists entered into the fray, all texts dealing with the subject ended up being condemned, a fact that often brought with it condemnation of the Taoists themselves along with their other works. These battles for supremacy were sometimes intense, and the Taoists were not the only ones to suffer. Emperor Wuzong's proscription of Buddhism in 845 seems to have in part been inspired by the Taoist Zhao Guizhen.

Still, these quarrels did not involve everyone, and exchanges and meetings between Taoists and Buddhists remained frequent in all periods. At all times there were Taoists who considered Buddhism a complementary discipline parallel to their own—sometimes inferior but not incompatible with it. We have seen (and shall continue to see) that Taoism never stopped borrowing from Buddhism. This was done in ways that were not openly admitted and thus often difficult to disentangle. As a result, the borrowings are not fully understood and have been little studied.

Emperors organized public debates between adherents of the two religions, and the outcome was often important to the participants because the victors gained official protection. Such debates affected both ideologies (and their formulation). The confrontation of concepts and doctrines became more profound and more articulated and affected the evolution of the two religions. This fact is revealed by Buddhist as well as Taoist sources. These official debates were backed up by constant individual contacts. Many Taoists, like Tao Hongjing, maintained close relations with the Buddhists.

There were also frequent cases of conversion from one religion to the other. As early as the *Zhen'gao*, we have reports of Taoists converting to Buddhism, and vice versa. The famous sixth-century critic of Taoism, the Buddhist Zhen Luan, had been a Taoist adept. Yixing, one of the most famous Buddhist monks of the eighth century, had had a Taoist master (a fact the Buddhist sources do not note), and he was equally versed in Taoist and Tantric practices. Certain mountains, like Tiantai, which gave its name to a Buddhist school, or Lushan, center of Lingbao Taoism, sheltered both Taoist and Buddhist communities that lived side by side in harmony.

Throughout the centuries, even during the most furious conflicts, voices were raised from both the Taoist and the Buddhist camps affirming the fundamental identity, despite all the differences in form and methods, of Buddhism and Taoism. Among others we have the example of the Buddhist Sun Chuo (ca. 300–380), partisan and protégé of the Taoist Wang Xizhi (321–79). Sun maintained that the Buddha incarnated the same wisdom as did Confucius and Laozi. We also have Taoists like Zhang Rong (late fifth c.) and Ma Shu (522–81), who "loved the Buddhist texts, Laozi, and the *Book of Change*," and the master of Du Guangting, who taught the "great elixir," drawing parallels with Buddhist teachings (DZ 296, 40.13b–14a). Under the Tang, this line of thought continued and became stronger, both among Taoists and among Buddhists.

Consolidation

For Taoism, the Tang was a period of consolidation and integration. Externally elements of Buddhism were incorporated, while internally the various trends that had grown up over the previous centuries began to merge. The Tang Taoists in this respect were simply continuing the work begun during the fifth century, but they went about it much more methodically and systematically. They increased the number of hagiographic collections, classified texts, and inventoried the heavens, celestial palaces and their descriptions, the gods of the heavens and the human body, holy places and earthly paradises mentioned in those works—all "born spontaneously from the Breath" (DZ 1123, 14b–15a). Great ritualists like Zhang Wanfu (ca. 711) and Du Guangting, to mention only two, fixed the order of the liturgy as well as the rules governing progress up the hierarchical ladder of the priesthood, the pattern of monastic life, priestly vestments, the production of statues and paintings, the form of cult objects, and the recitation of texts. There was also significant activity in the field of laboratory alchemy, and at the same time an interiorization of these procedures and the beginnings of interior alchemy. Finally, the basic concepts of the religion were both deepened and given definition.

Many written works resulted from these efforts. They took the form of collections that tried to integrate and coordinate the earlier traditions. Here I shall give only a few titles from among many;

these works cannot be categorized, as far as their content is concerned, within any of the preceding traditions. After the *Wushangbiyao*, of the sixth century, we have other thematic anthologies such as the *Sandong zhu'nang* and the *Daomen jing faxiang cheng xuci* in the seventh century and the *Yi qie daojing yinyi miaomen youqi* of the eighth. Other works, such as the *Benjijing*, the *Daojiao yi shu*, and the *Xuanmen dayi*, from the sixth and seventh centuries, are dedicated to theoretical matters and are based on works that have not survived (their number, however, attests to the intellectual activity of the period).

One good example of efforts to sum up, synthesize, and organize Taoist doctrine is the *Daojiao yi shu*, among the earliest of these methodical presentations. Like earlier works along these lines, it relies on Buddhist precedents, including the dialectic of the Mādhyamika, but its authors understand them much better than did earlier compilers. It is an effort to construct a coherent theoretical view of Taoism, on the basis not only of traditional texts, like the *Daodejing* and the writings of the Shangqing and Lingbao schools (from which the compilers assembled scattered quotations and tried to fit them together) but also of more modern texts that had already begun this effort at synthesis. These include works like the *Benjijing*, the *Xishengjing*, as well as others that have not survived, like the *Daomen dalun* and works by the Xu, Meng, Song, and Xuanqing Masters of the Law. The *Daojiao yi shu* proceeds by rereading certain basic texts and interpreting selected phrases in the light of mental techniques and concepts assimilated from Buddhism. In this respect, Buddhistic speculations tended to be accepted in preference to data provided by the Shangqing and Lingbao texts, even if the cosmology presented is inspired primarily by those texts. Thus we see a curious combination of Taoism and Buddhism: from Buddhism were taken the dialectic of existence (*you*) and non-existence (*wu*), of illusion and reality, along with valuable conceptual tools like *ti*, substantive basis, and *yong*, operation, ideas that permit two aspects of the same principle to be joined. From Buddhism came also a certain part of the cosmology and scholasticism that permeates all contemporary texts of this type: for example, the three worlds, the "four greats" (earth, water, fire, and wind), which, when amalgamated with the Five Agents, give six principles, with the addition of the wind to the latter.[2] The six Buddhist states of awareness (*mano-vijñāna*) were equated with the six Chinese senses (*qing*). At the same time, the structure of paradise was based on the Shangqing tradition but reshaped to fit the taste of the times: three primordial heavens (the "three pure ones"), each in turn giving rise to three heavens, and each of these engendering three more; by adding the first nine to the next 27 one reaches 36, the number of Shangqing heavens. The fundamentally Taoist ideas of "chaos" and "stimulus and response" or resonance (*ganying*) were preserved. The concept of the Void took on several meanings, enriched by Buddhist connotations. The Void is that indeterminate state of the primordial Chaos in which nothing can be distinguished, a state at once the point of emergence and the ultimate end of things; it is also the spiritual emptiness that must be achieved during meditation; and finally it is also defined, in the purer tradition of the Mādhyamika, as "wonderful void" (*miao you*) encompassing at once negation (*wu*) and affirmation (*you*) in the form of potentiality: neither physical form nor obstacle, but the possibility of being one, neither void nor passageway but the possibility of being one. The "product of the Tao," the ultimate realization toward which the Taoist adept strives, was defined positively as permanence, joy, ego, and purity, a direct borrowing from the concept of nirvana in the school of Buddhism from Tiantai, the mountain on which Buddhists and Taoists lived together in harmony.

The writers of these texts sought to define a certain number of major terms more precisely. The word Tao was glossed as *li* (norm, structural explanation for things); transcendent, since it exists at a time before everything ("prior to Heaven," *xiantian*); without cause ("born of the non-born," "spontaneous," uncreated, having its root within itself); and ungraspable, invisible, and inaudible. And yet it is immanent in that it is universal, extensive, or pervasive (to use the anglicism by which François Jullien translates into French the otherwise untranslatable word *tong*).[3] "There is nowhere that it does not exist." The Tao's most striking characteristic, in fact—

and this is in the direct Taoist tradition—is to reconcile contradictions: it is immanent and transcendent, withdrawn, "secret," closed in (*si* "closed in on itself," says the *Yinfujing*), but also ubiquitous, widespread, broad, and immense. Its ability to assume new forms, to change, and to renew itself is another obvious trait. Through this quality, it can engender and bring to perfection, be "father and mother," "ancestor," source of all life, at once immobile and giving life ("in the Tao there is both motionless wisdom and moving spirit," says the *Yi qie daojing yinyi miaomen youqi,* 1b). It is formless, but can contain all forms, all possibilities. In the often evoked and quoted words of the *Daodejing* 21, "In it are the essences, in it all promise."

In fact, in order to compete with Buddhism even as they drew on it, the Taoists turned to their own classics, beginning with the *Daodejing* and the *Zhuangzi,* and they remained remarkably close, throughout their borrowings, to the ideas basic to their own philosophy. The ultimate truth, or more precisely its achievement, was expressed in terms that connote freedom, an opening that allows the play of the various parts among themselves ("the void, *kong,* is the way the Tao operates," says Du Guangting), a transition (*he*), a free circulation (*tong*), an absence of restraints (*wu'ai, wuzhi*): "That which comes without moving, and that goes without sign of haste," says Sima Chengzhen, citing the *Zhuangzi.* Whether they are describing the Spirit (*shen, xin*) or the Tao, the terms used are very similar. And, beginning with this fluidity, this possibility for transference, we also have light and serenity but not motionlessness. There is no quietism; on this point there is total unanimity. Instead correct action emerges from a lack of action, a motionlessness that is the root of life and its creative movement; a darkness that contains everything that is possible; a forgetting that is rather a lack of mindfulness; a beginning, the origin of one of those confused inceptions by which Taoists like to explain progressive organization, slow gestation; the void that is mystery, but the mystery of life; the "marvel" (*miao*), the puzzle behind the Origin that has no foundation, that has "no antecedent" (*wuxian*). It is the expression of amazed non-knowing.

Integration of Buddhism

The Buddhist contribution to this labor of reflection was to provide the Taoists with conceptual tools and more developed ways of
expression, especially the tetralemma of the Mādhyamika.[4] The
Void, or "absence" (*wu*), is the absence of absence, the transcendence of the two correlative ideas of presence (*you* or existence)
and absence (*wu* or non-existence), which results in a twofold synthesis expressed in two separate ways. On the one hand, we have
the *miao you*, "wondrous existence," including and presupposing
non-existence and based on it, and on the other, we have the *zhen
wu*, "true non-existence," which includes its opposite, existence.
This is pure Buddhism. But Tang Taoists handled this dialectic
with a new ease and applied it to all sorts of contradictory concepts to achieve a union of opposites where the "golden mean" can
be located. Zhuangzi and the School of Yin-Yang and the Five
Agents clearly paved the way for this.

A new school grew up around the *Daodejing*, in the form of
commentaries on it as well as on the *Zhuangzi*, and a new term
appeared based on the *Daodejing*, whose dialectical thought could
easily adapt to this formulation. This term appears in the name of
the Chongxuan school (the "double Mystery"), whose basic premises went back perhaps to the fourth century, but whose main representatives were Cheng Xuanying (ca. 650) and Li Rong (second
half of the seventh c.). The expression *chongxuan*, around which
this way of thinking crystallized and which was often used at this
time in many different texts, was inspired by a phrase in the first
chapter of the *Daodejing*, "mystery and yet again mystery." This
phrase suggests a double movement of the spirit, both on the
theoretical and conceptual planes as well as on the existential and
mystic planes: a double "forgetting," a forgetting of that which has
been forgotten, or a double rejection, a rejection of rejection itself
in a triumphant affirmation. It is a deepening of the "mystery" in
two steps, going beyond belief in any absolute form of existence
(the error of those who believe in the absolute, the "eternalists")
and going beyond the idea of nothingness (the error of the nihil-

ists). This results in the paradoxical realization of the reality of that existence we call illusory, a reality much more true in that it is recognized as "illusory," in a liberation of all attachment to any single opinion. It is a matter of not adhering to any single belief, no matter what it is, of not reaching the belief that nothingness exists. Nothingness is only a means, whose end is not the annihilation of *you*, of existence, and vice versa. These two truths must be formulated jointly, first one on top of the other, and then blended into a single identity: emptiness is fullness, and vice versa. The logical point of view that cannot accept two opposing truths at the same time and can accept them only in sequence must be abandoned so that each can be perceived through the other. Once again, all this clearly derives from the Mādhyamika, but is perfectly assimilated and applied to Taoist texts and ideas. (It should be noted here—and this is ironic—that both Buddhists and the Taoists reject precisely what the neo-Confucianists, firm in their ignorance of the two faiths, have accused them of believing.)

This methodological process was also used to resolve an old debate that had occupied the Chinese throughout their history: the relationship between the word and reality (here, the ultimate reality, the Tao). Thus the Taoists were able to explain a fundamental paradox in their philosophy: both Laozi and Zhuangzi spoke of this relationship and even claimed that "he who knows does not speak," that the Truth can be neither spoken nor transmitted. As explained in the *Daojiao yi shu* (DZ 10, 5a), once again citing the first chapter of the *Daodejing* (the Tao is unnamable and namable), the impossibility of giving a name can arise from the fact that nothingness has no "body" that one can "evoke" (names are given in order to assume control) as well as from the fact that a name can be applied to concrete existence insofar as it is "illusory," without a true substrate. On the other hand, the possibility of naming can in turn be applied to nothingness because of its real character, and to concrete existence just because it has a concrete character that lets us understand it.

It is in this way that a route toward the justification of discourse opens up.

The Classifying of Schools and Texts

But, just as with the Buddhists, the Taoists then faced another difficulty: that of reconciling all their various paths (voices). As we have seen, the various schools of thought had multiplied. Very early on people began to feel the need to organize them. Some texts from the Shangqing and Lingbao traditions had already started to do this on the basis of a hierarchical order. Lu Xiujing had continued and had given a decisive push to this tendency, which was continued by Tao Hongjing and became a characteristic of Tang Taoism. There began a long reflection on the texts, on their nature and their respective worth, leaning on and developing further the grandiose vision of this process bequeathed by the Shangqing school. Bibliographic categories were drawn up, and various levels of worth established among the Revealed Canons (*jing*), talismans, "formulas" transmitted by masters, essays and commentaries, collections of precepts, registers intended for ordinations, cosmic diagrams, "methods" or technical treatises, hagiographies, and other writings.

The basic division of the texts of the *Daozang* into three caverns or grottoes (*sandong*) was patterned after the Buddhist Tripitaka, a principle of organization that reached its full development under the Tang. This division has other roots going far back in the history of Taoism. It shows up first in certain Shangqing texts and was developed by Lu Xiujing on the basis of the *Jiutian shengshen zhangjing*, a basic Lingbao work. It provided a cosmological and theological basis for a hierarchical ordering of the various schools in relation to each other. This classification, however, was the product of the southern schools and omitted the Celestial Masters school, which was integrated into the system only later. The hierarchical classification of schools and their texts was constructed on the basis of this tripartite division. The triad, under many different aspects, was an idea already firmly anchored in Taoist thought and one that, because of its position as a central axis in the systems of thought of all schools, furnished a common foundation for their cosmology, theology, and patrology.

Many sources, many traditions, were present and had to be coordinated. On the one hand was the theory of the *sanhuang*, the Three August Ones: the Heavenly August One, the Earthly August One, and the Supreme August One (Taihuang). Promoted by the advisers of Qin Shihuangdi, this triad had been transformed into the Three-One among the *fangshi* around the Han Emperor Wu: the Heavenly One, the Earthly One, and the Supreme One (Taiyi). In the *Sanhuang wen*, one foundation for the traditions current among Tang Taoists, the Three August Ones had become the August Ones of Heaven, Earth, and Man, with the last the median element, at the juncture of the first two, instead of transcending them as did the Supreme August One. This triadic principle is thus at work on a double level: a Supreme Unity divides into Heaven and Earth, and Heaven and Earth rejoin each other in Man. For their part, the Celestial Masters had placed at the origin of the world three Breaths—*xuan*, *yuan*, and *shi* ("mysterious," "original," and "initiating")—tied to the Three Originals, the Sanyuan, which, as we have seen, became objects of meditation at the same time as they constituted the triple axis of a vast network of correspondences including the Three Officials of Heaven, Earth, and Water, the Three Luminaries, the three cinnabar fields, and the like.

During succeeding cosmic eras, three supreme gods, each reigning over a separate heaven, sent out in turn three teachings, or "three caverns," which correspond to the three southern schools. In descending hierarchical order they were the *zhen* (real) cavern gathering together the Shangqing texts, the *xuan* (mysterious) cavern for Lingbao texts, and the *shen* (divine) cavern for the tradition of the ancient seekers for immortality. Texts multiplied, and "annexes" (*fu*) were added to these caverns: the *Taixuan fu*, centered on the *Daodejing*, was added to the Shangqing Dongzhen; the *Taiping fu*, based on the *Taipingjing*, was added to the Dongxuan; the *Taiqing fu*, holding alchemical texts, was added to the Dongshen, as was eventually the *Zhengyi fu*, which held the texts of the Celestial Masters. Thus were constructed the three vehicles: the "great vehicle" dealing with the "three voids" or Three Originals, the "middle vehicle" teaching how to meditate on the bodily spirits and the circulation of breath, and the "lesser vehicle" dedicated especially to alchemy, the use of talismans, and mastery over demons and spirits. (This basic formulation varies according to the text.) Of course, these three caverns with their annexes, as well as the three deities from whom these teachings derived, are really only one. Everything is brought together under the ancient meditation on the Three-One, which follows the same schema as that on *you* (existence) and *wu* (non-existence). Buddhist dialectic is also applied: the three are at the same time the One and the not-One, neither One nor the not-One, at the same time Three and not-Three, neither Three nor not-Three.

Everything grows out of the Tao, which, at the beginning of the world, "sent down indications to stir a response to an impetus" (*ganying*) and then divided into three. This formulation derives from two basic theories. One of them, the basis of Taoist thought and that of the *Xici* (Great Appendix to the *Book of Change*), calls for the action of Heaven and the Sage—an action that is never dictated by any personal will, which is a "spontaneous response" to an incitation—that is to say, part of the natural order of things; the *Daojiao yi shu* presents a highly elaborated version of this theory. The other is the idea of the indication or trace, an ancient Chinese idea reinterpreted in the light of Buddhism: here the teaching is only an indication of the truth, a revealing hint, not the truth itself, but only an individual, incomplete expression of it that serves as a guide and must be surpassed; it is a veil marred by what is relative, through which the Absolute may be glimpsed. The Scriptures are the "word" or the letter, the opaque vehicle, outside the Root, but they are related to the Root in two ways: one of participation, since they are connected to their Root and their Exemplary Cause, the Tao, and one of analogy, since they are the thread that guides one back to the Root. These indications have "come down," have been granted; the term used (*chui*), according to an ancient explanation found in a similar form in the *Taipingjing* (p. 275), means first of all "to hang" and is traditionally used of the heavenly bodies "suspended" in the sky, which are the civilizing element of organization, "writing" (*wen*).

According to other versions, Yuanshi tianzun himself, the Celestial Venerable One of the Original Beginning, changed into the Three Lords, who are his three "transformational bodies," three different forms that he assumed to disseminate three distinct sets of teachings at three different periods. But these three bodies and these three teachings are really only one, which is his "true body"; they are only three for opportunistic reasons, appropriate for "different times." This idea and its formulation bring together, on the one hand, an ancient body of Chinese thought that is found especially among the Legalists and, in a germinal form, in Confucius and in a developed form in the *Huainanzi*, which preaches accommodation to the "times" and a certain opportunism, and on the other, the Buddhist teaching theory of the *upāya* (*fangbian*), "useful means" to impart understanding, means by which the teaching is adapted to the listener and thus can take different forms according to the circumstances and the audience. This theory, as well as that of the apparent and transformational body (*nirmāna-kāya*), can be found widely in Tang Taoist texts (especially in chaps. 2 and 9 of the *Benjijing*) and was there used, following the example of Buddhism, to justify the divergencies that distinguish the various texts and sometimes even give rise to contradictions among them. The form taken by the teaching or the appearance that the gods (Yuanshi tianzun or Laozi) give to the "body of response" for the use of the believer is a function of the adept's ability to accept, see, and understand.

The Three Teachings are associated systematically with three controlling characteristics of human beings: Breath, Spirit, and Essence (*jing*). In this specific context, Breath is the coarsest form of exterior appearance, corresponding to the sense of touch; Spirit is related to hearing and space; Essence, highest in this scale, is connected with vision and light. These three controlling characteristics, which originate in the three cinnabar fields, illustrate three ways of knowing. But the limit of human knowledge is recalled by a phrase from the *Daodejing* (chap. 14) describing the inaccessible nature of the Tao: Breath, Spirit, and Essence are the Three Originals that are found in the three cinnabar fields and are called the Impalpable (for touch-Breath), the Silent (from a word that also designates anything sparse, scattered, so expanded and distant that one cannot apprehend it, for hearing-space-Spirit), and the Indistinct (for vision-Essence).

In other texts the Three Lords are themselves only "traces," indications, this time of the Three Originals or the Three Primordial Chaoses that preceded them (and here we often find one of those long enumerations of various kinds of Chaos under different names, evoking the entire void, which were born spontaneously one from the other). The Lords appear one after another, and each emerges "through transformation" (and not by generation) from the particular Chaos of which he is the "indication." They are the Lords of a teaching, and they are at the origin of the Principles of the World. To them correspond three Breaths (almost identical to the three Original Breaths of the Celestial Masters), which energize the universe. They are at the same time forms of energy and masters of Truth, and thus they occupy a medial position between the various forms of primordial Chaos, which are also Voids, and the cosmos. Just as the text both precedes the world and founds it in the Shangqing theories, here the Lords both deliver a form of teaching and give shape to the world that begins in a chaotic state of indifferentiation and pure potentiality. It is through the book, and thus through knowledge, that Heaven and Earth are built up, and that light (Yang) and darkness (Yin) are separated from each other. These Three Lords have been identified with the triad of supreme gods in the liturgy: Yuanshi tianzun, Taishang daojun, or Very High Lord of the Tao, and Taishang laojun, the deified Laozi. The domains of the Three Lords are the Three Pures, the supreme heavens with which they are sometimes identified.

In fact, beyond the 32 heavens of the *Durenjing*, which form the "three worlds," there are the four heavens of "seed men" (a legacy from the Celestial Masters tradition), which suffering can no longer reach, then the Three Pures, and finally the supreme Daluo ("great net," an expression derived from the *Daodejing*) heaven, whose description is inspired by those given of celestial places in Shangqing texts. Various degrees of holiness are associated with these heavens. Ancient distinctions (never explained in any consistent form in previous texts) of "saints" (*sheng*), "true men" (*zhen*), and "immortals" (*xian*) are taken up again, with certain refinements and modifications.

The classification system adopted for texts also governed the gradual rise of Taoists up the priestly scale. Initiation could begin at age seven for boys and ten for girls. Those who did not marry could become monks or nuns at the age of fifteen. At the time of their ordination, Taoist masters received a complete set of texts corresponding to one of the sections of the Canon. Texts from the Celestial Masters, considered as both inferior and containing all the others (in potential form), constituted the lowest step. At the top were the Shangqing texts, held to confer the highest form of initiation. The initiation began with the Celestial Masters texts (the *Zhengyi*) and then sequentially involved those connected to the *Sanhuang wen* along with the group collected around the *Daodejing*, the Lingbao texts, the *Sandong* ("three caverns") group, and finally, at the highest level, the Shangqing texts. This progressive initiation on the ecclesiastical scale was measured in terms of liturgical knowledge and implementation of what had been learned, both externally and internally.

The Masters make up the religious community and constitute one of the "three treasures," at the same level as the Tao and the scriptures. They are enthroned in a solemn ceremony during which their place in the religious world is established, a place marked by a precise affiliation within a geographical area (*zhi*) that connects them to the sacred mountain to which their meditation chamber is attached.[5] This place is also heavenly, since it is determined as a function of their date of birth and the position of the stars on that date. To sum up, it is located both in space and in time, in the sky and on earth, in the external world and in the prayer room of the priest. The master then undertakes to transmit "civilization" or the art of transformation (*hua*, a word that contains both meanings), to work for the salvation of humankind, to pray for rain and good weather, and to carry out ritual ceremonies. He receives a *lu*, a register, which is the list of all the supernatural powers under his command. This register is qualitatively like the royal talismans that attest to the mandate the ancient sovereigns had received from Heaven.

The cult offered to the masters takes the form of a triple triad: the first consists of the first three Celestial Masters (Zhang Daoling, his son, and his grandson); this is echoed in the second, made up of the current Celestial Master, his father, and his grandfather, and in the third, the personal triad of every master, consisting of his own master, and the master of his master and his master's master in turn. The relationship between a master and his disciple is expressly compared to that between a father and son, because, it is said, it is the master who gives life to his disciple. This cult is thus built on the basis of a religious patriline and on the model of the cult of ancestors, which also works over a span of three generations.

Within this system, several kinds of masters are distinguished, by specialties: doctrine, ritual, monastic discipline, or interior purifications. Hermits and exorcists are classed separately.

Neiguan

The Tang era was also significant as the period when a new trend in mysticism started to appear. Represented by many texts, of which the most important date from the seventh century, there rose up a great current that I can present only briefly here and that, for convenience, I shall call simply *neiguan*, "interior meditation." It developed a form of silent meditation without visualizations, intended to empty the spirit and unify it with the Tao rather than to culminate in ecstasy and flight into the heavens. Once again under the influence of Buddhism, the conception of meditation and contemplation took a completely new turn. Whereas in the Shangqing techniques "oblivion," the halting of thought, was only a conditional state, a break with the ordinary world, it now became a technique in its own right and accompanied speculations on the reality of the world and nothingness. Certain ancient terms received new definition: thus "deliverance" came to mean liberating the spirit from all concepts and all idea of gain and loss, so that there would remain nothing, not even the absence of anything (*Benjijing*, 2, Paris, 1960, p. 26); "to leave the family" (*chujia*) means leaving the world of existing things, freeing oneself with respect to religious and moral precepts. The true precepts were those that could not be observed or transgressed, and the higher-level adept did not withdraw from the world because he had no fear of being soiled by it. Meditation on texts involved two steps: concentrating and then freeing oneself from meditation and recognizing that in the "law" (*fa*, doctrine) there are fundamentally no texts (this idea dates from the sixth century and so predates the famous formulation along these lines found in Chan or Zen). Similarly, meditation on the master consists in first contemplating him mentally and then having no mental image at all (*Benjijing*, 2, p. 30). This tendency reveals one of the methods that Taoists used to try to reconcile Taoism and Buddhism. The interest of this attempt lies not only in the way that the Taoists articulated these two religions, one in relation to the other, but also in the fact that this method of achieving an assimilation with Buddhism still permitted the Taoists to refine even further, near the end of the Tang, a completely original set of ideas that would become inner alchemy (*neidan*). In this effort we can see once again that when they borrowed things (and, unlike the Buddhists and neo-Confucianists, they acknowledged their borrowings, frankly citing the Buddhist texts they drew from), the Taoists still remained true to their roots and the distinctive quality of their orientations. They always returned to Laozi and Zhuangzi and retained their identity and fundamental qualities.

The *Neiguanjing* (*Scripture of Inner Contemplation*) is a short treatise that would later become a widely cited text. It is especially interesting in the way it inserts Buddhist data into a Taoist matrix. This text is largely dedicated to the contemplation of the gods of the body, a practice completely within the Taoist tradition, which has never lapsed into the kind of introspection common to Western mystics. The analysis is totally Taoist: the Primordial Breath animates a body constructed along the model provided by the School of Yin-Yang and the Five Agents; the gods of the human body are those we have already encountered; the body is a microcosm—the eyes are the sun and the moon, the hair the stars, and so on. With its constant subtext of meditation on rebirth, an intimately related theme, the text begins by describing the forming of the embryo, a recurrent motif in Taoism already taken up in chapter 7 of the *Huainanzi* and one found in many other Taoist works (for example, in the *Yebao yinyuan jing*, DZ 336, 8.1a-b, where this development of the embryo is related to the Nine Heavens; or in the *Chujia yinyuan jing*, DZ 339, 16b). Then it lists the gods of the body, those gods in the Shangqing register also found in the body, and the spirits of the five viscera. Next, it discusses the *xin*, which is in this context both the physical organ (the heart) in which affectivity and intellect reside, and the spirit itself. It is here that Taoism and Buddhism merge: man at birth is pure, a commonplace in the Chinese tradition, which sees the source of all troubles and errors in the emotions. The emotions are also considered as the source of the six forms of awareness (*shi*) of Buddhism, and they are also at the root of all faulty and partial opinions. Thus, it is necessary to seek out the origin of this awareness (*shi*), which is within the *xin*, and then the origin of the latter, which lies within the idea of the self, which in turn emerges from desire. Here we are face to face with Buddhist introspection in its most developed form. Still, the text stops short in that it does not consider any of the Buddhist methods for destroying this awareness and idea of the self but returns to the "emptying of the spirit."

Although this concept had been preached by illustrious thinkers of former times, it had later been ignored by Taoism. Immortality is achieved through the Tao and the Tao comes from oneself if the *xin* is pure. The end of the text thus preaches the emptying of the *xin*, the placating of the spirit (*shen*): the Tao will then come automatically. Laozi is cited and Zhuangzi evoked. Those who work on their bodies, exercise their will, and stir up their spirit do not know what they are about. However, Laozi appears at the end of the work and reiterates the basic Taoist position over the centuries by saying that his wisdom is not innate, that he had to work to attain the Tao. Implicitly, he is the model for meditation.

This text thus brings together two forms of meditation and, despite a short passage inspired by Buddhism, is based and eventually returns, contrary to its generally quietistic tone, to a call for "study." Taoism, throughout its history, is deliberately gradualist, which can be proved clearly in other texts in the *neiguan* tradition. Sima Chengzhen insisted on this need to work to attain the Tao, at the same time as he made clear that one must not push action too far, because this could harm the "fundamental nature" (*xing*); he also stressed, however, that one cannot expect to achieve the goal without ascesis, a delusion he warns beginners against.

At the heart of works on *neiguan* is a cluster of texts around the *Dingguanjing* (*Scripture of Concentration and Meditation*), a reference text that exists in many versions and is attached to the name of Sun Simiao (d. 682), and Sima Chengzhen's *Zuowang lun* (*Essay on Sitting and Forgetting*, a term from Zhuangzi), a text related to the former. Once more we can see the polyvalence of Taoist authors: Sun Simiao was an alchemist-physician, and Sima Chengzhen a patriarch of the Shangqing school who scorned neither the visualization practices of this school nor techniques for achieving immortality, as is proved by his works. These texts take up a number of basic points, such as the definition of the basic ideas of the *ming* (ordained life span), the *xing* (fundamental nature), the will (*zhi*), knowledge, factors in the fall of humanity, and the basic role accorded to the *xin* (heart-mind) in the process of freeing oneself.

All the texts under discussion here distinguish clearly several steps (five according to some, seven in others). These steps do not correspond to an ascent in the ecclesiastical hierarchy, but constitute rather an entirely personal progress revealed by no external sign; they make up a system of ascesis like that found throughout the history of mysticism.

The first level is the preparation for contemplation, defined according to rules and moral precepts as well as behavior patterns of the kind already found in Ge Hong: do not remain seated or standing for too long, do not work for too extended a period (Sima Chengzhen). It can also include following ancient prescriptions, for example, taking drugs (*Daojiao yi shu*, 1.21a). This stage is intended to ensure a primary purification and a beginning to serenity.

The *Dingguanjing* lists five stages that mark a progressive evolution from movement to quietude, beginning with the state of ordinary activity and reaching a state of total quietude in which the adept exists equally well in activity and in stillness. Only then do the seven steps that lead the mystic toward the "source of the

Tao" begin. The ancient categories are brought together. During the first step, one must "embrace the one and keep the mean." In the second, the devotee regains his youthful appearance. In the third, he reaches the state of an immortal, rises into the sacred mountains, and can fly through the air; celestial boys and maidens surround him and protect him. In the fourth step, he sublimates his body into breath, he gives forth light, he becomes a "true man" (*zhen*). In the fifth, his breath is refined into spirit, he is a "divine man" (*shen*); he can move heaven and earth, shift the position of mountains, and dry up seas. In the sixth, he refines his spirit and merges with the world of appearances, he changes shape according to circumstances and the needs of beings. Finally, in the last step, he is beyond the world of beings, he has reached the ultimate end.

The term *dingguan* itself needs some explanation. Like the binome *zhiguan* (*samatā-vipaśyanā*) adopted by Tiantai Buddhism, it goes back to a twofold spiritual attitude: *ding* is the concentration that brings a stability like that of the earth; *guan* is the kind of contemplation that puts into play intuitive wisdom (*hui, prajña,* insight) and shines with light, like Heaven. These two complementary aspects are always present in these texts. There is the negative or privative aspect, one of stasis, which brings about a rupture with the world and customary mental processes; here it is associated with the Earth, whose nature in the Chinese cosmological scheme is to be stable and which is classed in the Yin category, that of inward-folding motion. This aspect is completed by a positive one, *guan*, that of the spreading and light characteristic of Heaven and of the Yang. *Ding* and *hui* are trained by the observance of "precepts" (*jie*), to which certain Taoist texts append *shu*, that is, "methods," ancient practices, a triad of Buddhist origin. Huineng (638–713), a near contemporary of Sima Chengzhen, and Shenhui (668–760) explained things in this way within the Chan school: *ding* and *hui* are both necessary at the same time; if too much importance is given to *ding* (concentration), one sinks into a stupid contentment; if on the other hand only *hui* (insight) is cultivated, one ends up in enlightened madness (*kuang*). For the *Daojiao yi shu*, *ding* strictly speaking is an inherent part of *hui*. In other texts the *ding* has to be surpassed after it has been practiced, because it still involves discriminating mental activity.

Several states of the spirit (*xin*) play a basic role and are distinguished: one must get rid of the "attached spirit" but not the "emptied spirit," rid oneself of the "agitated spirit" but not the "luminous spirit," which is the Tao. No mindfulness can continue to exist, not even the desire for non-desire, not even a concentration on the void; as Sima Chengzhen points out, to become emptied, there must be nothing anywhere. Only at this price can lightness and luminosity be achieved; the distinction between true and false disappears, and the spirit enters into that "blind concentration," which, as we saw above, consists of light and illumination. The art is tricky: nothing can be sought out deliberately, and yet one must not expect that this free state will arrive of its own accord. There is, in a subtly shaded composition of "gradualism" and "suddenness," both effort and a state of grace, both innate and acquired capacities, an "orientation" that has to be given to the spirit, which is completely negative in that it consists of eliminating disorder without becoming attached to emptiness or obliterating the light (*Zuowang lun*, 3b–4a); one must not apply one's spirit to concentration, and yet concentration must not be eliminated (*Zuowang lun*, 12a).

The *xin* (here, the mind) must be contemplated with the *shen* (the spirit), and not with the body (*xing*), explains Du Guangting in his commentary on the *Qingjingjing* (DZ 759, 10a–b), another popular text during the Tang and the Song. The "idea" (literally, "mental idea" *xinyi*) "attracts the breath" that engenders the *shen*, but the mind should not be attached to anything, and there is thus no mental state that can be contemplated, that can "operate" (*yong*) or be exercised; in other words, "the *xin* is not this *xin* [the mentality of an individual]." And yet it is the lord and master of the abode that is the body—this is one of the basic tenets of Taoism. Without this place of residence, it cannot establish itself. Everything takes place as if there were no body and also no absence of the body! If one does not reach the state of "non-mind," how can one forget the body? It is a fact that the mind forgets the body that is "non-mind," and that "the body is not this body." To sum up in other words, that "forgetting" which is "non-mental" can come only through the mind. Emptiness, continues this commentator, is only an illusory "attribute" (*xiang*, a borrowing from Buddhism), an *upāya*, a pedagogical expedient that the Tianzun has set up for us in his great kindness (12a); it is only the "functioning" (*yong*) of the Tao (11a); in other words, it is only the laborious aspect of the spiritual exercise that leads to the Tao. One has to reach the state of "non-functioning," which is the "true void" and the true Tao. The "great void" is thus opposed to the "little void" achieved by non-action; one must reach the state where both "little" and "great" disappear, since the "great" exists only in contrast to the "little."

This group of texts agrees on insisting on two points that we shall find linked together in the following chapter on interior alchemy. The first is that one must not become attached to the void, not hypostatize it. (This idea comes from Buddhism.) The second is that one must exert effort both on the physiological and on the mental level, an idea deeply rooted in Taoist tradition that we shall see again in interior alchemy.

However, there is a problem in becoming attached to nothingness, in concentrating on the desire for non-desire—this is the great trap already evoked in the *Huainanzi* (chap. 11) where, well before the introduction of Buddhism, it was written: "He who constantly wants to be emptied cannot be emptied; he who does not seek emptiness becomes that way spontaneously." This sentence, as far as I know, is cited by none of the Taoist writers of the Tang, but its existence shows that they well could be predisposed to understand and integrate this doctrine so long developed by the Buddhists. We noted above the school of the "double Mystery" and its "double oblivion." When it comes to contemplation (*guan*), the Tang texts return to these ideas in many ways and, to this end, distinguish several forms and successive steps of contemplation. Some texts, like the *Daojiao yi shu* and the *Sanlun yuanzhi*, enumerate three time periods. First comes that of the contemplation of "illusory dharmas," which consists of meditation on the composite side of beings; the authors of these texts find it easy to illustrate this with an extract from chapter 2 of Zhuangzi. Next comes contemplation of the "real dharmas," and then that of the "universal void." Here the influence of Tiantai Buddhism is obvious. Yet another schema involves contemplation of *you* (existence), followed by that of *wu* (non-existence), and then that of the Tao of the middle—obviously under the influence of Mādhyamika and the school of the *Sanlun*.

We also find another pattern: mastery of the spirit by concentration on the One, which is only the "net" with which one catches fish (an image from Zhuangzi); then concentration on the "burned up spirit" (an expression from Zhuangzi), turned to ashes by the forgetting of the One; and finally the awakening to the "True One" and the "great concentration" (again a term from Zhuangzi). Some models are more elaborate. Du Guangting lists fourteen kinds of concentration, which he divides into three vehicles, to which he added that of the Sage, which crowns them all. The *Zuoxuan lun* recognizes fourteen different kinds, ranged in pairs of opposites so as to create a balancing effect. Under the Song this activity continued, and the *Daoshu* distinguishes five kinds of concentration.

The complementary and correlative relationship that unites *ding* (concentration) and *hui* (insight) is the same as that which binds together the body and the spirit, to such an extent that the two are placed into correspondence with each other. Concentration is connected with the body and with breathing exercises (which in this context are called by analogy *qiguan* "contemplation of the breath"), and insight is linked to the spirit (*xin* or *shen*) and to the "contemplation of the spirit." Although both are equally necessary, there is a ranking, like that between concentration and insight: the *Daojiao yi shu* holds that one must pass from the contemplation of the breath to that of the spirit. The *Sanlun yuanzhi* (11b) claims that exercising the breath leads to longevity, whereas exercising the spirit, which consists of "sitting and forgetting," ensures salvation (*miedu*); here again there is no quietism. The achievement of the desired condition of calm tranquillity lies both in action, "becoming transparent," and in non-action, in "shedding light" (7a).

All these speculations lead up to those of interior alchemy, which began to take shape at the end of the Tang and developed fully during the Song. We shall see there the pair *ding*-body and *hui*-spirit under the forms of *ming* and *xing*. It should, however, be emphasized that they coexist with the ancient methods of visual meditation dealing with subtle, imaginary physiology. For example, Du Guangting, in his commentary on the *Qingjingjing*, moves with the greatest of ease from one methodology to the other without seeing any contradiction between them, taking up, after long presentations on non-attachment, the absorption of solar and lunar effluvia. His commentary is also interesting in that it verifies the existence at this early date of themes and terms seen as belonging specifically to interior alchemy.

Finally there is the *Yinfujing*, a short anonymous treatise that had a wide influence. Although probably dating from the second half of the sixth century, it was not widely read until a Taoist contemporary of Emperor Xuanzong, Li Quan (ca. 743), wrote a commentary on it. He promoted the text to such an extent that the earliest version of it we possess is accompanied by his commentary. From then on, this work was often commented on and constantly cited. It became a reference work and provided Taoism with a certain number of key terms. In the version edited by Li Quan, it is divided into three sections, each with its own title: the first is dedicated to the Tao and to the immortals and to the "preservation of the One" (*baoyi*); the second to the law, the state, and peace; the third to "methods" (*shu*) concerning war and ensuring the victory of armies: according to later Taoist tradition, the nation (*guo*) and war are understood metaphorically as referring to the individual and the battle for interior peace. Like its title (taken by Li Quan to mean "union with the Dark Yin"), the work is rather enigmatic, and this may account for its popularity. Under the Song it was most often understood in terms of *neiguan* or interior alchemy. It gives the *xin* a position of central importance: it is the "mover" or fundamental mechanism (*ji*) of man. The Five Agents are "thieves" in that they are at the origin of the opening onto the exterior world and distract from the interior life. Li Quan interpreted this text in a traditional fashion with, nevertheless, a clear tendency toward closing off the exterior world and an extreme interiorization. Man is "the most numinous thing on earth," according to the revered formula, because he can "turn his light onto his own nature and totally understand the Prime Origin." However, this understanding comes through an understanding of the mechanisms of this world—the interplay of Yin and Yang and the Five Agents and of the calendrical cycles for which a study of the *Book of Change* is basic. This is because wisdom and holiness lead man not to take the initiative, but rather to follow the natural and heavenly order. Although the text cites the Confucian classics, it gives Laozi, Zhuangzi, the hidden sages, and the Yellow Emperor prominence and precedence over the Confucian sages Yao and Shun.

8

Under the Song and the Yuan:
Interior Alchemy

The Song dynasty was a period of troubles and instability, a time when China was threatened by invading barbarians. They defeated the Chinese armies decisively in 1126 and thereafter occupied the north, cutting Chinese territory in half. The response to these events was a reactionary moralizing and nationalistic movement that not only led to a renewal of Confucianism but also benefited Taoism, the repository of traditional values and a spiritual refuge in time of troubles. Death and demons were everywhere, and exorcisms were needed to fight them. This need fueled the growth in popularity of new forms of rituals. Despite the reported debauchery and charlatanism of some individual practitioners, Taoism now played an important role in the preservation of traditional moral values, and its influence was strengthened by its humanitarian activities in this time of troubles and distress among the people.

Taoist practitioners benefited from the support of emperors, especially Zhenzong (r. 997–1022), who claimed a Taoist deity among his ancestors. He protected Wang Jie (980–1020), the producer of alchemical gold, established a laboratory in the Hanlin Academy, and gave official rank to prominent Taoists to put them

on par with the bureaucrats. Taoists were also supported by Huizong (1100-1125), the emperor-aesthete promoted by Li Lingsu to
the rank of incarnate deity and patron of the new Shenxiao revelation into which he was initiated. Huizong also built Taoist temples
in his capital and throughout the empire, presented tripods to the
Shenxiao school, awarded honorific titles to prominent living
Taoists, and participated in Taoist ceremonies. He created Taoist
schools and insisted on the need to study Taoist texts in preparation for the official examinations, in an attempt to harmonize
Taoism and Confucianism. In addition, it was not uncommon for
famous Confucians of the period to practice Taoist meditation
techniques—for example, Su Shi (1037-1101) wrote descriptions
of them (see, e.g., *Daoshu* 35, 5b-9a), and Zeng Zao (ca. 1131-93),
the author of the *Daoshu* (*Pivot of the Tao*), an important Taoist
work, wrote a treatise on music, traditionally a Confucian art.

Taoist texts were collected, and efforts were made to establish
an authoritative canon of received works. From the beginning of
the dynasty, emperors ordered that Taoist texts scattered during
the confusion of the Five Dynasties be sought out. A Taoist Canon
was published in 1019 on imperial orders, under the supervision
of Zhang Junfang (fl. 1008-29). He was the author of another important collection, the *Yunji qiqian* (finished around 1028-29),
compiled at the request of Zhenzong. A century later, at the urg-
ing of Huizong, a new Taoist Canon was produced; this was the
first one to be printed. It was destroyed at the time of the Mongol
invasion of Beijing, but in 1244 another, more complete one was
compiled and reproduced in more than a hundred copies. In 1281,
following disputes with Buddhism, all Taoist works were condemned to be burned; only a few fragments were spared. The present Taoist Canon (*Daozang*) was compiled in 1444-45. Meanwhile, various great liturgical and other encyclopedias were
produced, such as the *Daoshu* of Zeng Zao and the *Xiuzhen shishu*,
two works devoted largely to interior alchemy. Collections of
works as well as monographs multiplied: hagiographies, histories
of monasteries and sacred mountains, general histories of Taoism
usually said to be produced under the patronage of Laozi himself
(such as the *Hunyuan shengji*, DZ 770, and the *Youlong zhuan*, DZ

774), anthologies, and commentaries on the great Taoist classics like the *Dadong zhenjing,* the *Durenjing,* the *Jiutian shengshen zhangjing,* the *Daodejing,* and the *Zhuangzi.* The commentaries were disseminated by famous Taoist priests like Chu Boxiu in 1270 and Li Daochun (fl. 1290).

In southern China three great centers were pre-eminent: that of the Celestial Masters at Longhu Shan, that of the Lingbao school at Gezao Shan, and that of Mao Shan. Apart from the new forms of ritual, which I shall not discuss here, developments took place in two directions. The first, based on concepts surrounding the Taiyi (the Supreme Unity), the Zhen Dadao (the Great True Tao), and the Jingming zhongxiao (Pure Light, Loyalty, and Filial Piety), was a movement toward moral renewal combined with therapeutic action. The other line of development, interior alchemy, signaled a rebirth that was much more intellectual in tone. We shall return to interior alchemy after a brief glance at a few traits of the first trend.

The two first currents in this more practical trend, those centered on the Taiyi and the Zhen Dadao, first appeared in northern China. They were essentially dedicated to therapeutic practices— by means of talismans in the first case and by prayers and exorcism in the second—and did not leave texts. The Taiyi movement was popular under the Jin emperors (the Jürchens) and the Yuan (the Mongols) and disappeared about the middle of the fourteenth century. The Zhen Dadao movement, on the other hand, seems to have limited its activity to lower-class circles and ceased to exist during the Yuan.

The Filial Piety movement was actually the resurgence of a cult whose first known appearance dates to the fourth century of our era. It reappeared on several occasions, in particular under the Tang, which officially recognized it toward the end of the dynasty. It was centered on a legendary saint of Sichuan, Xu Sun, who was supposed to have lived at the turn of the third and the fourth centuries and was famed for cleansing the region of an evil dragon, fighting against popular "wild cults," and demonstrating a truly exceptional level of filial piety. He was associated with another saint, Wumeng, also legendary but supposed to have died in 374

A.D., and equally famous for his filial piety. This cult, centered at Yulong guan, a temple located on Mount Xi in Jiangxi, benefited from the patronage of Huizong, who saw in this temple a symbol of Chinese unity against the Jürchens. Great processions there drew thousands of the faithful at the mid-autumn anniversary of the celestial apotheosis of the saint. In 1224, a personal appearance by the saint gave new impetus to the movement, gained it many followers, and led to the building of new sanctuaries. This renewal was strengthened by the activities of Liu Yu (1257–1308), who can be considered the true founder of the Pure Light movement (Jingming dao) in the fourteenth century. Followers of this movement exalted the virtues of purity, loyalty, and filial piety (*zhongxiao*). These virtues, which attained a cosmic quality, were most widely understood to imply loyalty, respect, and obedience toward the ruler, father of the people. For this reason, the movement took on the role of guardian of the social order and political stability. It found adherents largely in intellectual circles and among officials, but later it gradually evolved in the direction of popular Taoism. During the Ming, its adherents turned more and more toward liturgical activity, incorporating alchemical and magical elements. The cult of Xu Sun continues in a vital fashion today, especially in Taiwan.

Interior Alchemy, or Neidan

By far the most important innovation in the Taoism of this period, however, was the development of "interior alchemy." This practice, which had much earlier origins, now contributed significant new elements to Taoism. It both represented the mystical side of the religion and complemented the existing liturgical side of Taoism, essentially that of the present-day Celestial Masters.

The term "interior alchemy" conforms to long-established usage. This expression is an arbitrary designation for a widely followed movement still in existence today. At the outset it was not designated by a specific term, except perhaps *jindan* (literally, "golden cinnabar"), a term also used to refer to laboratory alchemy. "Interior alchemy" is an approximate translation of the term *neidan*, which means "inner cinnabar" and contrasts with *waidan*, "outer cinnabar." The two terms were used with varied meanings by the ancient Taoists and have no precise meaning except in context. The term *neidan* usually signifies a later phase of development, more inward-turning and more sublimated than the preceding phase, the *waidan*. In the absence of any specific name, modern authors (Chinese as well as Western), now use the term *neidan* to designate "interior alchemy," in contrast to the "exterior alchemy" in which the practitioner seeks to produce a transformative substance by means of laboratory techniques. Although it is sometimes difficult to distinguish the two, given the similarity of the language used, the fundamental difference is that interior alchemy does not seek to produce a particular physical substance and is above all a technique of enlightenment including a method of controlling both the world and oneself and a means of fashioning (*zaohua*) and hence understanding in the sense of an existential and intellectual integration.

There is also a clear distinction between interior alchemy and the breathing and gymnastic exercises, which, as we have seen, are not specifically Taoist and were also practiced at this time by the Confucianists and by people claiming no particular religious affiliation. The distinctive trait of interior alchemy, its own special character, lies in the completely original speculation on which it is founded. It is largely this feature that gives interior alchemy its position in the history of Taoism, which, as we have seen, had by this time integrated Buddhist speculations. In anticipating neo-Confucianism, to which it made important contributions, it constituted a completely Chinese and Taoist response to Buddhism by filling the gap left by Taoism's great pragmatism. It thus provided an outlet for those with a bent toward intellectual speculation who were not satisfied by visionary meditations of the Shangqing type. Faithful to the basic spirit of Taoism, it managed to preserve the physiological and visionary training Taoists had traditionally sought while training the intellect. This speculative element defines the movement and is an essential part of it, as the authors of its texts repeat insistently. It was in large part based on the style of

Book of Change exegesis popular under the Song, which was one of the factors in the intellectual reconciliation of Confucianism and Taoism.

The second aim of the movement was to achieve a synthesis between the various disciplines that already existed in Taoism (a large body of well-chewed-over material) and the two other great currents in Chinese thought, Buddhism and Confucianism. The interior alchemy authors often did this by citing basic Confucian and Buddhist texts. As we have seen, Tang Taoists had tried to synthesize the Three Teachings, in the belief that the three had one single root and goal. This idea was also expressed in similar terms in certain Buddhist texts, but it was within Taoism that it was the most openly and clearly asserted.

Within the framework of this conjunction of diverse elements, interior alchemy texts are always characterized by these features:

1. a concern for training, both mental and physiological, with the mental aspect often tending to predominate;
2. a synthesizing tendency bringing together various Taoist elements (breathing exercises, visualization, alchemy), certain Buddhist speculations and methods (speculations on the *wu* and the *you*, Chan *gong'an*—the koans of Japanese *zen*), and references to Confucian texts;
3. a systematized use of the trigrams and hexagrams of the *Book of Change*, already used metaphorically in laboratory alchemy and ritual; and
4. references to chemical practices, of a purely metaphorical nature, following an interiorized interpretation we have already seen in less developed form in the Shangqing school.

Every interior alchemy text uses chemical terminology (at least the words for lead, mercury, water, fire, furnace, and cauldron) and connects these terms to the trigrams of the *Book of Change*. This joining of trigrams and chemical terms is the distinctive element that distinguishes interior alchemy from the ancient breathing exercises that are still the subject of many treatises being written today. All the texts using this double system of referents are fired by the same synthesizing spirit described above, and it is thus possible to consider them a coherent group, despite divisions by school, which are actually more formal that real.

The basic nature of this line of Taoist thought and practice is didactic. The masters insist on this so often that there can be no doubt on this score. They try to explain their mystical experience and to induce it in their adepts. They do this not only by means of ancient physiological methods but also by harnessing the mind to disentangle knotty problems and break logjams, in order to make themselves mentally and spiritually more supple. These mental exercises are an analogue of breathing techniques at the physiological level. Like visionary meditation, interior alchemy is an operative discipline, a creative act, a process to be carried out, that is both redeeming and regenerative. Its inevitable result is the birth of the fetus, the new man. But this didactic nature means that interior alchemy texts are often unlike earlier ones. With only a few exceptions, they are not *revealed* texts. They are essays, poems dedicated to a disciple, friend, or visitor (some of these texts have been incorporated into liturgy), or teachings by various masters, transmitted in the form of disciples' notes (*yulu*, dialogues, following an ancient genre used as early as the *Taipingjing* and much in vogue among Song neo-Confucianists). The nature of the documents has significant consequences that we must take into account as we try to understand the doctrine or the message transmitted: the texts are often of uneven quality (on both the spiritual and the intellectual plane), and sometimes even contradictory, because they do not always address the same readers.

To simplify, in every alchemical operation the adept starts without reference points, markers, or limits (Chaos); he begins by establishing and delimiting a series of reference points, which he then manipulates, moves around, endows with life, encloses, and weaves together. He finishes by uniting them at the Center, where they fuse, where he "links" them, and where they produce ever "purer," more interior forms. He repeats the same operations with these purified forms until he "leaps into the Void." He has reconstructed the ill-made, disordered world in which he lives by beginning from a *tabula rasa*; only later does he recognize the norma-

tive, conceptual, and purely utilitarian—in a sense, factitious—
nature of his reference points. We can see how all this derives
from Zhuangzi. The ultimate goal is no longer illustrated and incarnated by the
somewhat fantastic image of the Saint. References to this figure in
interior alchemy texts are rare, abbreviated, and scattered. As we
shall see below, Wang Zhe denied that such operations can result
in bodily immortality, and his disciple Qiu Chuji told Genghis
Khan that the elixir of immortality does not exist. The ultimate
truth is the unity between the Tao and the world (see, e.g., DZ
1067, 8.5b–6a) and the Tao and the *xin* (human spirit). One must
seize upon and live this moment of eternity, the moment when the
world was born, before the division into two, the time of the coincidence of the two opposed poles, the unknowable human *sum-
mum* (*ren zhi ji*; DZ 1067, 5.11b). It is an exercise, as the authors
reiterate, in "producing existence [*you*] from non-existence [*wu*]"
(see, e.g., DZ 1310, 2.2b) or "matter" (*zhi*) from the non-matter that
gives rise to it (DZ 249, 1.6a), of channeling the "natural spring"
(*tianji*) of the world (DZ 1090, 11a). In other words, far from taking
refuge in the sterile "void," a goal that they constantly stigmatize
and that they are accused of seeking, the Taoists do the opposite:
they undertake an act of re-creation. They seek, as Buddhism
taught them, the fusion between the "positive path" and the
"negative path." This was stated by Bixuzi (DZ 241, 4a) when he,
like all the masters, warned adepts not only against the "useless
void" (*wankong*) but also against a dedication to "spontaneity,"
which, in the name of Laozi, found favor during the third and
fourth centuries in certain circles that believed one should follow
all one's urges: "The void," he says, "this means that one can neither see nor hear [ultimate reality]; spontaneity [*ziran*] means that
one can move forward and grasp it [*yingqu*]."

History

Interior alchemy took shape so gradually that we cannot assign a
precise date to its birth. According to one interpretation, it was
born when the north was ruled by non-Chinese, and those who
had received a Confucian education sought refuge in Taoism

rather than enter their service. These people brought an intellectual and cultivated element to Taoism. This interpretation, which
seems based on the supposition that no "cultivated" element previously existed in Taoism, derives from the misunderstanding the
religion has always faced, even though its adherents throughout
history have included highly educated people and those of great
culture. Furthermore, well before the invasions of non-Chinese,
the interior alchemy movement was in existence and had produced major works. In fact, neo-Confucianism benefited from the
joint contributions of Buddhism and Taoism in its own renewal.

Interior alchemy texts. The most ancient writings referred to in
texts on interior alchemy are the *Cantongqi (Token of the Concor-
dance of the Three)*, of which there are several versions in the *Daozang*, and the *Guwen longhu jing* (DZ 996), both attributed to Wei
Boyang, a legendary immortal who supposedly lived in the second
century A.D. The date and exact attribution of these texts remain
unanswered questions. There are references dating to the Han to a
text called *Cantongqi* and ascribed to Wei Boyang, but it is doubt-
ful that this was the work of that name extant today. All we can
say of the current work is that it existed under the Tang, and from
then on it was widely cited and commented on. The great Zhu Xi
wrote a commentary on the *Cantongqi*, a work as sybilline as it is
famous. Like all subsequent interior alchemy works, this text min-
gles philosophical aphorisms and concrete images. It was interpreted as a work on practical alchemy, but its many images were
later to become part of the basic repertoire of interior alchemy
texts. The metaphors strewn throughout it were constantly used
by the masters, for whom it became a fundamental reference. Such
metaphors include the cauldron, the oven shaped like the "setting
moon," "black mercury containing the flower of gold" (or "of metal," since the word *jin* can mean either), the "original Essence," the
"river chariot," "fire phasing," the "dust on the shining window,"
and many others that we shall have occasion to see again. The interior alchemy masters also seem to prefer the *Cantongqi* as a
source for more philosophical terms of wider usage, such as "original nature," "master the *you* through the *wu*," along with borrowings from Laozi, for example, "before Heaven and Earth," "higher

virtue has no virtue," "one looks at it [the Tao] and does not see it," "a tool is useful only in its lack of content."

However, the first clearly dated texts presenting articulated features of interior alchemy as defined above go back to the eighth and ninth centuries, illustrated, for example, by certain passages in the work of Wu Yun (d. 778; DZ 1051, 2.20a-b). The essential elements of interior alchemy are clearly well in place by the time of Cui Xifan's (fl. 940) *Ruyao jing* (*The Text for Entering the [Realm of] Elixirs*, DZ 135), the object of many commentaries and a constant reference for later authors.

Chen Tuan (ca. 906-89) was one of the first significant writers on interior alchemy as such. Only a few quotations and many references in the texts of others survive from his works. He was the disciple of one Mayi—a Buddhist according to some sources and a Taoist according to others. He is considered the heir to a tradition of studying the *Book of Change* unknown to the official exegetes of the Han and the Six Dynasties. It was summed up in a formulation that attests once more to the astonishing continuity of the Taoist tradition. To each part of the body were attributed numbers the same as those assigned to them in the sexual ritual of the Celestial Masters referred to earlier. What was formerly a sexual ritual is presented here as a science emerging from the *Book of Change*.[1] It is also from Chen Tuan that we get the famous diagram of the Taiji—the circle divided into black and white comma shapes—which occurs in an earlier version in a Buddhist text[2] and which Zhou Dunyi (1017-73) later employed. It was also Chen Tuan who formed the connecting link between Taoism and neo-Confucianism, through Zhou Dunyi and Shao Yong, who saw him as an important transmitter of Han traditions to the Song neo-Confucianists.

The *Wuzhen pian* of Zhang Boduan (d. 1082) is, with the *Cantongqi*, the basic reference text for interior alchemy. Since it includes an exposition of the entire procedure, it has been the object of many commentaries and is constantly cited.

Schools of interior alchemy. It is only with the beginning of the twelfth century that we can begin to speak of schools, albeit in carefully qualified terms. Several minor currents can be distinguished, such as the Zhenyi (The True One) and the Zhenyuan (The True Origin). The main lines of development, however, were those called the Zhong-Lü, the northern Quanzhen school, and the "school of the South."

The Zhong-Lü line (the name is an abbreviation formed from the names of Zhongli Quan and Lü Dongbin) goes back to Zhongli Quan, a figure who, in the manner of the Taoist saints, is supposed to have reappeared several times, many centuries apart. He supposedly lived under the Han, was active under the Jin in the fourth century, and appeared many times to famous masters of the Tang and Song dynasties, including Lü Dongbin, who was himself later to become legendary and considered a master by all interior alchemy schools. Lü seems to have lived in the ninth century and was a disciple of Cui Xifan (mentioned above). None of this prevented reports of frequent reappearance at later dates. (Zhongli Quan and Lü Dongbin became popular figures; as members of the group of the famous "eight immortals," they turn up as characters in Yuan theatrical productions.) The Zhong-Lü school did not take shape, however, until the Song. We know of it from anonymous texts of uncertain date, of which the most important are the *Ling-bao bifa* (prior to the twelfth century, translated by Farzeen Baldrian-Hussein), the *Chuan Dao ji*, and the *Huizhen ji*, all of which exist in several versions in the *Daozang*. Compared with other interior alchemy schools, this group gives more importance to breathing techniques and much less to the speculative side of things, but its texts certainly must be ranked among those of interior alchemy as defined above.

In the northern part of China, then occupied by the Jürchens, there appeared a school called Quanzhen (the fundamental Truth), otherwise known as the Golden Flower movement. Started by one Wang Zhe (1123–70), this movement can be termed a school since the founder established five separate congregations in 1167 and 1168. His teaching began in Shanxi and then spread into Shandong. It seems to have been limited to the poorer sectors of the population. It was only in 1183, well after Wang Zhe's death, that this movement started to be called Quanzhen, the name it retains to this day. The school's teaching is characterized by a strong emphasis on interiorization (the true journey is the inner one, the palaces to be built are inside the body, and so on) and insists on finding a happy medium between motion and stillness, between effort and spontaneity. It denies that there is a point in seeking bodily immortality; the spirit must rise above this world. This was the first movement in Taoism to require celibacy, and the founder established monasteries modeled after Chan establishments and governed by strict rules. Wang Zhe promoted a syncretism uniting the Three Teachings. He was strongly opposed to wine, sexual intercourse, anger, and the love of wealth—probably in reaction to the presence of the Mongols and their habits—and he integrated into his system both the Confucian virtues and Buddhist methods, extolling the reading of both the Confucian classics (especially the *Classic of Filial Piety*) and Buddhist sutras (the *Heart Sutra*). He preached poverty and asceticism, in direct contrast to the corruption and the wealth reportedly current among the Taoists of his time.

Seven of his disciples, the "seven true ones," became especially important. One of these was Ma Danyang (1123-83), the second patriarch of the school, who propagated the teaching of the master. Many women were accepted into the school, which grew quickly and benefited from the patronage of Jürchen rulers. Another of the group of seven, Qiu Chuji (1148-1227), was summoned by Genghis Khan, who wanted to know the secrets of longevity. His stay at the Mongol court brought great prestige and popularity to the Quanzhen school. While there, he managed to negotiate a stay of execution for the Chinese people by which two or three million lives were saved, as well as the promulgation of an edict protecting the monks of the school and giving them preeminence over all other religious groups—actions that brought many new adherents. The synthesizing character of the school attracted the educated, and thus the little sect that had found its original membership largely among villagers spread to all classes of society, even to the highest levels of the government. Its popularity peaked in the second half of the thirteenth century, but after 1225 it began to suffer from the attacks of Buddhists. In a misuse of the power over other religious groups that the imperial court had given them, they accused the school of persecuting them. Great doctrinal debates were held at the court, with the emperor as arbiter; during the course of these debates, the quarrel over the *Huahujing* (see Chapter 7) was revived, resulting in the defeat of the Taoists. Kubilai then ordered all Taoist texts except the *Daodejing* to be burned.

The Quanzhen school revived during the fourteenth century, but with its original asceticism relaxed. By this time the Celestial Masters had regained an unquestioned pre-eminence, and this may be why members of the Quanzhen school carried out great rituals and dedicated themselves more and more to exorcism. At the same time, the school's leaders moved away from their fundamental ideals of poverty and withdrawal from the world and instead solicited the privileges of power and built themselves sumptuous palaces. While some abbots lived ostentatiously, the monks themselves led a life of prayer and gathering medicinal herbs. The monasteries of the school were still active at the beginning of the twentieth century, and their main temple, the Baiyun guan in Beijing, still survives. Under the Qing the school was superseded by one of its own branch movements, the Longmen school deriving from Qiu Chuji—a school that still exists and continues the interior alchemy tradition.

In the south, separated politically from the north after 1127, a distinct interior alchemy movement continued to develop. The terms and processes used, as well as their sources, were the same as those used in the north. The movement that started in the eighth century thus underwent separate, parallel paths of development, without any clear sign of direct relations between the two schools of the north and south before the unification of China under the Yuan. Like the "seven true ones" of the Quanzhen school, the southern group counts five patriarchs (Liu Haichan [d. ca. 1050], Zhang Boduan [d. 1082], Shi Tai [d. 1158], Xue Shi [d. 1191], and Chen Nan [d. 1213]). Unlike the Quanzhen school, this group established no contact with centers of power. Most of its masters wandered around the country, and despite the group's claims to go back to Zhang Boduan, nothing that could be called a real school developed before the time of Chen Nan and Bo Yuchan (fl.

1209–24), especially after the latter became a grand master of the thunder ritual.

One of the most interesting successors of Bo Yuchan was Li Daochun (fl. 1290), the author, among other things, of the *Zhonghe ji* (DZ 249). The school was highly syncretistic, and Li freely decorated his teachings with Buddhist quotations, especially from the school of the Prajñāpāramitā, along with exegeses of Laozi and the propositions of the Chan masters. He also commented on the *Taiji tushuo* of the neo-Confucian Zhou Dunyi (cf. DZ 1060 and 249).

It is not completely clear whether Li Daochun was associated with the Quanzhen school (to which he seems to refer [DZ 249, 3.28b]) or with the southern school, to which his master belonged. But by the time of Chen Zhixu (fl. 1329–36), alias Shangyangzi, a product of the Quanzhen movement, the north-south division had ceased to be meaningful. This is shown, for example, by the case of Zhao Yizhen in the fourteenth century: he was trained by two masters, one coming from the northern school, the other from the southern. The division was by now only a historical matter; in any case, the roots were the same. The examination of interior alchemy texts does not reveal any true doctrinal divergencies, as would be expected of a synthesizing pattern of thought. The most notable difference consists in the fact that the northern school preached retreat and celibacy, whereas the *Wuzhen pian* of Zhang Boduan, for example, made it clear that adherents of the southern school need not retire from daily life: Xue Daoguang (d. 1191) and Chen Nan were craftsmen, and southern adepts in general lived very much in the world as they spread their teaching. The northern school also put more emphasis on conventional moral behavior; its texts, especially the earliest ones, warn constantly against the dangers of wine, sex, a desire for wealth, and anger. Some of its masters, such as Ma Danyang, practiced severe austerities.

Later, when the history of these movements came to be written, writers tried to find doctrinal distinctions between them. Some, for example, started to claim, and still do, that the southern school began by "cultivating the *ming*," which they equated with physiological exercises, and continued by "cultivating the *xing*."[3] This

second term corresponds to mental and spiritual phases of education. But even if one accepts these meanings for the terms *xing*
and *ming*, they are interpreted differently in various contexts.[4] It is
revealing that modern historians (among them, Li Yuanguo and
Chen, Guofu) quite unconcernedly contradict each other on the
matter.[5] Thus, the whole interpretation of differences between the
two schools is open to doubt and ultimately of little relevance. The
Zhonghe ji of Li Daochun, who opposed the contemporary separation of the *xing* and the *ming*, states that one must first empty
one's spirit by practicing the mental disciplines of observing precepts, concentration, and wisdom (the *sila*, *dhyāna*, and *prajñā* of
Buddhism) so as to rediscover the original complete and luminous
state of the *xing*, and then purify the essence, the breath, and the
spirit to preserve the body and strengthen the *ming* for all eternity. At the same time he insisted that the *xing* and the *ming* cannot survive without each other (DZ 3, 1a). Elsewhere he did not introduce work on the *xing* and the *ming* until a higher, final step,
with these concepts not coming into play in the two first stages. As
for Qiu Chuji, of the northern school, he required work on the
ming (which is Yang in nature) by day and the *xing* (with its Yin nature) by night (DZ 244, 1.11b). Wang Zhe, the father of the Quanzhen school, as well as Li Tongxuan (thirteenth c.), from the same
school, maintained that the one cannot subsist without the other
(cf. DZ 1156, 5b; and 1151, 1.3b-4a). The truth is that for both
schools *xing* and *ming* are to be worked on conjointly and that any
division of them into "before" and "after" is artificial. As Li Daochun said, one speaks of *xing* and *ming* only insofar as one is
faced by a body, by an individual (*shen*), and only in the state of
duality that came about with the division of the Primordial Chaos,
the Taiji (DZ 4, 2b). That is to say, all this is simply a matter of
wording but makes no real difference in practice. In fact, while
admitting that the adept gives first place to physiological exercises, Li Daochun insists he must before all else find his tiny internal portion of the universal breath from before the cosmos; without this his undertaking will have no meaning, and this is a
spiritual matter. As a disciple of Bo Yuchan wrote, it is necessary

first of all to purify the body, but in order to purify the body, one must know the spirit (DZ 1308, 5b).

Some authors believed (as some still do) that the southern school, or a subgroup of this school, recommended sexual practices as a means of implementing the basic principle of alchemy that one must "join the Yin and the Yang." But this inference has still not been investigated seriously and remains purely hypothetical. Many statements in interior alchemy texts oppose such sexual practices. It is highly probable, however, that some individuals interpreted certain statements in the texts literally—a thing all masters warn prospective adepts against—and indulged in sexual practices, but it seems clear that this is not what the alchemical masters were proposing. Li Yuanguo reports that one sector of the southern school claimed that successful application of interior alchemy required a couple, on the principle that neither the Yin nor the Yang exists alone and that their crossing or mating is needed for existence. But this axiom can also be found much earlier, in an eighth-century text, for example, before the establishment of these "schools" (DZ 1083, 5b and 7a). It was also set forth by Xia Zongyu (DZ 146, 2.8b), whom Li Yuanguo puts into the opposite group in the southern school, which he refers to as "pure practice," as well as by that avowed partisan of celibacy Wang Zhe (DZ 1156, 5a). On the other hand, Chen Zhixu, whom Li classes with those who are supposed to have practiced sexual techniques (Li Yuanguo, p. 410), makes it clear that in alchemy one is not dealing with spermatic *jing*, but the *jing* "that predates Earth and Heaven" (DZ 1068, 3.2b–4a; also see 11, 8b–9a). Furthermore, he states explicitly that no ingredient needed in interior alchemy practice can exist outside the body (DZ 1068, 11.7a), the kind of statement on which Li Yuanguo (pp. 410–16) builds his attempts to define partisans of the school of "pure [i.e., sexless] practice."

One can, however, observe some fairly marked differences between the Zhong-Lü movement and the northern Quanzhen and the southern school. The Zhong-Lü movement placed much more importance on physiological exercise and less on speculation. This translates concretely into the fact that it did not refer to *ming* and *xing* and did not introduce the concepts of the spark of "Original Yang" or of the "Mysterious Pass," to which we shall return below. Its point of view was less mystical, and for this reason it was sometimes expressly criticized by the other schools (e.g., DZ 1090, 8b). Furthermore, the synthesizing streak is less marked in this movement; the other two schools have a strong tendency to borrow from Buddhism (close personal contacts between their representatives and Buddhist monks are reported frequently) and to use terms from neo-Confucianism, whose masters, contemporaries of their own first masters, they quote. The Zhong-Lü texts do none of this.

Origins of Interior Alchemy

Those who practiced interior alchemy made many spectacular innovations and often proclaimed a new way, rejecting all ancient practices as false, even "perverse." But in fact interior alchemy does not represent a rupture in the continuity of the Taoist tradition. In the Shangqing school, there was a movement toward interiorization that used alchemical vocabulary. A second-generation Lingbao text (from the early fifth century) gives us another indication of this evolution. In it is a discussion of the celestial flow that moves downward and the terrestrial one that rises up, of the Yin and the Yang that pass on their power and enter into resonance (DZ 361, 2.7b), one of the fundamental points of interior alchemy doctrine. Further on, it states, "The golden cinnabar [*jindan*] is in your body," and mentions the Original Essence (*yuanjing*) (DZ 2, 13a). We see here, in these early statements, not only all the basic problematics of interior alchemy but also, with this term *yuanjing*, a fundamental notion of interior alchemy, which added the Original Essence (*jing*) to the Original Breath already known from breathing practices.

Interior alchemy also continues the tradition of the *weishu*, with its exegesis of the *Book of Change*, its speculations on numbers, its representations of the world in the form of diagrams—all elements that make up an essential part of its discourse. The study of the *Book of Change* had been neglected by orthodox literary scholars but had never ceased in Taoist circles. Interior alchemy did not treat this ancient book as a divination manual, nor, in the style of Wang Bi, as a springboard for metaphysical and ontological reflections, but as a work of cosmology, describing the world in terms of symbols (*xiang*) and numbers (*shu*). In this the alchemists continued the Han tradition and were part of a tendency also developed by Song neo-Confucianism.

Laozi and Zhuangzi are constantly cited and loom large in the school. The cosmogonic system of Laozi was superimposed on that of the *Book of Change*, in spite of the contradictions between them: the *Book of Change* divided chaos (Taiji) into two, then four, then eight, and so on, whereas Laozi has the Tao giving birth to the One, then the Two, the Three, and the ten thousand beings—interior alchemy practitioners had no trouble reconciling the two very different points of view implied.

As we have seen, ancient techniques of alchemy and breathing practices were integrated into the system. This was done by re-reading all the competing ancient texts and interpreting them in a new light. Another contribution came from the movement toward interiorization that marked the Tang era, with its somewhat contemplative texts, those of the *neiguan* group and the *Yinfujing* in particular (with the latter cited very frequently). Finally throughout its development interior alchemy relied for support more and more frequently on Buddhism—Chan in particular, but also Tiantai—and on neo-Confucianism, both of them heavily indebted to Taoism. This did not prevent the alchemists from marking themselves off clearly from these two "teachings" and insisting on their own identity: the ultimate goal might be the same, they said, but the methods of achieving it were different.

The Word That Utters Silence

"The Tao conceals itself between word and non-word," says one text (DZ 522, 5a). Another distinguishes between the "discourse" (*tan*) expressed by all the alchemical metaphors, even by seated meditation or fasting, and "transmission by the spirit," which is true realization or illumination (DZ 1067, 8.4a–b). Alchemy thus reveals itself as the heir of Zhuangzi as it pursues his reflection on the relation between word and truth, a reflection also exploited by the Chan masters. Language is only a necessary vehicle that one must transcend. The texts often express forceful opposition to words and even images and concepts, and the perversions and distortions to which they lead when they are conflated with their referents. The masters repeat ad nauseam a statement from the Great Appendix to the *Book of Change* that coincides so well with the thought of Zhuangzi, at least in the way it was developed by Wang Bi: "symbols" (*xiang*) lead to the idea, but once the idea has been reached, the symbols must be abandoned. The images offered by Zhuangzi of the boat that one leaves on the riverbank once one has crossed over, of the net that one discards once one has caught the fish, are among their clichés. The alchemical masters, however, insist that one must use the boat to cross the river and work with symbols before abandoning them.

But if alchemists had already posed the problem of language in traditional terms, the solution proposed by the practitioners of interior alchemy was completely new. Language is both an indispensable tool and an obstacle; hence it has to be both created—and the interior alchemy movement sets up a new code—and destroyed, in a continual act of refutation. This process engaged the masters constantly. Their mistrust of language was accompanied by a profound faith in language. The method used implies that the adept can be remade through a new form of language, that a new language imposes the creation of new images, new relationships, and a new man. It is considered actively effective. At the same time, it is seen as shaking up existing mental and cognitive states; it is established not only to prevent the adept from accepting the things the discourse says, but also, as Li Daochun says, to enable the adept to "discover for himself" (DZ 249, 3.27a). In good Chinese fashion, the masters use the language primarily to reveal the relationships that exist among words, the spaces between words or images. Words and images are only markers or reference points. Abstract concepts and images are on the same level and are used in pairs, with the pairs then put into relationships with other pairs along the pattern, for example, of "A is to B as C is to D." Thus what is really revealed is the relationships among them, what separates or bonds A and B, or C and D, on the one hand, and the parallelism of the relationships A-B and C-D, on the other. Once this is done, A, B, C, and D themselves become unimportant. The equivalences set forth are those of connections, correlationships; the way words and concepts are used is always more important than their actual definitions, which are inevitably so multiple and contradictory that anyone who relies on them is quickly lost. No term has meaning except insofar as it functions with or in relation to another term or several others, because it is these relationships that are most important and unite the terms, along with the organization and functioning that gives rise to them. Thus, for example, the word *xin* (heart-mind) when opposed to *shen* (the body) designates the intellect, but used alone and in an absolute sense it designates the Center, the Heart of Things, or the Spirit. The pair Dragon-Tiger can refer to the pair of Breaths, from the liver and the lungs, or that of the Spirit (*shen*) and the Breath (*qi*). This is why no meaning can be given for a term except in a specific context. One must always keep this rule in mind and make it a firm principle, with the goal being to treat all signifiers—words and images used in relation with each other—systematically as tools, seeing them in terms of the meanings they carry without stopping to examine the provisional and contingent nature of their existence. The meaning that they carry in each setting is the important thing, but this tends to destabilize them since meaning is necessarily polyvalent and the system consists of inviting the adept to hold onto this polyvalence and all its ramifications.[6]

Furthermore, silence is constantly stressed, because only in silence can the Mystery (*xuan*) and the Marvelous (*miao*) be found, with the surplus of meaning always present and always fleeting. Thus the *Zhonghe ji* (DZ 249, 6.13a) states: "Silence is the word; fundamentally in the place where the word exists there is silence; the world is silent; that is the secret formula of alchemy." A preface to the *Wuzhen pian* takes up the same idea: "The Tao has no name; the sage gave it an artificial name [allusion to the *Daodejing*]. Names and words resemble silence. . . . The Tao is made manifest by words, and words are forgotten by the Tao."

In silence, in this "forgetting," interior alchemy can rely on all means of using and abusing language by going beyond it and twisting it, in a methodical system of twists and turns. Thus, the trigrams of the *Book of Change* offer a complete set of symbols, allowing a less discursive approach to that Truth to which interior alchemy wants to open itself. Diverted from their divinatory uses, the trigrams are taken as stylized, abstract forms of fundamental truths, as ways of speaking concisely, of bringing together several levels of truth in one single sign. This is very much in the line of the *weishu* of the *Book of Change* for whom the trigrams are "ancient writing," ancient in the sense of close to the Original.[7] This economy of expression is compensated for, and opposed by, a burgeoning of freely multiplied metaphors used to designate a single datum with multiple facets, forming a configuration that can take shape in various settings. Innumerable metaphors and symbols are used, and here again we see the tendency of the Taoists to make use of symbolic thinking rather than intellectual speculation of the type used in the Mādhyamika, which is not, however, completely abandoned. Still, symbolic thinking is used to give words to the silence, which, if it remained in its raw state, could not be used to teach: so we have masses of poems and chants, paradoxes, contradictions, *gong'an* imitated from Chan, philosophical essays, dialectical games, and above all, as we shall see, a polyvalence of images as well as of words. Rediscovering the old procedures of the men of Han who transcribed the world on their divination tables, the masters also returned to cosmic diagrams (*tu*) and liked to depict their Great Task in drawings accompanied by captions that give to certain of the treatises the charm of a *Mutuus liber*. Their favored mode of expression is the *xiang*, a term heavy with meaning in the Chinese tradition and one signifying those images that Nature provides for us to see and decipher, the teaching that it thus offers for human understanding, the stars it hangs in the sky that form a "heavenly text" to be read, the delineations made on the earth by the mountains and the rivers that make up its veins. In interior alchemy this term *xiang* takes on almost the meaning of the simulacrum, the artifact, the depiction, the poor representation that reveals and reflects that which cannot be said. The master manipulates these puppets in every possible meaning as well as beyond meaning.

Alchemical language exists on two levels. It is both a language, with its own vocabulary, and a use of this language—a meta-language—that both renders the language effective and at the same time indicates its death by going beyond it. Along with this technique come others that complement it to make up an integral whole: texts on interior alchemy treat much more than this single form of discipline. It is only one of their teaching methods among many others (see, e.g., DZ 1052) or, to put it another way, the alchemical language is not the only one used.

The Circle, Surpassing

Beyond the notion of silence as surpassing language, another idea that confuses the spirit of the system is the concept of the circle, often used to illustrate the absolute or illumination. This idea is tied to the concept of the cycle, a reversible form of time. Leaving the familiar linear time that leads inexorably toward death, with its inevitable loss of energy, the adept "climbs back up the path of time," to use an image dear to interior alchemy, to find once more the Source from which he springs.

For the circle represents not only the constant repetition of cycles but also a return to the point of departure as the adept thus takes up life all over again. The circle also represents a return after having completed a loop, the discovery of identity between the beginning and the end that comes through experiencing diversity, the trip that is as important as the destination. The adept closes the circle by connecting the two complementary and mutually repelling poles, a connection, however, that does not blend them but keeps their binary nature intact; it is the principle of order and dynamism. The world is produced and disappears in the same moment of existence. Here, the circle is a symbol of a dynamic, moving unity, of complexity set up in the form of a loop, a "generative" form, as E. Morin has put it, "a looping form," where each stage is both the means to reach others and an end in itself, marking the "retrospective effect of everything as a whole on the individual moments and elements from which it emerged."[8] This binary nature is not a dualism but a polarity that is not to be abolished but integrated; it is constantly maintained and surpassed by the successive purifications that the adept passes through in the process of transformation. This cyclical process occurs in stages, in a time quite apart from linear time, a cyclical and achronic time during which the materials on which the adept works (lead and mercury, or body, breath, spirit, etc.) are progressively deepened, purified, exalted, in an upward moving, widening spiral that culminates in the universal and the ultimate truth and finally permits escape from the cycle of life and death.

All explanations of the alchemical task follow this spiraling movement. Progress is never linear but always truncated, punctuated by movements backward. Like the task itself, these explanations do not proceed in a straight line but in a labyrinthine fashion, with repetitions and returns to earlier points, circularly, repetitively, dialectically. The perpetual reiterations are never identical, thus suggesting a constant labor of renewal and enlarging of understanding.

The Symbolism of the Numbers in the "Book of Change"

The proliferation of symbols in interior alchemy makes any attempt to organize them seem futile. But in order to make an elementary explanation a little easier to follow—and recognizing the risk of oversimplification—I will explore the system of numbers and trigrams used in the texts, in a very schematic fashion.

The number One corresponds to the Taiji, the Supreme Pinnacle, and to the Tao, or to the *hundun*, original Chaos. The figure One is also symbolized by the ideas of *xin*, which can be translated as Spirit or Heart (in the meaning of Center), of *zhong*, Center, and *ho*, Harmony. It designates the vague, confused unity that ensnares most humans; at the same time, it is the complex but ordered unity that is the ultimate goal of alchemical work. It is the basic unity and the union of these two kinds of unity, that of existing unity and acquired unity; it is, finally, transcendent unity, always present in all diversity and throughout the task. The masters like to say that the task ends up by being "a single thing." The confused Unity or *hundun* (Chaos), or the Taiji, is itself the potentiality of Yin and Yang, a Unity that admits and permits the diversity for which it is the crucible, the womb of all possibility. This Taiji, a term drawn from the Great Appendix to the *Book of Change*, is one of the primordial forms of Chaos that, according to the *weishu*, succeeded one another in a slow, sequential gestation of the world in which it gradually took on concrete form.

The figure Two is represented above all by Yin and Yang, which themselves make up the totality of the interior alchemy task, itself regarded as "two things," according to the internal alchemy masters. All their statements, all the names that they give to their procedures, and all the transformations of these procedures, they say, can be reduced to Yin and to Yang—that is, to a basic binary nature that covers all possible interweaving polarities set into operation. The most common of these are the ideas of empty and full, movement and repose, constant and variable, remaining and disappearing, nature and passions, war and peace, hard and soft, black and white, shrinking and increasing (fire or activity), going up and going down, time and eternity, sacred and profane, body and spirit, and so on. (See, for example, the table drawn up by Bo Yuchan in DZ 263, 1.3a). And it is important to understand and keep in mind that each of these oppositions *always* involves the entire universe. In the symbolic language of alchemy, these principles are represented by Heaven and Earth, Dragon and Tiger, Water and Fire, Furnace and Cauldron.

Two also represents the principle of binary opposition, the principle of difference, without which there can be neither order nor, it follows, intelligibility (an idea often also expressed in Confucianism, in which a division into two rules the organization of society and culture), and without which there can be no dynamism. The masters continually repeat the statement of the *Huainanzi* that in isolation the Yin and the Yang remain sterile (see Chapter 5).

Two divides into Four, which represents an outgrowth and

repetition of the expansive and reproductive tendency in the first fission. There are four trigrams at the basis of the alchemist's work: Qian (three Yang lines), or pure Yang; Kun (three Yin lines), or pure Yin; Li (a Yin line between two Yang lines), or the Yang containing the Yin; and Kan (a Yang line between two Yin lines), the Yin holding the Yang. These Four make up two pairs, one vertical and the other horizontal. Qian and Kun are, in cosmological terms, Heaven and Earth, south and north; in alchemical terms, the Furnace and the Cauldron; and in human terms, the Spirit and the Body. Li and Kan are, in cosmological terms, the Sun and the Moon, east and west; in alchemical terms, the "ingredients," Mercury and Lead, Dragon and Tiger. Qian and Kun are the constants in the system (the "completed procedures," *chengwu*), and Li and Kan are the principles of resonance (*ganying*) and growth and exchanges (*jiaoji*). These two pairs stand in opposition to the variables (*bianhua*), which are represented by the hexagrams (cf. DZ 249, 4.18a) and give a pattern to the play of Li and Kan. According to another, complementary interpretation, the Furnace and the Cauldron are the Yin and the Yang (as binary principles), and the ingredients (Li and Kan) are the "interior and the exterior" (dedicated to exchanges); the "fire phasing" (represented by the variables) designates "measurement" (of the intensity of practice as a function of time; see DZ 1059, preface 3b).

Li and Kan are the most favored trigrams in the work of alchemical purification. Their shared quality is that each consists of two parts. In them, Yin and Yang have divided to give birth to two new, mixed forms. This concept distinguishes the ideas of the alchemists from those of Shao Yong, for whom Qian and Kun separately give birth to a Yin and a Yang. For the alchemists, they give rise to a Yang containing a Yin and a Yin containing a Yang. This is not simple fission but, so to speak, a form of sexual reproduction both of whose end products possess "genes" from the two parents. (In fact, Qian and Kun are called the Father and the Mother of the hexagrams, and the other trigrams the product of the desire of Qian for Kun and of Kun for Qian.) In a way, Li and Kan in themselves represent the Four in the form of a redivided division through conjunction of the Two, and various authors stress that this second division is produced by the *union* of the first pair, Yin and Yang. The inner line of each is, it is said, a product of the crossing of the first pair, the trace that each has left in the heart of its "child." Both Li and Kan attest that no Yang can exist without Yin, and no Yin without Yang. All A contains some B, and vice versa. Here the alchemists followed the Buddhists closely and incorporated their metaphysical notions: the Void contains the Full and vice versa. They rediscovered the *zhenwu* (true non-being) and the *miaoyou* (miraculous existence) and connected them quite naturally to the language of the *Book of Change.*

The first task of the alchemist consists in finding the "true Lead" and the "true Mercury," which are the Yin in the Yang, and, conversely, the kernel inside the fruit. On its first level, the alchemical task is carried out not on the obvious Yin and Yang, the upper Yang in Heaven and the lower Yin on Earth, but on the rising Yang that is below, grounded in the Earth, and the descending Yin that is above, coiled in the Yang. This is one of the features of the principle of "inversion," of the "inverted world," that controls alchemical practice. Unlike the usual observations among mortals, where the Yang rises to form Heaven and the Yin descends to form the Earth (cf. Chapter 5 on the cosmology of the *Huainanzi*), here the Yang is below and rises, and the Yin is above and descends. This idea, found in Zhuangzi, sees Yin and Yang as moving forces, compared to chariots; they are the inner lines of the Li and Kan trigrams, both indication and demand, sign of and desire for the first Unity. They make the world go round, permutate and crisscross, and seek to rejoin each other. Here the pair is no longer the visible and stable Yin and Yang, no longer fixed concepts, but their ungraspable operation.

The inner lines of Li and Kan are also active principles within human hearts. The original, eternal Yang, predating the formation of Heaven and Earth, tends to rise from below toward heaven, to the top of the head, whereas the original Yin tries to descend from the top into the lower depths. In physiological terms we have "the fire [Yang] in the kidneys [Yin]" for the trigram Kan, and "the water [Yin] in the heart [Yang]" for Li.

It was well understood that the binary system alone was not

enough. By itself, it would remain sterile and turn on its own axis. Alchemy infused into this binary tendency the more holistic thinking expressed by the idea of the Five Agents, a system of exchanges, resonances, correspondences, and relations in contrast to the system of binary oppositions found in the *Book of Change*. Li Daochun saw the Five as "the transformation of the primary Two," that is, their dynamic manifestation (DZ 251, 8a). He spoke not of the Four but of the Five, because the Center-One plays an integral role; it is this One, the "fifth" Agent, that allows the grouping to make a unified whole. This notion is behind the importance in interior alchemy of the Agent Earth, the "intermediary," the agent that links the pairs. It is the mute actor, the silence, a place unfixed and impossible to locate in space (transcendent) where the combination and joining of opposites takes place. It does not need to be more exactly defined and is spoken of only in its role as a mediator of conflicts. It is the Three of Laozi, giving birth to all things, and, as a central harmony, it is a cosmic principle exalted by both Laozi and Huainanzi.

The alchemists thus used the cosmogony of both the *Book of Change* and the *Daodejing*, even though they appear contradictory at first sight. In the first system, the One divides into Two, which divides into Four and then into Eight—a multiplication by successive divisions employed by Shao Yong for which the most common term used is that of *fen*, "divide." On the other hand, Laozi states that the One "gives birth" (*sheng*) to the Two and then to the Three. The term used by alchemical texts in this case is either *sheng* or *hua*, "transform." Li Daochan tended to use the term *liang* (pair), rather than *er* (two), because it suggests, according to him, a "coupling"; it is through union, he said, that there arises *gan* (impetus, emotion, resonance), and thus *biantong* (transformation and extensive communication, pervasiveness).

Thus we see that procedures in interior alchemy use different and apparently contradictory systems to arrive at complementary visions of the world: on the one hand, binarism and a system of division of 1 into 2, 4, 8, and so on; and on the other, a process of emanation in the slow, gestational emergence of the world and a dialectical system of 1, 2, and then 3. Within all this, we find also the principle of resonance and relations that lies at the heart of Five Agents thought.

Procedures

Interior alchemy is thus concerned with maintaining polarity while constantly going beyond it, by putting into action sequences of procedures that both establish a binary quality and deny it in order to transcend it. Of course, there are well-known procedures that consist quite simply in stating that the binary values make up a single whole (Laozi) or in denying their ultimate duality and considering it illusory (as in Buddhism). But although interior alchemy occasionally calls on these procedures, they are not typical if only because they do not allow one to cling to binarism except by declaring that the illusion of duality is a necessary step on the road to union and thus giving it an anagogic value, as is done in Buddhism. The unique characteristic of the interior alchemy masters, as opposed to the users of other techniques for achieving illumination, is that they put this binary nature into play, but, as an illusionist might do it, by manipulating it in a truly stunning fashion, showing it in all its aspects, so that whoever tries to follow all the twists and turns, comings and goings, is completely stupefied. Thus we see in action equivalences that superimpose on one another, contradict one another and mingle, crossings and unions of pairs, movements at once centrifugal and centripetal of contrary or similar principles, alternances, complementarities, contrasts, various changing doses of one element among others, the engendering and destruction of one principle by another or by itself, reversals of values, mutations of terms through equivalences, and changes or superimposition of levels for a single pair of principles. Opposition and reduplication are mingled.

The "invention" or "identification" of the ingredients or materials used in the task, "true Lead" and "true Mercury," Dragon and Tiger, is achieved by extraction, union and begetting, and enwrapping—operations that are similar and presented as such. "Within the Mystery there is another Mystery," says Laozi, a statement often quoted by the masters, who then add, "In the breath there is another Breath," "In the body there is another body." The more one draws out the inner essence of something, the more "pure" and "real" the resulting element is.

Each of the elements in the task is at once the product of another element and the begetter or perfecter of it, with one containing the other, enwrapping it: it "keeps" it, in the sense of protecting it, or "veils" it. The processes of conception, gestation, and begetting or birth are constantly telescoped and mingled linguistically. The adept always follows the double procedure of distinguishing two aspects—One and the Other, Water and Fire—and joining them. Giving birth and completing are so much the same thing that, in the language of interior alchemy, union, perfection, nourishment, and begetting are synonyms, and one may as easily say of the Water of the True One that it "carries" or contains the Breath of the Correct Yang as that it combines with it. Metal gives birth to Water and is its "mother," according to the cycle of begetting in Five Agents theory, but Metal is also within Water. Thus, say the masters, the "mother" is contained in her child, the begetter is the begotten. In the same way, the spirit is the "mother" of the body and is also hidden within it. Water is born of Breath and vice versa, motion is born of stillness, and vice versa (DZ 1156, 5a). Fire is in the Water (in physiological terms, "breath, the male element, which is in the *jing* [which is in the kidneys]"), just as the sun emerges from the sea; and conversely there is water in fire (in physiological terms, "the water that is in the heart"), since water cannot become steam by itself—fire is also necessary (cf. DZ 249, 3.26a).

Water rises; fire descends. This is what the masters call the "reversal" of ordinary phenomena, and historians of religion the "hierogamic exchange of qualities." Thus the trigram Li, considered usually a Yang trigram, is Yin for the alchemists, and the trigram Kan is masculine; this means not only that the inner line predominates (it is Yin) but also that values are "reversed" (*jiandao*). In an analogous fashion, men must take special care to treasure the *jing* of their kidneys, which corresponds to their *po*, Yin soul, and women must preserve the blood of their hearts, which corresponds to their *hun*, Yang soul. All must nourish their complementary principles. Each person, at all levels of the task, contains his opposite, her complement, which itself was contained within its opposite at an earlier time. It is impossible to explain in brief here all these interactions involving coproduction, compensation and antidotes, mutual devouring and integration, connivance, joining and separating, and recapitulations and returns. (On this subject, see my 1993 work on interior alchemy.) We see equivalences and movements from concrete to abstract and vice versa. Just as the matchmaker fades out of the picture when two people marry, there is a complete obliteration of the unifying totality in the presence of the resulting relationship, even though it has initiated and nurtured it.

Dragon and Tiger fight each other (*zhan*), twist around (*pan, rao*), unite (*he*), crisscross (*jiao*), respond to each other (*ying*), exchange and transform (*bian*) into each other, "acquire each other reciprocally" (*zhi*). They rise and fall, crossing over on the way, just as the cosmic Yin and Yang go up and come down. Each principle, when it reaches its culmination, reverses and turns into its opposite. The earthly Yang contained by the Yin mounts to Heaven just as the Spirit contained within a bodily mass can escape and fly upward, as light is reborn stronger as the days begin to grow longer during winter, as the sun rises in the morning, as sexual energy is raised into the brain during sexual exercises. At the same time, the celestial Yin contained within the Yang moves downward, as represented by the Water of the heart. This Yin water is born of the excess of Yang represented by the Yang Breath of the Yang heart. (This is not the only possible reference point for this Yin within the Yang; we can, for example, talk of the saliva, a fluid Yin principle, inside the Yang head.) Just so, at the beginning of summer, at the solstice, the days start to shorten and night begins to encroach on light.

Duality is constantly redoubled; it is a double, diametric dualism. These pairings can be horizontal, between the liver (Yang, Dragon) and the lungs (Yin, Tiger); or between the *po* Yin souls and the *hun* Yang souls. They can also be vertical, for example, between the kidneys (Yin, Kan) and the heart (Yang, Li), or the head (which plays the same role as the heart but at a higher level), or between the Yin fluid essence of the body (*jing*) in the north and the Yang spirit in the south. This duality is reflected even in the Center, where the earth is represented by two cyclical signs, one connected to Kan and Lead, and the other to Li and Mercury (*Shangyangzi*, DZ 1067, 6.1a–3b). It also appears in the double level maintained throughout the task: on the one hand, the human and bodily level, represented by the *jing* or "humors," the breath of breathing, and mental activity; and on the other hand, the level of eternity represented by the *jing*, the Breath and Spirit that are cosmic and even pre-cosmic.

The terms used take on different meanings according to the linkages established and the dimensions on which the linkage takes place. The attribution of meaning is systematic, because it is part of the method employed. Often, however, it is implicit, because a spirit of subtlety, flexibility, and versatility of understanding has to come into play. Thus, *xing* (basic nature), when it is paired with *qing* (the emotions), refers back to a "horizontal" dimension and corresponds to the Yang east (and the emotions to the Yin west); it is located at the middle level in the vertical, three-story scale, cosmic in dimensions, made up of Heaven, Earth, and Man. Between Heaven and Earth, when paired with the *qing*, it is connected to the Human dimension represented by the psychic level (*yi*, or "creative idea"), in opposition to the two levels of earthly physicality (*shen*, the body) and celestial spirit (*xin*; DZ 249, 3.4a–7a). When paired with the *ming*, however, it belongs to the metaphysical dimension, along with Lead and Mercury (DZ 249, 3.9b), which can also in their turn be understood in a bodily dimension.

Times, Fire Phasing

Thus, the motions and transformation of the "two principles" define the object of the alchemical task rather than the principles themselves, which provide only the framework and the instrument for these changes. The hexagrams of the *Book of Change* symbolically measure the times of these interactions, and the four basic trigrams represent the raw materials and the formal principle behind their use. The hexagrams represent motion and evolution; they mark the *tempo* of the task, the "fire phasing," that is to say, the rhythm of the action.

The alchemists organize the hexagrams into two main groups that constitute two times, the first of "yangization" and the second of "yinization," following a sequence peculiar to them not present in the *Book of Change*, even though it can be found in the *weishu*.[9] Beginning from the first hexagram, Fu, which is that of awakening Yang, with a single Yang line at the bottom and five Yin lines, the point of departure corresponding to the north or the northeast, Yang grows continually, passing through hexagrams that variously contain two, three, four, and five Yang lines, until it reaches the hexagram Qian, that of complete Yang. This process of increasing the Yang principle is one aspect of the "countercurrent" (*ni*) still practiced by alchemists. In the normal run of things, a young man of sixteen possesses a maximum amount of potential Yang vitality, which he gradually loses; when this is completely exhausted, the human being becomes "pure Yin" and dies (see, e.g., DZ 1068, 7.5a–b). This natural process is reversed by the alchemists, who accumulate Yang. But instead of starting from a stock of "pure Yang," as does the ordinary young man of sixteen,[10] they start from a simple "allocation of Yang." This is a clear sign that this is not ordinary Yang, certainly not simple semen, as, for example, Liu Ts'un-yuan[11] has held; nor is it a matter of sexual practices intended to preserve Yang. As the text we have just cited puts it, along with many other texts, we are here dealing with "true Yang." The situation is reversed, and the basic material is completely different.

One reaches the Qian hexagram, Heaven, when pure Yang has been achieved, when the "brain has been restored," that is to say, when the Yang line of Kan has risen to replace the Yin line of Li (to the south and upward), which gives, in the system of the trigrams, three Yang lines. When this pure Yang is achieved, there is a momentary halt in the labor, a pause before a turn in the inverse direction. Then, beginning from the hexagram Gou, the inverse of Fu (a single rising Yin line at the bottom, with five Yang lines above), yinization proceeds to Kun, complete Yin, the Earth (see, e.g., DZ

249, 2.3a and 3.19a). The period of yangization is one of activity (*youwei*), that of yinization one of stillness (*wuwei*, non-action). Shangyangzi (DZ 1067, 5.5a–b) called this yinization time "Yin alchemy" (literally, "Yin cinnabar," *yindan*). During this time, he said, one works with "interior" ingredients, as opposed to the former time of using "exterior" ingredients. That is to say, during this time one relies, for example, on breathing techniques. Here is the paradigm for one of the many understandings of the terms "interior alchemy" and "exterior alchemy," or "Yin cinnabar" and "Yang cinnabar."

Total yinization, represented by the trigram Kan, signals a return to the root and to stillness. It is the "exhaustion of the Tao [that is to say, of the task] and the return to the Kun-Origin." One reaches the moment when "the six Yin [lines] are exhausted and the Yang has not yet emerged." "Heaven and Earth being not yet separated, the divine immortals complete their Elixir in this moment." For, adds Yu Yan (1258–1314), Yang is not born from the hexagram Fu but from Kun, the Great Yin (DZ 1005, 6.7b–8a).

This course of events is related to phases of the waxing and waning moon, in a clear symbolism of light increasing or decreasing, as well as to the cyclical signs (the earthly branches indicating the time of day) and the seasons of the year. The alchemists rediscovered the cosmological reference points of the Han and encapsulated the dimensions of the year, the month, and the day, one inside the other. The task can be completed either in a year, a month, or a day, or, to put it differently, the same task goes on simultaneously on various scales, in nested phases one inside the other. A yinization period in the daily cycle can come to an end within the framework of a yangization period in the annual cycle. The growing and decreasing proportions of Yin and Yang are also expressed in terms of dosages of Lead (Yin) and Mercury (Yang), or of activation of Fire (Yang) and use of Water (Yin).

"Fire phasing" represents the variation in the system; the masters have always kept the details of this process secret. It cannot be revealed in any precise fashion and can be transmitted only orally from master to disciple, since its very nature is to be unfixed and to depend finally on each particular case presented by the work undertaken by an individual disciple. It constitutes the ungraspable element, always in motion, the essential dynamism of the whole, of which only the structure and the general orientation can be traced, as I have just done in brief.

In any case, fire phasing has nothing to do with time as measured by the cyclical signs, years, months, and days, fixed in precise fashion by various authors. So it was stated by Bo Yuchan (DZ 263, 6.3a). Fire phasing, says a commenter on Zhang Boduan, is not the observation of the hours of *zi* (midnight, hour of complete Yin) and *wu* (noon, hour of complete Yang), winter and summer solstices (with the same symbolism). Purification does not happen at the hours of *mao* or *you* (corresponding, within the day, to the equinoxes, a balance of Yin and Yang). In the human being, the fire that moves upward and "around the sky" spontaneously has times of speeding up and slowing down and times of purification. This cannot be connected with seasonal rhythms (no. 262, 5, 9a).

The Stages

Time and the principle of mutation that it symbolizes and makes concrete also enter into the idea of stages or steps. Three stages are generally distinguished, from the coarsest to the most subtle. First, there is that of the *jing* (essence, fluid, liquid principle) or the *shen* (body); according to various texts, *jing* has a physiological connotation as a vital power of subtle and potential state (see, e.g., DZ 1017, 37.10a). Reference is often made to Laozi's statement (*Daodejing* 21) that *jing* is the promise of life contained in Chaos. The second stage is that of *qi* (breath, energy); the third is that of *shen* (spirit). All the oldest Taoist texts, for example, the *Taipingjing*, refer to *jing, qi,* and *shen,* but do not always give the terms the same meaning. To formulate the stages in a dynamic perspective, which is the most accurate way of looking at them, the first stage goes from the *jing* to the *qi*, the second from the *qi* to the *shen,* and the third from the *shen* to the Tao or to the Void. Often interior alchemy texts attach a qualifying statement: this is not the ordinary *jing*, the spermatic essence or fluids of the body, nor is it *qi* in the sense of the breath of respiration, nor even ordinary *shen*, that of discursive thought. But none of these qualifications prevents one at certain times from working with these "ordinary" manifestations.

At each of these three stages the practice is the same, but the "ingredients" on which the alchemist works are refined and consequently change. Thus, even when the same terms are used—Lead, Mercury, Dragon, Tiger—they do not designate the same realities. The operations carried on—purification, extraction, combination, and so on—are repeated almost identically, but the procedure is directed into a rising and widening path culminating in infinity. The authors use parallelisms and even conflate the paradigmatic sequence with the syntagmatic chain so that the succeeding episodes and various materials are treated as interchangeable and identical.

Some thinkers, like Li Daochun (see, e.g., DZ 249, 2.6a–b), tie the three stages to "fire phasing." The first step, from *jing* to *qi*, is the initial moment of awareness or "gathering" of the spark of eternal Yang found in the depths of man, in the center of the Kan trigram of water (fluid, *jing*). This is considered either as lying in the lower part of the body, in the kidneys or lower cinnabar field, or as transcendent and not to be located specifically. It is the first mover of the whole task, that is, the desire to carry out the work of taking control and the ability to see the direction the work must take are the necessary first steps in the task. (Certain authors speak of the *yi*, the creative idea, the intention, and make of this the *ji*, the inner source.) We are dealing with the realization that there are such things as the *jing*, *qi*, and *shen*, they make up a single unit, and they are not the coarse *jing*, *qi*, and *shen*, which are only elements of "external" alchemy (DZ 249, 2.6a), that is, the elements of the classical Taoist techniques for circulation of the breath. In other terms, inner alchemy begins where exercises on the "coarse" breath, that of respiration, end. At this stage, it is a matter above all else of recognizing the "moment" (*shi*) of awakening and catching it ("as one catches a thief"; DZ 240, 2.13b). It is the moment indicated by the hexagram Fu and the cyclical sign *zi*, of rebirth, and by the "gathering" of the "true" ingredients, the moment that begins the alchemical dynamic and its retrograde evolution, the "reversal," the return from later, worldly time to an earlier time, that of alchemy, the time of eternity before Heaven and Earth existed, the time of pure Yang and pure Yin.

The second stage, the movement from *qi* to *shen*, is often given a precise meaning by exterior alchemy. This is the step of yangization. It moves, as we have just seen, from the hexagram Fu to Qian. Here one makes ingredients go around, up, and down; one activates them. In other words, it is the implementation of what was discovered during the first stage, the repetition of the initial "gathering," purifications in the form of extractions, and an ever more profound interiorization achieved by the repeated combining of the two basic principles, always under differing aspects. This is often described in great detail using both physiological and alchemical terms; it is the phase of "action."

But the task does not stop there, for a third step has to follow, one that is less discussed. This is the return to the void or to the Tao, or to the "original nature," or even to the motionlessness that underlies action, the inaction that follows the activity represented by the conscious practices carried out up to this point. This second part of fire phasing is yinization in the sense that Yin is the principle of immobility and invisibility. For Li Daochun, it is symbolized by the Yin line of the Li trigram, a lack of image and thus mental emptiness. The adept is compared to the dragon who guards the pearl, to a chicken who broods on her egg, to a fish in the water, and in this stage, action becomes so subtle and tenuous that it is compared to the delicate "cooking of little fish" referred to by Laozi. In Li Daochun's diagram (DZ 249, 2.2b) the stage of *shen* in the void, represented by a simple circle ◯, is in the middle, between the designs that represent the first stage ◉, which is at the bottom, and the second stage ⊙, at the top. This ultimate stage, which for one text consists in returning to the *ming* (physical, bodily nature) from the *xing*, is essential: if one does not "collect" the true void and does not practice non-action, one has completed only half the task. To collect is to concretize (DZ 240, 15b). The true void, once again, is said by all the masters not to be nothingness (the "useless void") but a state of complete darkness and stillness from which light and movement burst forth. "That which alchemy [*danjia*] calls the void [*xuwu*] is neither non-mental [*wuxin*] nor non-thought [*wunian*] nor the 'dead wood and the burnt cinder' [an expression from Zhuangzi describing the ecstatic state]," wrote Yu Yan (DZ 1005, 5.6b), for whom these states are only stages.

These three stages, Li Daochun tells us (DZ 249, 2.5a), represent only external alchemy, in a usage of this term peculiar to himself. Other authors express the same idea by saying that the three stages are only ways of speaking, heuristic distinctions. In interior alchemy all that matters is the spark of "true eternal Yang" represented by the inner line of the Kan trigram, which is in fact the inner line from Qian, pure Yang, as it enters into union with Kun, pure Yin, its counterpart. The essential is to consolidate it and to "return" it (that is, to recognize it for what it is) to the "ancestral breath," which is not that of physical breathing but the original Breath, the cosmic Yuan Qi.

Subitism, Spontaneity

With this apparent denial of the actual existence of the stages, we now confront the problem of subitism, or instantaneous vision similar to that in Buddhism. This problem was broached by interior alchemy authors, but in their own particular way. Obviously these authors, like all those from whom they derive, go against the grain of the truly instantaneous strain of traditional Taoism in their gradualism, as they develop and describe a form of teaching, cultivation, and education that can only be long and progressive. But this does not prevent them from insisting that a "sudden grasping," to use the term coined by Rolf Stein, is essential and must always accompany the process of mental ascesis: an intuitive, global vision that is the concretizing of the unity underlying, accompanying, and looming over the inherent duality of word and deed. Thus, Chen Nan, among others, stated that all is contained in oneness, at "one single time, which is one single place, and one single thing" (DZ 1090, 14a). Li Daochun explained that the time (*shi*, the moment of initial opening when one must "collect") is not really time, but neither is it outside time, without which one could not begin the task (DZ 249, 3.31a).

This "moment," described as blinding, when "suddenly" (*huran*) something emerges that "transports" (*haoran*, the word used by the Confucian philosopher Mengzi), is most often described as an opening, a "mysterious pass" (*xuanguan*, recalling the *sanguan*, the "three passes" of the vertebral column in subtle physiology), called the Opening One of the Mysterious Pass or the Mysterious Female by Laozi. This Pass, say these authors, is not to be found, as the ancient breathing techniques taught, in the cinnabar field or between the kidneys, and in fact it has no precise location: an unplaceable opening in an eternal time, that is, outside time, which is "so big that nothing is outside it, and so small that nothing is inside it" (a formula traditionally applied to the Tao; DZ 240, 2.11b). Everything is in it, the winter solstice (the moment when breathing exercises or alchemical work must begin), the ingredients, fire phasing, purification, the knotting of the embryo, and deliverance: the beginning, middle, and end. Zhang Boduan here added, adopting the same attitude as that found in Chan, that this opening cannot be transmitted except "by the heart and the mouth," that is, directly by a personal drive (DZ 263, 5.4a–b).

Radicalism and globalism—the unity inherent in the process of alchemical work—are expressed in a thousand ways, too varied to be reported here. And Li Daochun is not the only one to insist on this moment (*ke*), the "single thought," which must be eternally repeated. In its tininess it has the tenuousness of a single thought, but in its vast expansiveness it can hold the world. In this moment can be completed the work of a year, but inasmuch as it is constantly repeated, it fits into the length of a year and undergoes a slowing-down through fire phasing (DZ 249, 4.3b). By its constant presence, the moment—a denial of history and binarism, an expression of the permanence of oneness throughout multiple development—is part of the permanent negation of the entire system, a negation intrinsic to the system. But all the authors also insist on the progressive work to be accomplished—on the production of the world (*zaohua*), on the process to be followed, which is just as important as the goal to be reached and which moves through the use of the symbols (*xiang*) of external alchemy, which one must not take literally and must finally reject and surpass.

In this they clearly differ from the adherents of Chan. The latter, they say, grasp only the *xing*, the "original nature" in its purity, intuitive, and immediate vision. The practitioners of interior alchemy criticize Chan for rejecting all exterior practices, and they welcome, as we have seen, both breathing exercises and ritual. The Chan adepts neglect *ming*, which, in the language of the interior alchemists, represents the resistant, corporeal, weighty part of human beings. It is this part of our makeup that requires constant work, a vocation that also involves the "incarnation" or concretization of the primordial celestial intuition. A conflation of *xing* and *ming* is needed, a joining of activity and stillness into the "non-action that is action." Without the *ming*, the *xing* bogs down in an inactive, futile void; without the *xing*, the *ming* cannot arrive at "non-action" (DZ 1067, preface 2b; see also 15b). Interior alchemy adepts want to join instantaneity and gradualism, spontaneous intuition and ongoing effort, into a synthesis that is an "acquiring of the innate" with a view to fixing an innate presence that is otherwise fugitive and immaterial. They regard themselves as "Yang spirits," completely unlike Chan monks, whom they call "Yin ghosts," incapable of truly incarnating and concretely manifesting their vision. This follows from the idea that ghosts (*gui*) belong to the domain of the invisible, the Yin, and human beings to that of the visible, the Yang (see DZ 263, 47.15a).

Noumenal and Phenomenal Worlds

The necessary conjunction of the instantaneous and the gradual, of eternity and the moment, is represented by the conjunction of the *xiantian* and the *houtian*, the *xing* and the *qing*, or the *xing* and the *ming*. The *xiantian* (literally, "before heaven") is the world of *noumena*, "before heaven and earth," the eternal world of the innate (the "original nature," *xing*), of which man holds within him, even before his birth, a tiny piece called the "spark of the original

Yang," a light that appears above the furnace, like the light of the moon when the clouds suddenly part, in "a blinding moment without time" (DZ 240, 2.13a–b). It is the domain of non-action. The *houtian* is the world of phenomena, the "later world" of passions (*qing*)—which waver and change—of movement, of change, represented also by the term *ming*. This is the world of action (see, e.g., DZ 005, 5.3b).

Above all one must rediscover in quietness what we possess of the *xiantian*, the "original nature" (*yuanxing*), the true heart-mind (*zhenxin*), which is found in the straying *xin* (heart-mind) and is not distinct from it (DZ 240, 2.19a–b—on this last point the author of this text differs from both the Buddhists and the Confucianists). Those who have not understood the principle of "before Heaven" but try to make the *jing* fluid and the *qi* breath "move up and down" are only charlatans teaching "illusory alchemy" (*huandan*). In other words, they lack the "moment," the fermenting agent, the spark of original Yang, which is the only tool, the driving force behind the sought-for refinement, the dimension of eternity. Nevertheless, he continues, the "light of the original *jing* [fluid]" cannot appear without the "light of the everyday *jing*." In the same way, the original spirit (*shen*) can do nothing without the spirit of everyday life (*riyong shen*, the spirit of "everyday use"). This line of thinking rejoins, in a more imaged and probably more lived fashion, that of Wang Bi, for whom *you* (existence) emerges from *wu* (non-existence) but who added that the *wu* cannot manifest itself without the *you*.

We have a good example of the paradoxical attitudes beloved of the alchemical masters in a text by Chen Zhixu in which he reversed the facts. He explained that the "method of the *houtian*" is that of non-activity: the spark of Yang from the time before the formation of the world that gave birth to all things should simply be protected from all attack. On the other hand, he says that in the domain of *xiantian* (before Heaven) the desire of Qian for Kun and that of Kun for Qian give rise to the mixed trigrams Li and Kan and reveal themselves as resembling human desires; hence the alchemical task should be to reverse the process, to re-establish Qian and Kun in their purity (DZ 1068, 11.8b–9b).

The Interaction of the Different Levels

Complementary to the temporal ideas of stages, or fire phasing, a more spatial dimension of levels and planes plays a permanent role. In the *Zhonghe ji* (DZ 249, 3.6b–7a), for example, Li Daochun first distinguishes three levels: that of the Taiji, where the duality is that of Heaven and Earth, which is the cosmological level; that of the *Book of Change* with the pairing Qian/Kun; and that of the Tao, with Yin and Yang. Here the level of the Tao is thus the level of metaphysical principles and the level of the *Book of Change* that of their application. Li Daochun then proceeds from these three levels to three others: that of human beings, that is to say, as we can see from the language used, that of the psycho-physiological domain; that of symbols (*faxiang*); and that of alchemy (*jindan*). At each level in this second group, the three levels in the first group are repeated. On the human level, the level of Heaven/Earth is expressed in terms of *xing* (form) and *ti* (body, substance); the level of Qian/Kun in terms of nature (*xing*) and passions (*qing*); and that of Yin-Yang in terms of spirit (*shen*, which is Yang) and breath (*qi*, which is Yin, in relation to *shen*). On the level of symbols are, in the same order, the pairs dragon/tiger, horse/bull, and (sun) crow and (moon) hare. On the alchemical level, the pairings are cauldron/furnace, Metal/Earth, lead/mercury.

Earlier in this text (3.4b), Li distinguishes three different levels that make up three "ways" (*dao*) on the level "of the person" (*shen*): the way of the Heart (corresponding to Heaven), with the pairing spirit/breath; that of the Body (*shen*) corresponding to the Earth, or to materiality, with the pairing "form" (*xing*) and "substance" (*ti*); and the way of the Idea (*yi*), which plays the role of the Center in alchemy, with the pairing *ren* (sense of humanity) and *yi* (sense of duty). These three features of Heart-Body-Idea, which form a trio related to Heaven-Earth-Man, are a borrowing from Buddhism, which is thus integrated into the triadic classification system of Taoism and traditional China. We have here once again one of the procedures used by Taoism to integrate Buddhist notions.

In another work Li Daochun (DZ 251, 2.11a–b), commenting on

the *Taiji tushuo* of Zhou Dunyi, distinguishes between the bodily level and the psycho-physiological level (the *xingming*). On the bodily level the eight basic trigrams of the *Book of Change* are matched with the natural physical elements that the *Book of Change* assigns them: Heaven-Earth, Water-Fire, Thunder-Wind, Mountain-Lake. On the psycho-physiological level, these same trigrams stand for different features (five of which are traditionally connected with the five viscera): body, mentality (*xin*), essence (*jing*), soul (*shen*), the Yang *hun* soul, the Yin *po* soul, idea (*yi*), and breath.

To this layering of stages corresponding to points of view that complement each other are added further distinctions of levels corresponding to the level at which the adept works, depending on his degree of awareness of himself and the world. A table in the *Zhonghe ji* (DZ 249, 2.12b–17a) sums these levels up in three "vehicles," in addition to a fourth, predominating and unique one (*zui yi sheng*). In the first, lower vehicle, the Furnace and the Cauldron are the body and the spirit; the ingredients are the Essence (*jing*) and the Breath; Water and Fire are the heart and the kidneys; the Mysterious Pass is located between the navel and the kidneys. The goal consists of fusing the Five Agents. From the evidence we have, this involves psycho-physiological techniques translated into alchemical and physical terms. This level is developed mostly in texts from the Zhong-Lü school.

At the second, middle level, Qian and Kun correspond to the Cauldron and the Furnace, and Kan and Li to Water and Fire. The Five Agents are the five psycho-physiological features mentioned above (*jing, shen, hun, po,* and *yi*); the Tiger and the Dragon stand for the body and the spirit (*xin*); the "true seed" is the Breath (*qi*); fire phasing is measured out in seasons through the course of a year; the Mysterious Pass is located in the *niwan* (in the brain, thus at the summit of the body, no longer down below). The goal consists of uniting the Essence and the Spirit (*jing* and *shen*). This is a method of nourishing life (*yang ming*), and the dimension is less physical and more psychological.

At the third, the upper level, the Cauldron and the Furnace are

Heaven and Earth; Water and Fire are the sun and the moon; the Dragon and the Tiger stand for "nature" (*xing*) and the passions; the Mysterious Pass is the Heart (the center). The goal is reached when nature and passions are united. Here, the dimension is more exclusively cosmic and psychic. The "life" that is to be "consolidated" is called *sheng* and no longer *ming*, which has physical connotations.

The unique and predominating fourth vehicle is clearly patterned after the Unique Vehicle of Buddhism. Here the Cauldron is the Great Void; the Furnace, the Taiji; the cinnabar foundation is serenity, its mother non-action; Lead and Mercury are the *xing* and the *ming* (the two poles, spiritual-heavenly and physical-earthly, of the personality); the Water and Fire used are concentration (*ding*) and insight (*hui*). The goal is reached when *xing* and *ming* fuse. There is no longer any bodily element involved, except in a general way in the term *ming*.

Another example of this division into "vehicles" can be found in a text (DZ 276, 14a–15b) by Niu Daochun (late thirteenth century) of the northern school. For him, in the "great vehicle" the Furnace is the "great void," and the Cauldron is "the true void"; the ingredient is "awakening" (*yuanming*, a Buddhist expression, literally "perfect, round light") and the activating fire is the celestial light. In the "middle vehicle" the Furnace is the trigrams Qian and Kun, the Cauldron is Yin and Yang, the ingredients are "true Lead" and "true Mercury," and fire is the "true Yang." In the "little vehicle" the Furnace is the body; the Cauldron, the *xin* (the spiritual center); the ingredients, Breath and Spirit; the fire, luminous awareness. The lowest level of the little vehicle takes the body as the furnace, the viscera as the Cauldron, *jing* (here spermatic essence) and blood as ingredients, and the circulation of the breath as fire. Here we see the physiological techniques that characterize most particularly the Zhong-Lü school among the schools of interior alchemy.

Thus we have schemas (there are others of the same type; see, e.g., DZ 263, 4.1b–2a) that outline the system in a clear fashion. Most of the time in the texts, however, the various levels are mingled because of a double didactic procedure. First, the master is addressing disciples with varying levels of skill, and each of them (according to the main basic didactic principle of Buddhism) understands according to his own ability: thus, a single word may be understood in various ways. In addition, from the point of view of the basic, ultimate unity of all that is said, these various levels coexist and, eventually, fuse into one and are thus neutralized by one another and incomplete by themselves.

Here we see the Buddhist system of *panjiao* (classification of the teachings) and *yuanjiao* (comprehensive teaching) being applied in alchemical work and to Taoism in an original fashion. The various practices and schools of Taoism are reunited in a hierarchical whole that culminates simultaneously in the wiping out of the hierarchy and its unifying synthesis into a unitary globalism that transcends them all.

At whatever level it is practiced, however, alchemy always seems to contain both a speculative and theoretical part and an experimental part, a praxis. This praxis may be physical, as in the Zhong-Lü school, but it may be simply mental, psychic, and purely mystical, as at the third level and the "supreme" level. The basic distinction between interior alchemy and the respiratory practices lies in this feature.

To sum up, the essential difference between interior alchemy and Chan, according to the Taoist authors, lies in the fact that internal alchemy begins "at the bottom," in the *ming*, the "resistant," opaque, physical or psycho-physiological part, in experimentation and the real of the concrete; only later does it move toward the *xing*, which is connected with the domain of speculation and abstraction (*wu xing*, without physical form). Moving from abstraction (*xing*) toward the concrete (*ming*) is like trying to catch the moon in the water (DZ 240, 2.12a–b). One must make the *xing* grow out of the *ming*, that is, one must work on the *xing* that resides in the *ming*. This is the first stage in the growth of Yang; then one must return to the *ming*, beginning from the *xing*. This is what in this context is involved in yinization, the return to the physical world (DZ 240, 2.15b). Thus, the loop is closed after a long detour. It is this detour, this journey, that the interior alchemy masters consider the defining quality of their discipline. Although it is unlike ancient Taoist practices as well as those of Chan and neo-Confucianism, the Taoists reiterate that all derive from the One Source and all have the same ultimate goal.

Conclusion

Today Taoism is reduced to two extreme, complementary tendencies: ritual and interior alchemy. Ritual lies entirely in the hands of the Celestial Masters, who officiate on Taiwan as well as on the mainland when the situation permits. It fulfills an extremely important social role; the Masters preside over local festivals, funerals, and expressions of popular religiosity. Ritual helps people to cope with mental threats—demons, hallucinations, and the like—as well as physical ones, especially sickness. The Celestial Masters are both exorcists and healers. The popular nature of this strain of Taoism has grown constantly, as I have briefly indicated. Continuing a development already well under way under the Song, it has assimilated more and more cults addressed to local popular gods. Strong "shamanistic" elements have been incorporated into it as well: the grand master is accompanied by a medium. However, although the ritual is vastly different from that seen in earlier texts, it is still the direct heir of a long history. Its practitioners are aware of this, even if they know little about writings on ritual and its great variety through time.

The outward form of these ceremonies and, to a certain degree, the spirit in which they are conducted are certainly not the same as those of the major official ceremonies carried out by the great masters under imperial orders. A strong dramatic element— paper horses and messengers, firecrackers, little comic plays, all giving the atmosphere of a popular festival that is somehow still an integral part of the ceremony—gives the ritual a somewhat different tone. But the same texts are recited, and it is not hard for the informed spectator to identify them. The establishment of the sacred area and the gestures of the head priest follow the same symbolic rules. We are in the same world. The "interior altar," the role of silent recitation and meditation, and the interior ritual still survive and remain quietly central and predominant.

But this popular setting should not lead us to forget, as certain ingrained attitudes might suggest, the "literary" nature of Taoism that complements this setting. Michel Strickmann surprised the scholarly world when he showed that under the Six Dynasties the Shangqing revelation spread widely throughout aristocratic circles. This is a tendency that has always existed in Taoism, and the "literary" strain can reveal itself in many fashions. The biographies of Taoists reveal that they had often had literary training, that they developed as Taoists while retaining their standing among their literary brethren. When writers produced works in honor of Taoist friends, they included epitaphs praising their literary talents and culture. The Taoist masters themselves were often talented poets, and their works teem with references to the Confucian classics, the *Shijing*, the *Zuozhuan*, the *Zhongyong*, and reveal their precise knowledge of both Confucian and Buddhist texts.

It is mainly among the masters of interior alchemy, who belong generally to the Quanzhen school, that this tradition has persisted. Y. Yoshioka, who visited a monastery belonging to this school in 1940, described the austere life led there, consecrated to praying, chanting texts, and gathering herbs. These monasteries, of which some examples survive in Taiwan, were vacated in China but are now being occupied again, at least in certain cases, by a few monks. It seems that the true tradition of interior alchemy has been maintained principally, both in Taiwan and in mainland China, among those masters who have withdrawn to temples located in the mountains, going back generally to the Longmen school (the "dragon's gate," a school supposedly founded by Qiu Chuji). They are part of a line of transmission with a list of masters that has been carefully preserved. No serious study has been made of this transmission, but it seems that the techniques taught are unquestionably in a direct line from the originals.

These techniques, however, tend to be confused with simple breathing techniques, called *qigong* ("breath work"), which are extremely popular in Taiwan and mainland China and about which much has been published. This development accentuates the physiologic aspect of interior alchemy, to the detriment of cosmological speculations and spiritual and intellectual training, in some cases to the point of obscuring them completely. As a result, some publications that claim to be about interior alchemy treat it as no different from *qigong*, which belongs more to the general stock of things Chinese than it does to Taoism proper. This practice, however, is only the most obvious visible phenomenon and does not preclude the continued existence of pure interior alchemy.

Thus, starting from a worldview with roots deep in the Chinese history, a view that took form under the Han, Taoism has built up, both in its liturgy and in its meditative practices, a method based on images, one that allows the faithful to emerge from the "chaotic" state of symbiosis with the world and define their place within it before transcending it. Taoist language has always done this through images and symbols; there is never any true theoretical and methodical development in it, and it has swallowed up the more conceptual language of Buddhism, blending it with that of the *Book of Change*. However, we should not allow ourselves to be fooled about this language. Its map of the world is in itself a theory, an ontology, and an epistemology, a whole grouping of propositions on the structure and development of reality, and manipulation of this map is a reflection on the knowledge it puts forward.

The cosmic wanderings of visionaries, copied by the priest as he paces out the liturgical area, conjoining himself to and echoing the First Unity that diffuses and multiplies itself throughout the world; the art of disappearing into non-being because it includes being and is the only way of transcending life and death; astonishment before the emergence of thought and light; the integration of doubt and the rejection of demoniac forces that incarnate false thinking; the taking over of a language considered halting and values assumed to be relative—Taoism is a complete world and its history is a complete human history, containing everything since the emergence of human beings on earth and their desire for transcendence. It is a history that throughout the centuries has preserved a single identity. Through all its variations, this firm identity has allowed Taoism to renew itself constantly and at various levels, where we can still see its features being perpetuated or re-emerging. Its syncretic nature, its multiple facets, are in no way opposed to a unity of inspiration and a continuity that we can follow easily through all its avatars. This inspiration and continuity mean that without knowing Han cosmology, one cannot understand either Song or modern alchemical texts, or even the modern liturgy; and without knowing the pattern of development of Taoism, a great deal of their meaning will be missed.

Unlike other religions, we must look for the fundamental structure, the unity, and the continuity of Taoism in its cosmological discourse and not in its pantheon, which is always proliferating and almost without structure, changing with time and along many lines. In the history of Chinese thought, Taoism was the harbinger of Han cosmological thought, which maintained itself through Taoism in the face of the revolution wrought by Buddhism. Buddhism brought to China a more conceptual, more rhetorical discourse, a more linear pattern of thought, a deep-seated anti-cosmological vision—all elements that would give birth in China to an opposing current represented by the School of Mystery and later by Neo-Confucian thought. This countercurrent resulted in the great seventeenth-century criticism of cosmological thought. But Taoism survived as an active oppositional embodiment of correlative, "morphological" thought based on a theory of universal empathy and of cosmic correspondences and interactions, working on a trinary system, itself growing out of the binary system of the *Book of Change.* As an active, living entity, it has evolved constantly by adapting, enriching, and developing itself through constantly renewed internal and external alluvia. It is remarkable that never, at any time, did it close in on itself. Throughout its history, it has faced up to various challenges, even some that could have threatened the fundamental organization of its world. Perhaps because it was weaker in terms of the power relationships that structure society, it is the only one of the Three Teachings to openly assimilate elements from opposing currents and engage in dialogue with them. Taoism cites them, borrows terminology and ideas from them, works them over—sometimes refashioning them—and assimilates them. It has enriched itself at their expense, enlarging and extending itself, without ever abandoning its own cosmological vision and without ever forgetting its goal: to sublimate humanity and not to leave it behind.

Perhaps Taoism has been able to survive because from its origin Taoists have regarded their cosmological discourse as a formative tool, a method intended to shape human beings and thought, and because Taoism does not claim to give an exact accounting of external, "worldly" reality. Pragmatically, didactically, the basic tool rendered necessary services: healing and achieving illumination. Reality, whether ultimate or external, was held to be unknowable; the center of attention is humankind—human beings and the world, human beings in the world—and it is they who must be "saved." Taoism does not describe. It teaches a way of seeing, feeling, and distinguishing and reconciling things. Then, like the artisan of Zhuangzi, Taoists manipulate this tool to the point of going beyond ("forgetting") that mastery. Taoism either marginalized itself or was pushed into a marginal position. But, there too, it seems that it simply continued its original tradition and vocation, without losing any of its strong vitality, as is attested by its presence in all periods and throughout all levels of society.

Deeply nominalist, like Buddhism but unlike Confucianism and Legalism with their realistic tendency, Taoism has, since its origin, set at the basis of its discourse the powerlessness of the word and of thought. Taoists have always considered that the images they borrowed from Han thinkers and with which they built their fantastic visionary structures were only images, a conventional "language" that they must transcend. This may be why the deconstruction characteristic of the literate classes' speculations on cosmology could not affect them—it was carried on in the name of a scientific and rational truth or reality which is not that of Taoism. Thus, the contradictions inherent in the cosmological system that Taoists adopted could not upset them. The truth of Taoism does not lie in description but in efficacy, in psychic resonance, and the meaning to be found in its language is not descriptive but mystical and religious, that is to say, operative within human awareness. Its usefulness is connected not to rational coherence, but to ritual efficacy, which makes us part of a cosmological movement and a moving context with which we are able to move and transform ourselves along the lines of the continual transformations of the primordial Unity, to go beyond ourselves, and to move toward the ever-present Origin.

Reference Matter

Notes

Introduction: Definitions and Controlling Concepts

1. L. Kohn, *Taoist Mystical Philosophy: The Scripture of Western Ascension* (Albany: State University of New York Press, 1991).

2. R. Stein, "Religious Taoism and Popular Religion from the Second to Seventh Centuries," in H. Welch and A. Seidel, *Facets of Taoism* (New Haven: Yale University Press, 1979), pp. 53–81.

3. M. Meslin, *L'expérience humaine du divin* (Paris: Editions du Cerf, 1988), pp. 260–71.

4. See particularly K. M. Schipper, "Taoist Ritual and Local Cults of the T'ang Dynasty," *Zhongyang yanjiyuan guoji Hanxuehui yilun wenji* (Taiwan), pp. 101–16, reprinted in M. Strickmann, ed., *Tantric and Taoist Studies in Honour of R. A. Stein*, vol. 3, *Mélanges Chinois et Bouddhiques* 22 (1985); and H. Doré, *Recherches sur les superstitions en Chine* (Shanghai, 1921), vol. 6, chap. 2.

5. E. Zürcher, *The Buddhist Conquest of China*, 2d ed. (Leiden: Brill, 1959), p. 87. The *Xuanxue*, or School of Mystery, was a group of thinkers belonging to the intelligentsia of the second and third centuries. With their metaphysical tendency, completely new to China, they speculated on "non-being" and "being" (see Chapter 7), but there was nothing religious in their thought. They based themselves mainly on Laozi, Zhuangzi,

and the *Book of Change* and tried to make a synthesis between "philosophical" Taoism and Confucianism.

6. This idea is very "modern" and corresponds closely to the idea of "contradictory duality" in S. Lupasco (*Du devenir logique et de l'affectivité* [Paris: Vrin, 1935]; new ed. [1973], vol. 1). Yang may be compared to the notion of "extensivity" and Yin to that of "intensivity" explained in that work. Along the same lines, the explanations of E. Morin of "organizational opposition" is a very enlightening approach (see *La méthode*, vol. 1, *La nature de la nature* [Paris: Editions du Seuil, 1977], esp. pp. 118–23 and 228, where he takes up Yin and Yang specifically).

7. See F. Jullien, *Procès ou Création* (Paris: Seuil, 1989). Jullien has made himself the spokesman for neo-Confucianists; unfortunately he adopts their viewpoint on Buddhism and Taoism and does not take into account their complete misunderstanding of these religions.

8. See J. Lagerwey, *Wu-shang pi-yao* (Paris: Ecole française d'Extrême-Orient, 1981), pp. 89–90.

9. See J. Lévi, *Les fonctionnaires divins* (Paris: Le Seuil, 1989), pt. 3, "Identité et bureaucratie divines," pp. 203ff, where everything that Lévi says can be applied to the Taoist adepts who also *shou* the gods, in the sense of "observing a cult," "watching over a territory" (p. 211), and collect them (pp. 211–12); but with this qualification, that the emperor that Lévi speaks of "assembles" under his banner only certain gods, the "god officials" above whom he places himself, but not Shangdi, the supreme God.

10. See R. Stein, "Aspects de la foi jurée en Chine," *Annuaire du Collège de France*, 1966–67, pp. 411–15, and 1967–68, pp. 453–57.

11. See A. Seidel, "Imperial Treasures and Taoist Sacraments: Taoist Roots in the Apocrypha," in M. Strickmann, ed., *Tantric and Taoist Studies* (Brussels: Institut belge des hautes études chinoises, 1983), 2: 291–371.

12. See J. Lévi, "Les Fonctions religieuses de la bureaucratie céleste," *L'Homme* 101 (1987): 35–58.

Chapter 1 The Warring States

1. See A. Waley, *The Way and Its Power* (New York: Grove Press, 1958), p. 178nn3–4; and R. G. Henricks, "The Philosophy of Lao tzu Based on the Ma-wang-tui Texts: Some Preliminary Observations," *Bulletin of the Society for the Study of Chinese Religions* 9 (1981): 59–69.

2. P. Demiéville, "Enigmes taoïstes," in *Choix d'études sinologiques* (Leiden: Brill, 1973), pp. 141–48.

3. E. Chavannes, *Mémoires historiques de Se-ma Ts'ien* (Paris: Maisonneuve, 1967), 3: 436-37.

Chapter 2 New Elements Under the Han

1. See E. Chavannes, *Mémoires historiques de Se-ma Ts'ien* (Paris: Maisonneuve, 1967), 3: 463-66.

2. Ibid., 2: 125.

3. *Jinwen* was a hybrid of Confucianism and cosmological theories and speculations based on Yin-Yang and Five Agents theories. Its aims were to establish a way of governing in accord with the rhythms of the universe as they are described by these theories, to decode the warnings sent by a Heaven that was seen to control the acts of men, especially the ruler, and to sanction them insofar as they conformed to morality and the good functioning of the cosmos.

4. The *Yijing* (*Book of Change*) is well known to Western readers, who have at their disposal many translations of this text. Traditionally this text was dated to the Zhou dynasty, but the texts were put into shape between the fourth and the first century B.C. It contains hexagrams (six lines, either solid, *yang*, or broken, *yin*, whose combination is felt to represent all possible situations) accompanied by concise, enigmatic texts, along with commentaries made up of more or less deformed divinatory sentences that often have nothing or little to do with the texts. It has been considered both a manual of divination and a cosmological work giving in cryptic form all the workings of the universe. It is part of the heritage of Confucianists, who include it among their classics, as well as of the Taoists, who have always made it an object of contemplation.

5. See also "Les quatre canons de l'empereur jaune," trans. J. Lévi, in *Dangers du discours* (Aix-en-Provence: Alinéa, 1985), pp. 171-80.

6. A. Seidel, *La divinisation de Lao Tseu dans le taoïsme des Han* (Paris: Ecole française d'Extrême-Orient, 1969), pp. 50ff.

Chapter 3 The Celestial Masters

1. H. Maspero, *Taoism and Chinese Religion* (Amherst: University of Massachusetts Press, 1981), pp. 381-82.

2. Here and elsewhere the numbers given after the titles of texts in the Taoist Canon (*Daozang*) are those given in the catalog published by the Ecole Française d'Extrême-Orient. Such numbers will be preceded by the abbreviation DZ to distinguish them from other parenthetical references.

3. The School of Mystery, influenced by Taoism, adhered to the idea of

withdrawal from society, an attitude fundamentally opposite to Confucian tradition. They also exalted spontaneity and creativity. The School of Names, closer to Confucianism and Legalism, considered as essential for personal development an individual's involvement in society. This school favored political values and methods that assured order.

4. See K. M. Schipper, "Neighborhood Cult Associations in Traditional Tainan," in G. W. Skinner, ed., *The City in Late Imperial China* (Stanford University Press, 1977), pp. 651–76.

Chapter 4 Ge Hong and His Tradition

1. This reference is to Ware's translation of the *Baopuzi*, as are the parenthetical references later in this chapter.

2. It has been claimed that there exists also an ideal of "non-intervention" in Confucianism, but the difference is that this depends on a respect for the rites and morality established by the Sage-Founders of civilization. Here, it is simply by adjusting oneself to the Tao that everything falls into place.

3. Ngo Van Xuyet, *Divinisation, magie et politique dans la Chine ancienne* (Paris: Presses universitaires de France, 1976), p. 193.

4. See H. Maspero, *Taoism and Chinese Religion* (Amherst: University of Massachusetts Press, 1981), and I. Robinet, *Taoist Meditation* (Albany: State University of New York Press, 1993).

5. See Marc Kalinowski, "Les traités du *Shuihudi* et l'hémérologie chinoise à la fin des Royaumes Combattants," *T'oung Pao* 72 (1986): 175–228 (especially pp. 203–4 where Kalinowski shows that the calculation of auspicious and inauspicious days discussed by Ge Hong requires a procedure that goes back to the third century B.C. In addition, the system mentioned on p. 191 is also found in the *Zhen'gao*, a Shangqing text).

6. For example, a whole passage from the *Baopuzi* (11.1a–b) is found in a *weishu* of the *Xiaojing* (Yasui Kōzan and Nakamura Shōhachi, *Ishō shūsei* [Tokyo], 5.57). This passage is also found in the *Wu fu xu*, 388, 2.2a. These reduplications confirm the links between this text and the *weishu*.

7. See Maspero, *Taoism and Chinese Religion*; and R. Van Gulik, *Sexual Life in Ancient China* (Leiden: E. J. Brill, 1974).

8. See Rolf Stein, *The World in Miniature: Container Gardens and Dwellings in Far Eastern Religious Thought*, trans. Phyllis Brooks (Stanford: Stanford University Press, 1990), especially pp. 1–116. (This book is the translation of the revision and expansion of Stein's "Jardins en minia-

ture d'Extrême-Orient," *Bulletin de l'Ecole française d'Extrême-Orient* 42 [1943]: 1-104.)

Chapter 5 The Shangqing School

1. See, however, the works of Edward H. Schafer; e.g., *Mirages on the Sea of Time: The Taoist Poetry of Ts'ao T'ang* (Berkeley: University of California Press, 1985).

2. See I. Robinet, *Taoist Meditation: The Mao-shan Tradition of Great Purity* (Albany: State University of New York Press, 1993), pp. 100-103 (trans. of *Méditation taoïste* [Paris: Dervy-Livres, 1979], pp. 155-60).

3. See M. Granet, *Danses et légendes de la Chine ancienne* (Paris: Presses universitaires de France, 1959).

4. Ibid.; and the translation of the *Shanhai jing* by R. Mathieu, *Etude sur le mythologie et l'ethnologie de la Chine ancienne* (Paris: Collège de France, 1983).

5. Granet, *Danses et légendes.*

6. See M. Kalinowski, "Les instruments astro-calendériques des Han et la méthode *Liu ren*," *Bulletin de l'Ecole française d'Extrême-Orient* 72 (1983): 309-412 (esp. pp. 346 and 412).

7. See E. H. Schafer, *Pacing the Void: T'ang Approaches to the Stars* (Berkeley: University of California Press, 1977).

Chapter 6 The Lingbao School

1. See M. Granet, *Danses et légendes de la Chine ancienne* (Paris: Presses universitaires de France, 1959).

2. See K. M. Schipper, *Le corps taoïste* (Paris: Fayard, 1982), pp. 33-45.

3. See U.-A. Cedzich, "Das Ritual der Himmelmeister im Spiegel früher Quellen" (Ph.D. diss., Julius-Maximilians-Universität, Würzburg, 1987).

4. See Yasui Kōzan and Nakamura Shōhachi, *Ishō shūsei* (Tokyo, n.d.), 1: 1 and 81.

5. See P. Andersen, "The Practice of Bugang," *Cahiers d'Extrême-Asie* 5 (1989-90): 15-53.

6. See R. Stein, "Religious Taoism and Popular Religion from the Second to Seventh Centuries," in H. Welch and A. Seidel, eds., *Facets of Taoism* (New Haven: Yale University Press, 1979), pp. 53-81.

Chapter 7 The Tang Period

1. See E. Zürcher, *The Buddhist Conquest of China*, 2d ed. (Leiden: Brill,

1959), chap. 6; A. Seidel, *La divinisation de Lao tseu dans le taoïsme des Han* (Paris: Ecole française d'Extrême-Orient, 1969); and L. Kohn, *Laughing at the Tao: Debates Among Buddhists and Taoists in Medieval China* (Princeton: Princeton University Press, 1995).

2. When the Taoists undertook these specifically Chinese assimilation processes, we should remember that they were doing what the Buddhists had already done under the Six Dynasties (316–589). At that time, in order to adapt better to Chinese culture, they had identified the Five Agents with their four elements (*mahābhūta*), and the five Confucian virtues with the five Buddhist moral principles (see A. Wright, *Buddhism in Chinese History* [Stanford University Press, 1971], pp. 37–38). Under the Tang they continued to work at this assimilation by setting up complex sets of correspondences (see. R. Birnbaum, "Introduction to the Study of Tang Buddhist Astrology," *Bulletin of the Society for the Study of Chinese Religions* 8 [1980]: 12ff).

3. F. Jullien, *Procès ou création* (Paris: Le Seuil, 1989), *passim*.

4. The tetralemma, or double dilemma, is a teaching process, an exercise of the spirit intended to become an existential experience; it translates a mystical truth that opens into the *epochè*. It requires that one transcend the opposition between negation and affirmation. One begins with the fact that every affirmation contains a negation of that which it is not; only the non-affirmation of whatever may exist of the particular can take into account the totality. Yet at the same time the particular must be retained, even the part of it that contains the negative-privative, because it cannot be excluded from the totality. All this is condensed into a four-part formula under the following pattern of abstraction: (1) affirmation; (2) negation (to reject the negative in every affirmation); (3) affirmation of the combined negation and affirmation; and (4) negation of these two. These positive and negative signs (+ and –) can be applied to all sorts of ideas, truth and non-truth, existence and non-existence, etc., and should lead to a going-beyond, a rejection of the entire system that is an integration of + and –, and vice versa; what the Taoists call *miao you* (marvelous existence) and *zhen wu* (true non-existence). "Marvelous existence" is "wondrous" in that it becomes extraordinary because it is affirmation as well as because it includes its opposite rather than denying it (both on the logical as well as the existential plane). Existence begins on the basis of "nothing," non-existence, which it must thus include, since this is what permits it to be. "True non-existence" is real in that it includes existence and thus acquires the status of a true affirmation; it is negation both by containing all affirmation, by being possible, and by its lack of particular-

ity—all that exists being essential both to each individual existence and to all, which implies that the idea of individual existence, even if it is real in the sense of necessary to life, is illusory, but also that this general correlativity is the source of life. For a longer and more scholarly development of these ideas, see, among others, the article on "Do" by J. May in the *Hobogirin* encyclopedia.

5. For a description of one such sacred mountain, see Edward H. Schafer's monograph *Mao Shan in T'ang Times*, Society for the Study of Chinese Religions, Monograph no. 1 (1980); 2d rev. ed. (Boulder, Colo., 1989).

Chapter 8 Under the Song and the Yuan

1. See *Fozu tongji* 44.274b (*Xuzang jing* ed.); cf. M. Kalinowski, "La transmission du dispositif des neuf palais sous les Six dynasties," in M. Strickmann, ed., *Tantric and Taoist Studies* (Brussels: Institut belge des hautes études chinoises, 1985), 3: 786-87.

2. In a work by the Buddhist Zongmi (780-841) we find a drawing consisting of half-black, half-white circles and illustrating the progressive purification of the *alāya-vijñana*. This prefigures the Taiji one and doubtless inspired it (DZ 48, pp. 411, 413). See I. Robinet, "The Place and Meaning of the Notion of Taiji in Taoist Sources Prior to the Ming Dynasty," *History of Religions* 1990: 406-7.

3. This use of these terms comes from separating the two elements of the Chinese binome *xingming*, which meant "life." In this way the physical aspect of life was distinguished from the psychic aspect.

4. For example, for Wang Zhe, the *xing* and the *ming* are located at the level of the "true breath," in direct opposition to the physiological level, which is that of the "breath and the blood" (DZ 1156, 2a).

5. See, e.g., Li Yuanguo who claimed that the northern school preaches the "cultivation" of the *xing* over that of the *ming* (*Daojiao qigong yangsheng xue*, Sichuan sheng shehui kexueyuan chubanshe, 1988, pp. 372 and 454ff); Chen Guofu asserts the contrary (*Daozang yuanliu kao*, Peking, 1962, p. 27).

6. In this regard we still need to find out whether *neidan* was simply developing and pushing to an extreme the poetic procedures of the Tang writers (see F. Cheng, *L'écriture poétique chinoise* [Paris: Le Seuil, 1977]).

7. See, e.g., Yasui Kōzan and Nakamura Shōhachi, *Ishō shūsei* (Tokyo, n.d.), 1A: 78-79.

8. E. Morin, *La méthode*, vol. 1, *La nature de la nature* (Paris: Le Seuil, 1977), p. 183.

9. See Yasui Kōzan and Nakamura Shōhachi, *Ishō shūsei*, 1: 141.

10. See M. Granet, *Etudes sociologiques sur la Chine* (Paris: Presses Universitaires de France, 1953), pp. 208-10.

11. Liu Ts'un-yan, *Selected Papers from the Hall of Harmonious Wind* (Leiden: Brill, 1976), p. 207.

Suggestions for
Further Readings

The following lists of suggested further readings are highly selective. I begin with a few books that treat Taoism in a general way or deal with modern practice. I then present, for each chapter, a selection of articles and books connected with the topics discussed in that chapter. Bibliographic data on works cited in the text are given in the endnotes. This list, therefore, supplements citations in those notes. It does not constitute in any way a comprehensive bibliography.

For an exhaustive bibliography on the entire field of Taoist studies, see Anna Seidel, "Chronicle of Taoist Studies in the West, 1950–1990," *Cahiers d'Extrême-Asie* 5 (1989–90). The bibliographies in this study have been brought up to date by Franciscus Verellen in his contribution entitled "Taoism" in "Chinese Religions: The State of the Field (Part II). Living Religious Traditions: Taoism, Confucianism, Buddhism, Islam and Popular Religion," *Journal of Asian Studies* 54 (1995): 322–46.

General Works

Kaltenmark, M. *Lao tseu et le taoïsme*. Paris: Le Seuil, 1965. English trans.: *Lao Tzu and Taoism*. Trans. Roger Greaves. Stanford: Stanford University Press, 1969.

Kohn, L. *Taoist Experience: An Anthology*. Albany: State University of New York Press, 1993.

Lagerwey, J. "'Les têtes des démons tombent par milliers': Le *fachang*, rituel exorciste du nord de Taiwan." *L'Homme* 27, no. 1 (1987): 101–16. English trans. in Tsao Peng-yeh and Daniel P. L. Laew, eds., *Studies of Taoist Rituals and Music of Today.* Hong Kong: Chinese University of Hong Kong, Chinese Music Archive, 1989, pp. 66–73.

Saso, M. *The Teachings of Taoist Master Chuang.* New Haven: Yale University Press, 1978.

Schipper, K. M. *Le corps taoïste.* Paris: Fayard, 1982.

Welch, H., and A. Seidel, eds. *Facets of Taoism.* New Haven: Yale University Press, 1979.

Zhao Bichen, *Traité d'Alchimie et de Physiologie taoïste.* Trans. C. Despeux. Paris: Les Deux Océans, 1979.

Chapter 1 The Warring States

Studies

DeWoskin, K. *Doctors, Diviners, and Magicians of Ancient China: Biographies of Fang-shih.* New York: Columbia University Press, 1983.

Harper, D. "A Chinese Demonography of the Third Century B.C." *Harvard Journal of Asiatic Studies* 45, no. 2 (1985): 459–98.

———. "The Sexual Arts of Ancient China as Described in a Manuscript of the Second Century B.C." *Harvard Journal of Asiatic Studies*, 47, no. 2 (1987): 539–93.

Kalinowski, M. "Les traités du *Shuihudi* et l'hémérologie chinoise à la fin des Royaumes combattants." *T'oung Pao* 72 (1986): 175–228.

Robinet, I. "Chuang tzu et le taoïsme religieux." *Journal of Chinese Religions* 11 (1983): 59–105.

———. *Les commentaires du Tao tö king jusqu'au 7e siècle.* Mémoires de l'Institut des hautes études chinoises. Paris, 1977, pp. 24–56.

Translations

Erkes, E. *Ho-shang-kung's Commentary on Lao-tse.* Ascona, Switz.: Artibus Asiae, 1956.

Graham, A. C. *Chuang tzu, the Inner Chapters.* London: George Allen & Unwin, 1981.

Hawkes, D. *Ch'u Tz'u: The Songs of the South, an Ancient Chinese Anthology.* Oxford: Oxford University Press, 1959.

Lau, D. C. *Lao Tzu, Tao Te Ching.* Harmondsworth, Eng.: Penguin Books, 1963.

Pastor, J. C. *Zhuang zi: Les chapitres intérieurs.* Paris: Le Cerf, 1990.

Rickett, W. A. *Kuan-tzu.* Hong Kong: Hong Kong University Press, 1965.

Watson, Burton. *The Complete Works of Chuang Tzu.* New York: Columbia University Press, 1968.

Chapter 2 New Elements Under the Han

On the *Fangshi* and the Immortals

DeWoskin, K. J. *Doctors, Diviners and Magicians of Ancient China: Biographies of Fang-shih.* New York: Columbia University Press, 1983.

Kalinowski, M. "Les instruments astro-calendériques des Han et la méthodes *Liu ren.*" *Bulletin de l'Ecole française d'Extrême-Orient* 72 (1983): 309–419.

———. "La transmission du dispositif des neuf palais sous les Six dynasties." In M. Strickmann, ed., *Tantric and Taoist Studies.* Brussels: Institut belge des hautes études chinoises, 1985, 3: 773–811.

Kaltenmark, M. *Le Lie-sien tchouan.* 2d ed. Paris: Collège de France, 1987.

Ngo Van Xuyet. *Divination, magie et politique dans la Chine ancienne.* Paris: Presses universitaires de France, 1976.

Robinet, I. "The Taoist Immortals: Jesters of Light and Shadow, Heaven and Earth." *Journal of Chinese Religions,* no. 13/14 (1985–86): 87–107.

Yü Ying-shih. "Life and Immortality in the Mind of Han China." *Harvard Journal of Asiatic Studies* 25 (1964–65): 80–120.

On the Huang-Lao School and Laozi

Seidel, A. *La divinisation de Lao tseu dans le taoïsme des Han.* Paris: Ecole française d'Extrême-Orient, 1969.

Huainanzi: Translations and Studies

Larre, C. *Le traité VII du Houai nan tseu.* Paris: Institut Ricci, 1982.

Larre, C.; I. Robinet; and E. Rochat de la Vallée. *Les grands traités du Huainan zi.* Paris: Le Cerf, 1993.

Le Blanc, C. *Huai-nan tzu: Philosophical Synthesis in Early Han Thought.* Hong Kong: Hong Kong University Press, 1985.

Le Blanc, C., and R. Mathieu, eds. *Mythe et philosophie à l'auve de la Chine impériale.* Montreal and Paris: Presses de l'Université de Montréal, 1992.

Robinet, I. "Des changements et de l'invariable, de l'unité et de la multiplicité, analyse comparative des chapitres 11, 13 et 18 du *Huainan zi.*" *Cahiers du Centre d'études de l'Asie et de l'Est* (Université de Montréal), 1990.

Wallacker, B. E. *The Huai-nan-tzu, Book Eleven: Behavior, Culture and the Cosmos.* New Haven, Conn.: American Oriental Society, 1962.

On Popular Religion

Seidel, A. "Geleitbreif an die Unterwelt—Jenseitvorstellungen in dem Graburkunden der späteren Han Zeit." In G. Naundorf et al., *Religion und Philosophie in Ostasien.* Würzburg, 1985, pp. 161–84.

———. "Traces of Han Religion in Funeral Texts Found in Tombs." *Dōkyō shukyō bunkai,* 1987, pp. 23–57.

Chapter 3 The Celestial Masters

Cedzich, U.-A. "Das Ritual der Himmelsmeister im Spiegel früher Quellen." Ph.D. diss., Julius-Maximilians-Universität, Würzburg, 1987; review by A. Seidel, "Early Taoist Ritual," *Cahiers d'Extrême-Asie* 1988, no. 4: 199–204.

Eichhorn, W. "T'ai-p'ing und T'ai-p'ing Religion." *Mitteilungen des Instituts für Orientforschung* (Berlin) 1957, no. 1: 113–40.

Kalinowski, M. "La transmission du dispositif des neuf palais sous les Six dynasties." In M. Strickmann, ed., *Tantric and Taoist Studies.* Brussels: Institut belge des hautes études chinoises, 1985, 3: 773–811.

Kaltenmark, M. "The Ideology of the *T'ai-p'ing ching.*" In H. Welch and A. Seidel, eds., *Facets of Taoism.* New Haven: Yale University Press, 1979, pp. 19–52.

Kandel, B. *"Taipingjing": The Origin and Transmission of the "Scripture on General Welfare." The History of an Unofficial Text.* Mitteilungen der Gesellschaft für Natur- und Völkerkunde 75. Hamburg, 1979.

Lagerwey, J. *Wu-shang pi-yao: Somme taoïste du VIe siècle.* Paris: Ecole française d'Extrême-Orient, 1981.

Maspero, H. *Le taoïsme et les religions chinoises.* Paris: Gallimard, 1971, esp. pp. 41–44, 318–30, 407–23. Trans. Frank A. Kerman, Jr., *Taoism and Chinese Religion.* Amherst: University of Massachusetts Press, 1981.

Mather, R. "K'ou Ch'ien-chih and the Taoist Theocracy and the Northern Wei Court, 425–451." In H. Welch and A. Seidel, eds., *Facets of Taoism.* New Haven: Yale University Press, 1979, pp. 103–22.

Stein, R. "Les fêtes de cuisine du taoïsme religieux." *Annuaire du Collège de France* 1971–72: 431–40.

———. "Quelques aspects des paroisses taoïstes." *Annuaire du Collège de France* 1968–69: 466–71.

———. "Remarques sur les mouvements du taoïsme politico-religieux au IIe siècle ap. J. C." *T'oung Pao* 50, nos. 1–3 (1963): 1–78.

Strickmann, M. "Therapeutische Ritual und das Problem des Bösen im frühen Taoismus." In G. Naundorf et al., *Religion und Philosophie in Ostasien.* Würzburg: Könighausen und Neumann, 1985, pp. 185-200.

Chapter 4 Ge Hong and His Tradition

Studies

Akahori, A. "Drug Taking and Immortality." In L. Kohn, ed., *Taoist Meditation and Longevity Techniques.* Ann Arbor: University of Michigan, Center for Chinese Studies, 1989, pp. 73-98.

Despeux, C. "Gymnastics: The Ancient Tradition." In L. Kohn, ed., *Taoist Meditation and Longevity Techniques.* Ann Arbor: University of Michigan, Center for Chinese Studies, 1989, pp. 225-62.

Engelhard, U. *Die klassische Tradition der Qi-übungen (qigong).* Wiesbaden: Franz Steiner Verlag, 1987.

———. "Qi for Life: Longevity in the Tang." In L. Kohn, ed., *Taoist Meditation and Longevity Techniques.* Ann Arbor: University of Michigan, Center for Chinese Studies, 1989, pp. 263-96.

Maspero, H. *Le taoïsme et les religions chinoises.* Paris: Gallimard, 1971, pp. 481-589. Trans. Frank A. Kerman, Jr., *Taoism and Chinese Religion.* Amherst: University of Massachusetts Press, 1981, pp. 309-430).

Needham, J. (and N. Sivin). *Science and Civilisation in China,* 4: 210-323.

Robinet, I. "Metamorphosis and Deliverance from the Corpse." *History of Religions* 19, no. 1 (1979): 57-70.

———. *Taoist Meditation: The Mao-shan Tradition of Great Purity.* Trans. Julian F. Pas and Norman J. Girardot of *Méditation taoïste.* Paris: Dervy-Livres, 1979. Albany: State University of New York Press, 1993.

Stein, R. "Les fêtes de cuisine du taoïsme religieux." *Annuaire du Collège de France,* Paris, 1970-71: 431-40.

Translations

Feifel, E. Trans. of chaps. 1-4 of the *Baopuzi:* "Pao-p'u-tzu *nei p'ien.*" *Monumenta Serica* 6 (1941): 113-311; 9 (1944): 1-33; 11 (1946): 1-32.

Huang, J., and M. Wurmbrand. *The Primordial Breath: An Ancient Chinese Way of Prolonging Life Through Breath Control. Seven Treatises from the Taoist Canon, the Tao Tsang.* Torrance, Calif.: Original Books, 1987.

Ware, J. R. *Alchemy, Medicine, and Religion in the China of A.D. 320; The Nei P'ien of Ko Hung.* Cambridge, Mass.: M.I.T. Press, 1966. Reprinted—New York: Dover Publications, 1981.

Chapter 5   The Shangqing School

Studies

Andersen, P. "The Practice of Bugang." *Cahiers d'Extrême-Asie* 5 (1989–90): 15–53.

Robinet, I. *Taoist Meditation: The Mao-shan Tradition of Great Purity.* Trans. Julian F. Pas and Norman J. Girardot of *Méditation taoïste.* Paris: Dervy-Livres, 1979. Albany: State University of New York Press, 1993.

———. *La révélation du Shangqing dans l'histoire du taoïsme.* Paris: Ecole française d'Extrême-Orient, 1984.

———. "La pratique du 'tao,' la transmission de textes sacrés, les paradis terrestres et cosmiques, la marche sur les étoiles." In *Mythes et croyances du monde entier: Chine.* Paris: Editions Lidis, 1986, pp. 369–98.

Stein, R. *The World in Miniature: Container Gardens and Dwellings in Far Eastern Religious Thought.* Trans. Phyllis Brooks of *Le Monde en petit: jardins en miniature et habitations dans la pensée religieuse d'Extrême-Orient.* Stanford: Stanford University Press, 1990.

Strickmann, M. "The Mao Shan Revelations, Taoism and Aristocracy." *T'oung Pao* 63, no. 1 (1977): 1–64.

———. "On the Alchemy of T'ao Hung-ching." In H. Welch and A. Seidel, eds., *Facets of Taoism.* New Haven: Yale University Press, 1979, pp. 123–92.

———. *Le taoïsme du Mao Shan, chronique d'une révélation.* Paris: Collège de France, 1981.

Translations

Andersen, P. *The Method of Holding the Three Ones: A Taoist Manual of Meditation of the Fourth Century A.D.* Studies on Asian Topics, 1. London: Curzon, 1980.

Kroll, P. "The Barrier of Heaven." *Etudes Asiatiques* 60, no. 1 (1985): 22–39.

———. "In the Halls of the Azure Lad." *Journal of the American Oriental Society* 105, no. 1 (1985): 75–94.

Porkert, M. *Biographie d'un taoïste légendaire: Tcheou Tseu-yang.* Paris: Collège de France, Institut des hautes études chinoises, 1979.

Schafer, E. H. "The Jade Woman of Greatest Mystery." *History of Religions* 17 (1978): 387–98.

Chapter 6 The Lingbao School

Ancient Lingbao

Bokenkamp, S. R. "Death and Ascent in Ling-pao Taoism." *Taoist Resources* 1, no. 2 (1989): 1-21.

———. "Sources of the Ling-pao Scriptures." In M. Strickmann, ed., *Tantric and Taoist Studies*. Brussels: Institut belge des hautes études chinoises, 1983, 2: 434-486.

Kaltenmark, M. "Ling-pao: Note sur un terme du taoïsme religieux." *Mélanges de l'Institut des hautes études chinoises*, no. 2 (1960): 559-88.

Zürcher, E. "Buddhist Influences on Early Taoism: A Survey of Scriptural Evidence." *T'oung Pao* 66, nos. 1-3 (1980): 84-147.

Messianic Movements

Schipper, K. M. "Millénarismes et messianismes dans la Chine ancienne." *Acts of the XXVIth Conference of Chinese Studies* (Ortisei-Ulrich, Italy), 1978, pp. 31-49.

Seidel, A. "The Image of the Perfect Ruler in Early Taoist Messianism: Lao tzu and Li Hung." *History of Religions* 9 (1969-70): 216-47.

———. "Le sutra merveilleux du Ling-pao suprême, traitant de Lao tseu qui convertit les barbares (le manuscript S 2081): Contribution à l'étude du Bouddho-taoïsme des Six Dynasties." In M. Soymié, ed., *Contributions aux études de Touen-houang*. Paris: Ecole française d'Extrême-Orient, 1984, 3: 305-52.

Ritual

Boltz, J. "Opening the Gates of Purgatory: A Twelfth-Century Taoist Meditation Technique for the Salvation of Lost Souls." In M. Strickmann, ed., *Tantric and Taoist Studies*. Brussels: Institut belge des hautes études chinoises, 1983, 2: 487-511.

Chavannes, E. "Le jet des dragons." *Mémoires concernant l'Asie orientale* 3 (1919).

Lagerwey, J. "Introduction to the History of Taoist Ritual Through the T'ang." Forthcoming.

———. *Taoist Ritual in Chinese Society and History*. New York: Macmillan, 1987.

Saso, M. *Taoism and the Rite of Cosmic Renewal*. Pullman: Washington State University Press, 1972; 2d ed., 1990.

Schipper, K. M. *Le Fen-teng: rituel taoïste.* Paris: Ecole française d'Extrême-Orient, 1975.

Schipper, K. M., and Wang Hsiu-huei, "Progressive and Regressive Time Cycles in Taoist Ritual." In *Studies of Time,* vol. 4. N.p.: International Association for the Study of Time, n.d.

Strickmann, M. "The Longest Taoist Scripture." *History of Religions* 17 (1978): 331-54.

———. "The Taoist Renaissance of the Twelfth Century." Address given at the Third International Conference on Taoist Studies (Unterägeri, 1979). *Proceedings,* forthcoming.

Chapter 7 The Tang Period

Barrett, T. "Taoism Under the T'ang." In Denis Twitchett, ed., *The Cambridge History of China,* vol. 3, *Sui and T'ang China,* pt. II. Cambridge, Eng.: Cambridge University Press, forthcoming.

Benn, C. "Religious Aspects of Emperor Hsüan-tsung's Taoist Ideology." In D. W. Chappell, ed., *Buddhist and Taoist Practice in Medieval Chinese Society.* Asian Studies at Hawaii, 34. Honolulu: University of Hawaii Press, 1987, pp. 127-46.

———. "Taoism as Ideology in the Religion of Emperor Hsüan-tsung (712-755)." Ph.D. diss., University of Michigan, 1977.

Köhn, L. *Early Chinese Mysticism: Philosophy and Soteriology in the Taoist Tradition.* Princeton: Princeton University Press, 1992.

———. *Seven Steps to the Tao: Sima Chengzhen's "Zuowanglun."* Monumenta Serica Monographs, 20. Nettetal: Steyler Verlag, 1987.

———. "The Teaching of T'ien-yin-tzu." *Journal of Chinese Religions* 15 (1987): 1-28.

Robinet, I. *Les commentaires du Tao tö king jusqu'au 7e siècle.* Mémoires de l'Institut des hautes études chinoises. Paris, 1977, pt. II.

Verellen, F. *Du Guangting (850-933), taoïste de cour à la fin de la Chine médiévale.* Collège de France, Mémoires de l'Institute des hautes études chinoises, 20. Paris, 1989.

Chapter 8 Under the Song and the Yuan
History and General Works

Boltz, J. M. *A Survey of Taoist Literature, Tenth to Seventeenth Centuries.* Berkeley: University of California Press, 1987.

Li Chih-ch'ang. *Travels of an Alchemist: The Journey of the Taoist Ch'ang-*

ch'un from China to the Hindukush at the Summons of Chingiz Khan.
Trans. Arthur Waley. London: G. Routledge & Sons, 1931.

Sun K'o-k'uan. "Yü Chi and Southern Taoism During the Yuan Period." In
J. D. Langlois, ed., *China Under Mongol Rule.* Princeton: Princeton University Press, 1981, pp. 212-53.

Thiel, J. "Der Streit der Buddhisten und Taoisten zur Mongolenzeit."
Monumenta Serica 20 (1961): 1-81.

Yao Tao-chung. *"Ch'üan-chen: A New Taoist Sect in North China During the Twelfth and Thirteenth Centuries."* Ph.D. diss., University of Arizona, Tucson, 1980.

Interior Alchemy

Baldrian-Hussein, Farzeen. *Procédés secrets du Joyau magique—Traité d'alchimie taoïste du XIe siècle.* Paris: Les Deux Océans, 1984.

Chang Po-tuan. *Understanding Reality: A Taoist Alchemical Classic, with a Concise Commentary by Lui I-ming.* Trans. T. Cleary. Honolulu: University of Hawaii Press, 1987.

Knaul, L. *Leben und Legende des Ch'en T'uan.* Würzburger Sino-Japonica, no. 9. Bern and Frankfurt: Peter Lang, 1981. (Special issue of *Taoist Resources* 2, no. 1 [1990], ed. S. Bokenkamp and L. Köhn [= Knaul]: entire issue dedicated to Chen Tuan.)

Robinet, I. "L'alchimie interne dans le taoïsme." *Cahiers d'Extrême-Asie* 2 (1986): 241-52.

―――. *Introduction à l'alchimie intérieure taoïste: de l'unité et de la multiplicité.* Paris: Le Cerf, 1995.

―――. "La notion de *hsing* dans le taoïsme et son rapport avec celle du confucianisme." *Journal of the American Oriental Society* 106 (1986): 183-96.

―――. "Original Contributions of *Neidan* to Taoism and Chinese Thought." In L. Kohn, ed., *Taoist Meditation and Longevity Techniques.* Ann Arbor: University of Michigan, Center for Chinese Studies, 1989, pp. 297-331.

―――. "The Place and Meaning of the Notion of Taiji in Taoist Sources Prior to the Ming Dynasty." *History of Religion* 1990: 373-411.

―――. "L'unité transcendente des trois enseignements selon les taoïstes des Sung et des Yuan." In G. Naundorf, K. H. Pohl, H. H. Schmidt, eds., *Religion und Philosophie in Ostasien.* Würzburg: Königshausen und Neumann, 1985, pp. 103-26.

Index

In this index, an "f" after a number indicates a separate reference on the next page, and an "ff" indicates separate references on the next two pages. A continuous discussion over two or more pages is indicated by a span of page numbers, e.g., "57-59." *Passim* is used for a cluster of references in close but not consecutive sequence. Certain concepts (e.g., *wu* [non-existence], or the relationship between Earth and Heaven) that recur throughout the book are listed here only selectively. Cross-references are given from the Wade-Giles versions of certain names and terms that may not be easily recognizable in their pinyin forms (e.g., from Pao P'u Tzu to Baopuzi).

Library of Congress Cataloging-in-Publication Data

Robinet, Isabelle.
    [Histoire du taoïsme des origines au XIVe siècle. English]
      Taoism : growth of a religion / Isabelle Robinet : translated by
    Phyllis Brooks.
         p.   cm.
    Includes index.
      ISBN 0-8047-2838-0 (cloth : alk. paper). — ISBN 0-8047-2839-9
    (pbk. : alk. paper)
      1. Taoism—History. I. Brooks, Phyllis. II. Title.
    BL1910.R63   1997
    299'.514'09—dc20   96-30127
                                           CIP

♾ This book is printed on acid-free paper

Original printing, 1997

Last figure below indicates year of this printing

07 06 05 04 03 02 01 00 99 98 97